Generative Artificial Intelligence

Scrivener Publishing
100 Cummings Center, Suite 541J
Beverly, MA 01915-6106

Industry 5.0 Transformation Applications

Series Editors: Dr. S. Balamurugan (sbnbala@gmail) and Dr. Sheng-Lung Peng

The increase in technological advancements in the areas of artificial intelligence (AI), machine learning (ML) and data analytics has led to the next industrial revolution "Industry 5.0". The transformation to Industry 5.0 collaborates human intelligence with machines to customize efficient solutions. This book series covers various subjects under promising application areas of Industry 5.0 such as smart manufacturing, intelligent traffic, cloud manufacturing, real-time productivity optimization, augmented reality and virtual reality, etc., as well as titles supporting technologies for promoting potential applications of Industry 5.0, such as collaborative robots (Cobots), edge computing, Internet of Everything, big data analytics, digital twins, 6G and beyond, blockchain, quantum computing and hyper-intelligent networks.

Publishers at Scrivener
Martin Scrivener (martin@scrivenerpublishing.com)
Phillip Carmical (pcarmical@scrivenerpublishing.com)

Generative Artificial Intelligence

Concepts and Applications

Edited by

R. Nidhya
Dept. of Computer Science & Engineering, Madanapalle Institute of Technology & Science, Madanapalle, India

D. Pavithra
Dr NGP Institute of Technology, Coimbatore, Tamil Nadu, India

Manish Kumar
Thapar Institute of Engineering and Technology, Patiala, India

A. Dinesh Kumar
KL Deemed To Be Univeristy, Vijayawada, Andhra Pradesh, India

and

S. Balamurugan
Intelligent Research Consultancy Services, Coimbatore India

Scrivener Publishing

WILEY

This edition first published 2025 by John Wiley & Sons, Inc., 111 River Street, Hoboken, NJ 07030, USA and Scrivener Publishing LLC, 100 Cummings Center, Suite 541J, Beverly, MA 01915, USA

For more information about Scrivener publications please visit www.scrivenerpublishing.com.

Wiley Global Headquarters
111 River Street, Hoboken, NJ 07030, USA

For details of our global editorial offices, customer services, and more information about Wiley products visit us at www.wiley.com.

Library of Congress Cataloging-in-Publication Data

ISBN 978-1-394-20922-4

Cover image: Adobe Firefly
Cover design by Russell Richardson

Set in size of 11pt and Minion Pro by Manila Typesetting Company, Makati, Philippines

Printed in the USA

10 9 8 7 6 5 4 3 2 1

Contents

Preface **xiii**

1 Exploring the Creative Frontiers: Generative AI Unveiled **1**
Generated Using ChatGPT
1.1 Introduction 1
1.1.1 Definition and Significance of Generative AI 1
1.1.2 Historical Overview and Development 2
1.2 Foundational Concepts 4
1.2.1 Neural Networks and Generative Models 4
1.2.2 Variational Autoencoders (VAEs) and Generative Adversarial Networks (GANs) 5
1.3 Applications Across Domains 7
1.3.1 Creative Arts: Music, Visual Arts, Literature 7
1.3.2 Content Generation: Text, Images, Videos 8
1.3.3 Scientific Research and Data Augmentation 9
1.3.4 Healthcare and Drug Discovery 10
1.3.5 Gaming and Virtual Environments 12
1.4 Ethical Considerations 13
1.5 Future Prospects and Challenges 15
1.6 Conclusion 16
Reference 17

2 An Efficient Infant Cry Detection System Using Machine Learning and Neuro Computing Algorithms **19**
Swarna Kuchibhotla, Kantheti Mohana, Alapati Yomitha, Sruthi Yedavalli, Hima Deepthi Vankayalapati and Kyamakya Kyandoghere
2.1 Introduction 20
2.2 Literature Survey 21
2.3 Methodology 23
2.3.1 Database 24
2.3.2 Feature Extraction 25

2.3.2.1 Short-Term Energy 25
2.3.2.2 Mel-Frequency Cepstral Coefficients 26
2.3.2.3 Spectrograms 27
2.3.3 Classification 29
2.3.4 Convolutional Neural Network (CNN) 29
2.3.5 Recurrent Neural Network (RNN) 31
2.3.6 Regularized Discriminant Analysis (RDA) 31
2.3.7 Multi-Layer Perceptron (MLP) 33
2.4 Experimental Results 33
2.5 Conclusion 35
References 35

3 Improved Brain Tumor Segmentation Utilizing a Layered CNN Model 39
Bilal Hikmat Rasheed and P. Sudhakaran
3.1 Introduction 40
3.2 Related Works 41
3.3 Methodology 42
3.4 Numerical Results 45
3.5 Conclusion 49
References 49

4 Natural Language Processing in Generative Adversarial Network 53
P. Dhivya, A. Karthikeyan, S. Pradeep and H. Umamaheswari
4.1 Introduction 54
4.2 Literature Survey 57
4.3 The Implementation of NLP in GAN for Generating Images and Summaries 61
4.3.1 Working of Sequence Generative Adversarial Network (SeqGAN) 61
4.3.2 Working of Generative Adversarial Transformer (GAT) 63
4.3.2.1 Steps to Incorporate NLP in GAN 64
4.3.3 Implementation of NLP in GAN 65
4.3.4 Generate the Image Using Textual Description 68
4.3.5 Text Summarization 69
4.3.5.1 Graph-Based Summarization 71
4.4 Conclusion 77
References 77

5 Modeling A Deep Learning Network Model for Medical Image Panoptic Segmentation 81
Jyothsna Devi Koppagiri and Gouranga Mandal
5.1 Introduction 81
5.2 Related Works 84
5.3 Methodology 85
5.3.1 Deep Masking Convolutional Model (DMCM) 85
5.4 Numerical Results and Discussion 87
5.5 Conclusion 91
References 91

6 A Hybrid DenseNet Model for Dental Image Segmentation Using Modern Learning Approaches 93
Pulipati Nagaraju and S. V. Sudha
6.1 Introduction 94
6.2 Related Works 95
6.3 Methodology 96
6.3.1 Dataset 96
6.3.2 Dense Transformer Model 97
6.3.3 DenseNet Model 100
6.4 Numerical Results and Discussion 100
6.4.1 Discussion 103
6.5 Conclusion 104
References 104

7 Modeling A Two-Tier Network Model for Unconstraint Video Analysis Using Deep Learning 107
P. Naga Bhushanam and Selva Kumar S.
7.1 Introduction 108
7.2 Related Works 109
7.3 Methodology 110
7.4 Numerical Results and Discussion 113
7.5 Conclusion 117
References 118

8 Detection of Peripheral Blood Smear Malarial Parasitic Microscopic Images Utilizing Convolutional Neural Network 121
Tamal Kumar Kundu, Smritilekha Das and R. Nidhya
8.1 Introduction 122
8.2 Malaria 124
8.2.1 Malaria-Infected Red Blood Cells with Types 124
8.3 Literature Survey 125

8.4 Proposed Methodology and Algorithm 130
 8.4.1 Proposed Algorithm 135
8.5 Result Analysis 135
 8.5.1 Dataset 135
 8.5.2 Preprocessing of Data 135
 8.5.3 Splitting of Dataset 137
 8.5.4 Classification 137
 8.5.5 Model Prediction and Performance Metrics 137
 8.5.6 CNN Learning Curves 138
8.6 Discussion 139
8.7 Conclusion 139
8.8 Future Scope 139
 References 140

9 Exploring the Efficacy of Generative AI in Constructing Dynamic Predictive Models for Cybersecurity Threats: A Research Perspective 143
T. Manasa and K. Padmanaban
9.1 Introduction 144
9.2 Related Works 145
9.3 Methodology 146
 9.3.1 Pre-Processing 147
 9.3.2 Classifier 147
 9.3.3 Optimization 148
9.4 Numerical Results and Discussion 149
9.5 Conclusion 152
 References 152

10 Poultry Disease Detection: A Comparative Analysis of CNN, SVM, and YOLO v3 Algorithms for Accurate Diagnosis 155
Spoorthi Shetty and Mangala Shetty
10.1 Introduction 156
10.2 Literature Review 157
10.3 Objectives 158
 10.3.1 Accurate Disease and Early Disease Identification 158
 10.3.2 Multi-Class Disease Identification 158
 10.3.3 Automation and Real-Time Disease Monitoring 159
 10.3.4 Better Accuracy 159
10.4 Methodology 159
 10.4.1 Dataset 159
 10.4.2 Data Preprocessing 160

10.4.3 Image Preprocessing 161
10.4.4 Data Augmentation 161
10.4.5 Extracting Region of Interest 162
10.5 Results and Discussion 165
10.6 Conclusion 169
References 170

11 Generative AI-Enhanced Deep Learning Model for Crop Type Analysis Based on Clustered Feature Vectors and Remote Sensing Imagery 173
B. Bazeer Ahamed, D. Yuvaraj and Saif Saad Alnuaimi
11.1 Introduction 174
11.2 Related Works 176
11.3 Methodology 178
11.3.1 Saliency Analysis 180
11.3.2 Saliency Region Analysis with Belief Networking 181
11.3.3 Group Analysis 182
11.3.4 Classification 183
11.3.5 Parameter Setup 183
11.4 Numerical Results and Discussion 184
11.4.1 Dataset 186
11.4.2 Classification Results and Discussions 187
11.5 Conclusion 190
References 193

12 Cardiovascular Disease Prediction with Machine Learning: An Ensemble-Based Regressive Neighborhood Model 197
Yuvaraj Duraisamy, Salar Faisal Noori and Shakir Mahoomed Abas
12.1 Introduction 197
12.2 Related Works 200
12.3 Methodology 200
12.3.1 Pre-Processing 200
12.3.2 Feature Selection 202
12.3.3 Classification 202
12.4 Numerical Results and Discussion 203
12.5 Conclusion 206
References 207

13 Detection of IoT Attacks Using Hybrid RNN-DBN Model **209**
Pavithra D., Bharathraj R., Poovizhi P., Libitharan K. and Nivetha V.
13.1 Introduction 210
13.2 Related Work 212
13.3 Methodology 216
13.3.1 Dataset Used 216
13.3.2 Data Preprocessing 217
13.3.3 Data Normalization 217
13.3.4 Multi-Class Classification 218
13.3.5 Splitting Dataset 219
13.3.6 RNN-DBN 219
13.4 Experiments and Results 221
13.5 Conclusion and Future Scope 224
References 224

14 Identification of Foliar Pathologies in Apple Foliage Utilizing Advanced Deep Learning Techniques **227**
Tamal Kumar Kundu, Smritilekha Das and R. Nidhya
14.1 Introduction 228
14.2 Literature Survey 229
14.2.1 Disease Detection Using Machine and Deep Learning Techniques (2015–2021) 229
14.2.2 Disease Detection Using Transfer Learning (2015–2021) 232
14.3 Different Diseases of Leaves 233
14.4 Dataset 236
14.5 Proposed Methodology 239
14.6 Data Analysis 240
14.7 Pre-Processing Technique 241
14.8 Data Visualization 242
14.9 Evolutionary Progression and Genesis of Model 242
14.9.1 Evolution Model 243
14.9.2 Model Performance 244
References 246

15 Enhancing Cloud Security Through AI-Driven Intrusion Detection Utilizing Deep Learning Methods and Autoencoder Technology **249**
P.V. Sivarambabu, Richa Agrawal, Arepalli Tirumala, Shaik Mahaboob Subani, Veeraswamy Parisae and S. V. L. Sowjanya Nukala
15.1 Introduction 250
15.2 Related Work 251
15.3 Proposed Methodology 253
15.3.1 DL-Based IDS for Cloud Security 253
15.4 Results and Discussion 254
15.4.1 Performance Analysis 258
15.4.1.1 Accuracy 259
15.4.1.2 Precision 260
15.4.1.3 Recall 260
15.4.1.4 F1 Score 261
15.4.1.5 AUC - Area Under the Curve 261
15.5 Conclusion 262
References 262

16 YouTube Comment Analysis Using LSTM Model **265**
Pavithra D., Poovizhi P., Rokeshkumar G., Bharathvaj T. and Mageshkumar M.
16.1 Introduction 266
16.2 Related Work 266
16.3 Literature Survey 267
16.4 Existing System 272
16.5 Methodology 273
16.6 Result and Discussion 275
16.7 Conclusion 280
References 280

Index **283**

Preface

Artificial Intelligence grows stronger every day, with Generative AI significantly boosting creativity. As a subset of Deep Learning, Generative AI enables machines to produce innovative content, taking creativity to unprecedented levels. Businesses are rapidly adopting this technology, extending its applications into diverse industries with customized solutions. It's an opportune time for businesses to strategically adopt Generative AI as it becomes a cornerstone of future innovation and success.

Generative AI is redefining the capabilities of machines to create and innovate. Unlike traditional AI, which analyzes existing data, Generative AI produces new and original content across images, text, music, and more by leveraging neural networks and deep learning techniques to learn patterns and relationships from vast datasets.

The applications of Generative AI are transformative. In creative arts, it assists in visual art, music, and literature, expanding artistic possibilities. Beyond the arts, it impacts industries like healthcare, aiding in drug discovery, synthetic medical imaging, and personalized treatment plans. In gaming and entertainment, it generates immersive virtual worlds and characters.

This book provides an understanding of generative models, neural networks, and data generation algorithms. It caters to students, developers, data scientists, and AI practitioners, exploring practical applications across domains such as art, music, text generation, and image synthesis. It also examines real-world examples of Generative AI's impact in industries like entertainment, healthcare, and design.

Chapter 1, generated by ChatGPT 3.5, explores the fundamental concepts, applications, ethical considerations, and future implications of Generative AI. It examines concerns such as bias, authenticity, and societal impact, concluding with an overview of future prospects and challenges.

Chapter 2 focuses on automatic infant cry detection, addressing the disparity between adults' speech-based communication and infants' reliance on crying. Highlighting the need for systems to alert parents, especially in their absence, the authors introduce Regularized Discriminant Analysis (RDA), which outperforms conventional machine learning methods. Results show heightened accuracy, enhancing remote baby monitoring and timely infant care.

Chapter 3 employs a CNN model trained on public datasets to achieve superior segmentation of tumor sub-regions. The model attains the highest dice scores for tumor core, entire tumor, and enhancement, outperforming existing architectures.

Chapter 4 highlights the integration of Natural Language Processing (NLP) within Generative Adversarial Networks (GANs) to enhance text generation and expand GAN capabilities. Applications include semantic understanding, text-to-image generation, and sentiment analysis, evaluated using datasets like CLINC150 and tennis_articles, with promising results.

Chapter 5 discusses advancements in panoptic segmentation, leveraging the Deep Masking Convolutional Model (DMCM) to analyze RGB data. The chapter reviews the historical evolution, evaluation metrics, models, and challenges while proposing future research directions.

Chapter 6 introduces the Hybrid DenseNet Transformer (HDNT) for dental image segmentation, trained on panoramic dental X-rays. HDNT achieves superior IoU and Dice coefficients, offering memory efficiency and suitability for clinical deployment to improve image analysis accuracy.

Chapter 7 presents a two-tier convolutional neural network (2T-CNN) framework for generating, predicting, and completing human action videos under various constraints. The approach generates posture sequences and utilizes them to produce high-quality videos, demonstrating superior performance compared to existing techniques.

Chapter 8 demonstrates how CNNs, a subset of Deep Learning, construct an advanced malaria detection system. Guided by a structured research methodology, the system surpasses human observation limits, offering reliable, precise diagnosis.

Chapter 9 integrates the Hybrid Learning Model (HLM) with Stochastic Gradient Boosting (SGB) to predict DDoS attacks with 99.2% accuracy, preventing disruptions and managing cyber threats. A comparative study with KNN (95% accuracy) further supports the model's efficacy.

Chapter 10 introduces a method for detecting chicken diseases using Support Vector Machines (SVM), Convolutional Neural Networks (CNN), and the YOLOv3 object detection algorithm. The integrated approach is evaluated on an extensive dataset of diverse chicken diseases, demonstrating remarkable accuracy and resilience in detection across various samples.

Chapter 11 explores learning-based methodologies for analyzing UAV-based remote sensing images to classify crops and plants. The study aims to help researchers and farmers choose optimal algorithms suited to specific crops and hardware configurations. By fusing deep learning techniques with UAV datasets, the authors enable accurate classification of various crop varieties while addressing key challenges and enhancing algorithm performance.

Chapter 12 examines key factors influencing cardiovascular disease, including family history, stress, and high blood pressure. Researchers propose an Ensemble-based Regressive Neighbourhood Model (ERN) for early CVD prediction, comparing its performance with alternative models. Accurate prediction is crucial due to the critical nature of CVD, and the study assesses various performance metrics to validate its approach.

Chapter 13 proposes a framework for detecting network intrusions by merging Recurrent Neural Networks (RNNs) and Deep Belief Networks (DBNs). Applied to the UNSW NB15 dataset, this model efficiently identifies and categorizes nine types of attacks, such as DoS, Exploits, and Reconnaissance, demonstrating promising results in securing IoT environments.

Chapter 14 introduces a system that simulates disease dynamics by integrating generative algorithms with traditional machine learning techniques. Combining models like CNNs, VGG-16, ResNet50, and SVM, the framework achieves high accuracy in disease classification, reducing human error and expediting the identification process.

Chapter 15 presents an AI-driven Intrusion Detection System (IDS) using Distributed Ledger Technology (DLT) and Auto-Encoders (AE) as feature extractors. Features are classified using CNN, RNN, and LSTM, achieving accuracy rates of 98.55%, 94.33%, and 95.08%, respectively, outperforming existing intrusion detection methods and enhancing cloud security.

Chapter 16 proposes a sentiment analysis system using Long Short-Term Memory (LSTM) RNNs with three layers. Beyond sentiment analysis, it introduces comment categorization, offering content creators segmented feedback for refining their videos. The system enables real-time analytics, revolutionizing online content analysis and fostering interactive content creation.

We offer our sincere thanks to all the authors for their timely support and for considering this book for publishing their quality work. We also thank all reviewers for their kind cooperation extended during the various stages of processing the manuscript. Finally, we thank Martin Scrivener and the Scrivener Publishing team for producing this volume.

The Editors

1

Exploring the Creative Frontiers: Generative AI Unveiled

Generated Using ChatGPT*

Abstract

Generative artificial intelligence (AI) stands at the forefront of technological innovation, captivating minds and pushing the boundaries of creativity. This paper delves into the realm of generative AI, exploring its foundational concepts, applications across diverse domains, ethical considerations, and the future implications it holds. The study navigates through the evolution of generative AI, highlighting its capabilities in generating content, fostering artistic expression, aiding in problem-solving, and revolutionizing various industries. Additionally, it examines the ethical implications associated with generative AI's advancements, shedding light on concerns regarding bias, authenticity, and societal impact. The paper concludes by envisioning future prospects and challenges that lie ahead in the fascinating landscape of generative AI.

1.1 Introduction

1.1.1 Definition and Significance of Generative AI

Generative artificial intelligence (AI) refers to a subset of AI that focuses on creating, generating, or producing new content, information, or data

* Footnote

Chapter 1 is generated using ChatGPT 3.5. To unveil the power of Generative AI this entire chapter has been generated using ChatGPT. ChatGPT (Chat Generative Pre-trained Transformer) is a pre-trained chatbot software developed by OpenAI launched on November 30, 2022 (initial release) and February 13, 2024 (stable release) that uses Natural Language Processing to support Prompt Engineering. This chapter talks about the revolutionary advancements in Generative Artificial Intelligence (GAI), focusing on the remarkable capabilities of ChatGPT. The advent of generative models has transformed the landscape of AI, enabling machines to not only comprehend human language but also generate contextually relevant and coherent responses. ChatGPT, based on the GPT-3.5 architecture, stands out as a prime example of the immense progress made in the field of Generative AI.

R. Nidhya, D. Pavithra, Manish Kumar, A. Dinesh Kumar and S. Balamurugan (eds.) Generative Artificial Intelligence: Concepts and Applications, (1–18) © 2025 Scrivener Publishing LLC

that mimics human-like creativity and innovation. Unlike traditional AI, which typically focuses on analyzing existing data to make predictions or decisions, generative AI is designed to generate new content autonomously.

The significance of generative AI lies in its ability to simulate human-like creativity, enabling machines to produce content that ranges from text, images, and music to videos and more. This technology has far-reaching implications across various domains:

Creative Expression: Generative AI allows for the creation of original artworks, music compositions, and literary pieces. This facilitates new forms of artistic expression and exploration.
Content Generation: It helps in automating the generation of content for various purposes, such as writing news articles, producing marketing materials, or creating realistic images and videos.
Problem-solving and Innovation: Generative AI aids in exploring new solutions to complex problems by generating diverse hypotheses and scenarios, contributing to innovation in research and development.
Personalization and Customization: It enables personalized content creation, catering to individual preferences and needs, thereby enhancing user experiences in various applications.
Data Augmentation and Simulation: In scientific research and data analysis, generative models assist in generating synthetic data, facilitating better analysis and understanding of complex systems.
Enhanced Realism in Virtual Environments: In gaming and virtual reality (VR), generative AI enhances the realism of virtual worlds, creating more immersive experiences for users.

Generative AI's significance also lies in its potential to transform industries by automating content creation, aiding in decision-making processes, and driving innovation. However, its development raises ethical concerns related to authenticity, bias, privacy, and ownership of generated content. Understanding and addressing these ethical challenges are crucial for responsible deployment and usage of generative AI in various fields.

1.1.2 Historical Overview and Development

The history of generative AI is an evolutionary journey marked by significant milestones in the field of AI and machine learning. Here is a brief historical overview:

Early Concepts (1950s – 1960s): The roots of generative AI can be traced back to the early days of AI research. Pioneers like Alan Turing laid the theoretical groundwork for machine intelligence and the concept of machines exhibiting creative behavior.
Rule-based Systems (1970s – 1980s): Early AI systems relied on rule-based approaches, where experts codified explicit rules for the computer to follow. While these systems were not inherently generative, they formed the basis for later developments.
Probabilistic Models (1990s – 2000s): Bayesian networks and probabilistic graphical models emerged, allowing machines to model uncertainty and generate probabilistic outputs. This era saw advancements in probabilistic modeling for tasks like speech recognition and natural language processing.
Rise of Neural Networks (2010s): With the resurgence of neural networks and deep learning, generative AI witnessed a significant leap. Variational Autoencoders (VAEs) and generative adversarial networks (GANs) became prominent; VAEs focused on learning latent representations of data for generative purposes, while GANs introduced a novel adversarial training framework for generating realistic data.
Recent Advancements (2010s – 2020s): The latter half of the 2010s and early 2020s marked rapid progress in generative AI. OpenAI's generative pre-trained transformer (GPT) models, starting from GPT-1 and evolving into larger versions like GPT-2 and GPT-3, showcased the power of large-scale language generation.
Diversification of Generative Models: The development of various architectures and techniques, such as transformer models, attention mechanisms, reinforcement learning, and fine-tuning strategies, expanded the capabilities of generative AI beyond language to images, music, and multimodal generation.
Ethical and Social Implications: Alongside technological advancements, discussions about the ethical implications of generative AI, including issues of bias, manipulation, and misinformation, gained prominence. Researchers and policymakers began addressing these concerns to ensure responsible use of generative technologies.

The historical progression of generative AI highlights the iterative nature of technological development, driven by advancements in algorithms, computational power, and data availability. This evolution laid the foundation for contemporary generative AI models and their diverse applications across industries, setting the stage for further innovation and ethical considerations in the field.

1.2 Foundational Concepts

1.2.1 Neural Networks and Generative Models

Neural networks serve as the backbone for many generative models within the realm of generative AI. These models leverage neural network architectures to facilitate the generation of new content or data. Here is an overview of how neural networks are used in generative models:

Feedforward Neural Networks (FNNs):

- FNNs consist of interconnected layers of nodes, passing information in a unidirectional flow from input to output.
- While not inherently generative, FNNs can be used in generative settings, especially in early rule-based approaches where explicit instructions guide the generation process.

Recurrent Neural Networks (RNNs):

- RNNs are designed to process sequential data by utilizing loops within the network, allowing information to persist over time.
- RNNs are employed in language generation tasks where context and sequence are crucial, but they face challenges in modeling long-range dependencies due to vanishing/exploding gradient problems.

Variational Autoencoders (VAEs) with Neural Networks:

- VAEs employ neural networks as encoders and decoders. These networks learn to encode input data into a latent space representation and decode it back to generate output data.
- The encoder and decoder networks in VAEs are typically composed of feedforward or convolutional neural networks.

Generative Adversarial Networks (GANs) with Neural Networks:

- GANs consist of two neural networks—the generator and the discriminator—working in tandem.
- The generator uses neural networks to transform random noise into data that resembles real data, while the

discriminator uses neural networks to distinguish between real and generated data.

Transformer Models:

- Transformer models, like the ones used in GPT series, employ attention mechanisms and self-attention layers to process and generate sequences.
- These models leverage neural networks to generate text, allowing for longer-range dependencies and capturing intricate patterns in the data.

Neural networks serve as the computational backbone for various generative models, allowing for the creation of sophisticated architectures capable of generating diverse and high-quality content across different modalities—such as text, images, audio, and more. The advancements in neural network architectures and training methodologies continue to drive innovation in generative AI, enabling the development of more powerful and versatile generative models.

1.2.2 Variational Autoencoders (VAEs) and Generative Adversarial Networks (GANs)

Variational autoencoders (VAEs) and generative adversarial networks (GANs) represent two powerful paradigms in generative AI, each with unique approaches to generating new content. Here's an exploration of their key characteristics and differences:

1. **Variational Autoencoders (VAEs):**
   - **Objective:** VAEs aim to learn a latent representation of data by mapping it to a lower-dimensional space and reconstructing it back to the original form.
   - **Architecture:** VAEs consist of an encoder and a decoder. The encoder maps input data to a latent space, producing mean and variance parameters that describe a probabilistic distribution. The decoder generates data from samples drawn from this distribution.
   - **Probabilistic Framework:** VAEs operate within a probabilistic framework, learning the underlying probability distribution of the data in the latent space.

- **Variational Inference:** VAEs use variational inference to train the model, optimizing a reconstruction loss and a regularization term that encourages the learned latent space to follow a specific distribution (often a Gaussian distribution).

2. **Generative Adversarial Networks (GANs):**
   - **Objective:** GANs aim to generate data by training two competing neural networks—an adversarial pair—where one network generates data (the generator) and the other evaluates its authenticity (the discriminator).
   - **Architecture:** GANs consist of a generator network and a discriminator network. The generator creates synthetic data from random noise, while the discriminator tries to distinguish between real and generated data.
   - **Adversarial Training:** GANs use adversarial training dynamics, where the generator aims to produce data that can deceive the discriminator, while the discriminator strives to become better at distinguishing real from generated data.
   - **High-Quality Outputs:** GANs are known for producing high-quality, realistic outputs, especially in generating images, by learning to capture complex data distributions.

Key Differences:

- **Objective:** VAEs focus on learning latent representation and probabilistic modeling, emphasizing data reconstruction, while GANs concentrate on generating realistic data by pitting a generator against a discriminator in an adversarial framework.
- **Training Dynamics:** VAEs optimize a reconstruction loss and a regularization term, while GANs use adversarial training without an explicit reconstruction objective.
- **Output Quality:** GANs often produce more visually realistic outputs, particularly in image generation tasks, while VAEs are versatile in generating diverse samples but might not achieve the same level of visual fidelity.

Both VAEs and GANs have contributed significantly to generative AI, offering distinct approaches to generating content and pushing the boundaries of creativity and realism in machine-generated outputs. Researchers continue to explore ways to combine and improve upon these models for even more powerful and diverse generative capabilities.

1.3 Applications Across Domains

1.3.1 Creative Arts: Music, Visual Arts, Literature

Absolutely, generative AI has made significant strides in revolutionizing the creative arts, contributing to music composition, visual arts, and literature in compelling ways.

Music Composition:

- **Melody Generation:** AI systems can compose melodies, harmonies, and entire musical pieces across various genres, offering composers new ideas and creative directions.
- **Style Imitation:** These models can emulate the styles of different composers or musical genres, creating music that resembles specific artists' styles.

Visual Arts:

- **Art Generation:** Generative AI generates visual art, including paintings, digital art, and even sculptures, exploring new styles, patterns, and aesthetics.
- **Style Transfer:** AI models can transform images or videos to resemble the artistic style of famous painters or artistic movements, blending styles in visually stunning ways.

Literature and Writing:

- **Text Generation:** AI writes stories, poems, and prose, generating content that mimics different writing styles or authors' voices.
- **Collaborative Writing:** Writers use AI as a tool for brainstorming, idea generation, and collaborative writing, expanding their creative possibilities.

Cross-modal Creativity:

- **Multimodal Art:** AI models merge different art forms, creating collaborations between music and visuals or generating art inspired by specific pieces of music or literature.

Generative AI's impact on the creative arts is not just about automation but also about collaboration and inspiration. It is offering new tools for artists, musicians, and writers to explore uncharted territories, experiment with styles, and push the boundaries of what is possible in their respective artistic domains. While some view it as a complement to human creativity, others see it as a catalyst for innovative expressions and novel artistic endeavors.

1.3.2 Content Generation: Text, Images, Videos

Generative AI's prowess in content generation spans across various mediums, transforming the creation of textual content, images, and videos:

Text Generation:
Natural Language Generation: AI models generate written content across diverse genres, from news articles, essays, and creative writing to product descriptions and summaries.
Chatbots and Conversational Agents: AI powers chatbots and virtual assistants, generating human-like responses for customer service, information retrieval, and conversation.

Image Generation:
Artistic Image Creation: Generative AI creates images, paintings, and digital art, often exploring unique styles, surreal landscapes, or mimicking specific artistic genres.
Photo Realism: AI generates realistic images, faces, objects, and scenes, often indistinguishable from real photographs, which find applications in graphics and visual media.

Video Generation:
Visual Storytelling: AI models generate videos and animations, aiding in visual storytelling, advertisements, and creating dynamic content for marketing purposes.
Face and Motion Synthesis: AI generates synthetic faces and human-like movements, contributing to video editing, special effects, and virtual characters in gaming and films.

Cross-modal Generation:
Text-to-Image Synthesis: AI models create images based on textual descriptions or captions, illustrating scenes or ideas described in text.
Image-to-Text Generation: AI generates textual descriptions or captions from images, enhancing accessibility and aiding in content indexing and retrieval.

Generative AI's ability to create content across multiple modalities has significantly impacted industries reliant on content creation. From automating routine content production to enabling new creative possibilities, these models have found applications in marketing, media, entertainment, and various sectors seeking innovative content solutions.

1.3.3 Scientific Research and Data Augmentation

Generative AI plays a crucial role in scientific research by contributing to data augmentation, simulation, and aiding in various research endeavors:

1. **Data Augmentation:**
   - **Synthetic Data Generation:** Generative models create synthetic data to augment limited or scarce datasets, enhancing training for machine learning models.
   - **Data Imputation and Enhancement:** AI helps fill in missing data points or enhances existing datasets by generating plausible data, improving the robustness of analyses and models.
2. **Simulation and Modeling:**
   - **Complex Systems Simulation:** AI-driven simulations model complex systems, such as climate patterns, biological processes, or physical phenomena, aiding researchers in hypothesis testing and scenario analysis.
   - **Predictive Modeling:** Generative AI contributes to predictive modeling by simulating various scenarios, predicting outcomes, and assisting in decision-making in fields like finance, healthcare, and logistics.
3. **Drug Discovery and Molecular Design:**
   - **Molecular Generation:** AI generates molecular structures and compounds, accelerating drug discovery by suggesting potential drug candidates or predicting their properties.

- **Biomolecule Design:** Generative models aid in designing novel proteins or biomolecules for various applications in medicine, bioengineering, and materials science.

4. **Genomics and Biomedical Research:**
   - **Genomic Sequences:** AI assists in generating synthetic genomic sequences, aiding in understanding genetic variations, regulatory elements, and disease mechanisms.
   - **Medical Image Synthesis:** Generative models generate synthetic medical images, contributing to training and validating medical imaging algorithms and enhancing diagnostic tools.
5. **Experimental Design and Optimization:**
   - **Experiment Design:** AI models aid in designing experiments by generating optimal experimental conditions, reducing costs, and improving efficiency in research.
   - **Parameter Optimization:** Generative AI assists in optimizing parameters for simulations or experiments, refining models and improving accuracy.

Generative AI's applications in scientific research and data augmentation have the potential to accelerate discoveries, overcome limitations in data availability, and drive innovation across various scientific domains. These models serve as valuable tools for researchers, enabling them to explore new hypotheses, simulate complex systems, and make advancements in diverse fields of study.

1.3.4 Healthcare and Drug Discovery

Generative AI has made substantial contributions to healthcare and drug discovery, revolutionizing processes and innovations in the field:

1. **Drug Discovery and Development:**
   - **Molecule Generation:** AI assists in generating novel molecular structures and compounds, predicting their properties, and accelerating the discovery of potential drug candidates.
   - **Virtual Screening:** Generative models aid in virtual screening by simulating interactions between drugs and biological targets, prioritizing compounds for experimental validation.

- ***De Novo* Drug Design:** AI designs new molecules with desired properties, optimizing drug candidates for efficacy and safety.

2. **Personalized Medicine:**
   - **Patient Data Analysis:** Generative AI analyzes patient data, including genetic information and medical histories, to tailor personalized treatment plans and therapies.
   - **Disease Modeling:** AI models simulate disease progression, aiding in understanding disease mechanisms and predicting treatment outcomes for individual patients.
3. **Medical Imaging and Diagnosis:**
   - **Image Synthesis:** Generative models generate synthetic medical images to augment limited datasets, enhance training of diagnostic algorithms, and improve accuracy in medical imaging.
   - **Diagnostic Support:** AI assists in diagnosing diseases by analyzing medical images, identifying patterns, and providing insights to healthcare practitioners.
4. **Drug Repurposing and Optimization:**
   - **Identifying New Uses:** AI models identify existing drugs that could be repurposed for different medical conditions, potentially expediting treatments for various diseases.
   - **Optimizing Drug Properties:** Generative AI optimizes drug properties, such as bioavailability and efficacy, aiding in improving existing medications.
5. **Biomedical Research and Genomics:**
   - **Genomic Sequencing:** AI analyzes genomic data, identifying genetic variations, regulatory elements, and disease markers, advancing understanding in genetics and personalized medicine.
   - **Biomarker Discovery:** Generative models aid in discovering biomarkers for diseases, facilitating early detection and targeted treatments.

Generative AI's applications in healthcare and drug discovery have the potential to significantly impact patient care, accelerate the drug development pipeline, and revolutionize personalized medicine. These advancements offer promising avenues for more efficient and effective treatments, leading to improved healthcare outcomes for individuals worldwide.

1.3.5 Gaming and Virtual Environments

Generative AI has profoundly influenced gaming and virtual environments, enhancing the gaming experience and enabling new possibilities in virtual worlds:

1. Procedural Content Generation (PCG):
Level Design: AI generates game levels, environments, and landscapes procedurally, offering diverse and dynamic gaming experiences without manual creation.
Terrain Generation: Generative models create realistic and varied terrains, landscapes, and worlds in games, fostering exploration and immersion.

2. Character and Asset Creation:
Character Generation: AI designs characters, non-playable characters (NPCs), and creatures, expanding the diversity and uniqueness of in-game personas.
Asset Creation: Generative models create assets, including textures, models, and animations, reducing development time and enhancing visual quality.

3. Adaptive Gameplay and AI Behavior:
Dynamic AI: AI-driven NPCs exhibit adaptive behavior, learning from player interactions and adjusting strategies, providing challenging and responsive gameplay experiences.
Procedural Storytelling: Generative AI creates dynamic narratives and storylines, adapting to player choices, offering branching narratives, and enhancing replayability.

4. Visual Realism and Graphics:
Realistic Rendering: AI-driven graphics engines generate realistic visuals, including lighting effects, textures, and visual effects, enhancing immersion in gaming environments.
Up-Scaling and Enhancement: Generative models enhance graphics by up-scaling lower-resolution assets, improving visual fidelity in games and VR.

5. Virtual Reality (VR) and Augmented Reality (AR):
Immersive Environments: Generative AI creates immersive VR/AR environments, offering realistic simulations and interactive experiences in virtual spaces.

Interactive Content: AI generates interactive elements and experiences, enhancing immersion and engagement in VR/AR applications.

6. Game Design Assistance:
Design Support: AI assists game designers by generating ideas, mechanics, and concepts, offering inspiration and aiding in game development processes.

Generative AI's impact in gaming and virtual environments extends beyond content creation, shaping gameplay dynamics, storytelling, and immersive experiences. These technologies continue to drive innovation in game development, paving the way for richer and more dynamic gaming universes.

1.4 Ethical Considerations

Ethical considerations surrounding generative AI cover a broad spectrum of concerns that arise from its capabilities and potential impact on society, privacy, fairness, and creativity. Here are some critical ethical aspects:

1. **Bias and Fairness:**
    - **Data Bias:** Generative AI models can inherit biases present in the training data, perpetuating societal biases in generated content or decisions.
    - **Fairness in Output:** Ensuring fairness and equality in the content generated by AI models, especially in sensitive areas like language, race, gender, or culture.
2. **Authenticity and Misinformation:**
    - **Fake Content:** Generative models can create realistic-looking fake content, raising concerns about misinformation, fake news, and the spread of disinformation.
    - **Detection and Verification:** Developing methods to detect and verify AI-generated content to prevent its malicious use or dissemination.
3. **Intellectual Property and Copyright:**
    - **Ownership of Generated Content:** Defining ownership and copyright laws for content generated by AI,

addressing the rights of creators and the legal implications of AI-generated work.

4. **Privacy and Data Security:**
   - **Data Privacy:** AI models trained on personal data may raise concerns about privacy violations and the potential misuse or exposure of sensitive information.
   - **Security Risks:** Guarding against AI-generated content used in phishing attacks, deepfakes, or other malicious activities that compromise individuals' security and privacy.
5. **Societal Impact and Employment:**
   - **Impact on Jobs:** The automation of content creation by AI may affect certain job sectors, necessitating the reskilling or redeployment of workers.
   - **Cultural Impact:** Understanding the cultural implications of AI-generated content and its influence on societal values, norms, and cultural expressions.
6. **Regulation and Ethical Guidelines:**
   - **Ethical Frameworks:** Establishing ethical guidelines and frameworks for the responsible development, deployment, and use of generative AI technologies.
   - **Regulatory Oversight:** Implementing regulations and policies to ensure the ethical use of generative AI and mitigate potential risks to individuals and society.
7. **Transparency and Accountability:**
   - **Explainability:** Ensuring transparency in AI models' decision-making processes and making them explainable to understand how and why certain content or decisions are generated.
   - **Accountability:** Holding developers, organizations, and users accountable for the ethical use and consequences of Generative AI technologies.

Addressing these ethical considerations requires collaboration among stakeholders—researchers, policymakers, industry leaders, and ethicists—to establish robust guidelines and frameworks that prioritize ethical principles, mitigate risks, and promote the responsible deployment of generative AI for societal benefit.

1.5 Future Prospects and Challenges

The future of generative AI holds immense promise, accompanied by several challenges that need addressing for its responsible and effective integration. Here is a glimpse into its potential prospects and the hurdles it faces:

1. **Advancements in Generative Models:**
   - **Improved Realism and Diversity:** Future models are expected to generate content with even greater realism and diversity, blurring the lines between AI-generated and human-created content.
   - **Multimodal Capabilities:** Advancements will enable models to generate content across multiple modalities seamlessly, integrating text, images, videos, and other forms of data.
2. **Ethical and Societal Challenges:**
   - **Ethical Guidelines and Regulations:** There is a need for robust ethical frameworks and regulations to govern generative AI, addressing issues like bias, authenticity, privacy, and intellectual property rights.
   - **Misuse and Malicious Use:** Combatting the misuse of AI-generated content for disinformation, deepfakes, and other malicious purposes requires continuous vigilance and countermeasures.
3. **Enhanced Creativity and Collaboration:**
   - **Human-AI Collaboration:** Enabling more seamless collaboration between humans and AI in creative endeavors, fostering new forms of artistic expression and problem-solving.
   - **Tools for Creativity:** Development of user-friendly tools that empower creators across various domains to leverage generative AI effectively without requiring extensive technical expertise.
4. **Personalization and User Experience:**
   - **Tailored Content Generation:** AI's ability to generate highly personalized and context-aware content, catering to individual preferences and needs in various applications.
   - **Enhanced User Experience:** Integration of generative AI to create more immersive, engaging, and personalized user experiences in gaming, entertainment, and other industries.

5. **Technological Challenges:**
    - **Scalability and Efficiency:** Scaling up AI models while maintaining efficiency and reducing computational costs remains a challenge, especially for larger, more complex models.
    - **Interpretability and Explainability:** Improving the interpretability of AI-generated content and ensuring models are explainable for better transparency and accountability.
6. **Bias Mitigation and Fairness:**
    - **Bias Reduction:** Addressing and minimizing biases in AI models to ensure fairness, inclusivity, and equity in the content generated across different demographics and contexts.
    - **Fairness in Output:** Striving for fairness in the output of generative AI, ensuring it aligns with ethical and societal norms without perpetuating stereotypes or prejudices.

1.6 Conclusion

Navigating these prospects and challenges demands a concerted effort from researchers, developers, policymakers, and society at large to harness generative AI's potential while responsibly managing its impact. Addressing ethical, technical, and societal aspects will be pivotal in shaping a future where generative AI contributes positively to diverse domains while upholding ethical standards and societal well-being. Generative AI stands at the forefront of innovation, reshaping industries, creative expressions, and problem-solving approaches. As it continues to evolve, the technology's potential remains vast, offering both promise and responsibility.

This transformative tool has demonstrated its prowess across diverse domains, from generating artistic masterpieces and assisting in content creation to aiding scientific research and revolutionizing healthcare and gaming. However, its advancement raises ethical considerations that demand careful navigation. Ethical frameworks, regulations, and responsible deployment are crucial to harnessing generative AI's potential while mitigating risks such as biases, misinformation, and privacy breaches. Collaboration among stakeholders—researchers, policymakers, industry leaders, and ethicists—is pivotal in establishing guidelines that prioritize ethical use and societal well-being.

The future of generative AI holds immense promise, with prospects of enhanced realism, personalized experiences, and improved collaboration between humans and AI. Overcoming challenges like bias reduction, transparency, and scalability will be instrumental in shaping a future where generative AI drives innovation while upholding ethical standards and societal values. Embracing this technology responsibly opens avenues for creativity, innovation, and problem-solving, paving the way for a future where generative AI augments human capabilities, fosters new discoveries, and enriches diverse aspects of our lives. As we navigate this transformative landscape, a balanced approach ensuring innovation while prioritizing ethical considerations will guide generative AI towards its full potential for positive impact.

Reference

1. https://chatgpt.com

2

An Efficient Infant Cry Detection System Using Machine Learning and Neuro Computing Algorithms

Swarna Kuchibhotla[1]*, Kantheti Mohana[1], Alapati Yomitha[1], Sruthi Yedavalli, Hima Deepthi Vankayalapati[2] and Kyamakya Kyandoghere[3]

[1]*Department of CSE, Koneru Lakshmaiah Education Foundation, Vaddeswaram, AP, India*

[2]*Artificial Intelligence Department, Mukesh Patel School of Technology Management and Engineering, NMIMS Mumbai, Maharashtra, India*

[3]*Institute for Smart Systems Technologies, University of Klagenfurt, Klagenfurt, Carinthia, Austria*

Abstract

Humans can communicate their emotions, distress, and discomfort through speech signals, but infants can only communicate their emotions through crying. Parents will try to recognize the reason behind their infant's cries, but most of parents will fail to find the reason in time. An infant cry sound detection system helps alert parents when their infant is crying. Detecting infant cries automatically is an essential step in the remote baby monitoring process for working parents. In this literature, several feature extraction and classification techniques have been used to detect infant cries, but most of the existing systems are not optimal for real time in terms of respond time and efficiency. In order to improve the performance, this work uses neurocomputing methodologies by extracting various features like the mel-frequency cepstral coefficients (MFCC), short-term energy, and spectrograms. Along with the existing algorithms such as linear discriminant analysis (LDA), multi-layer perceptron (MLP), recurrent neural networks (RNN), and convolution neural networks (CNN), the proposed regularized discriminant analysis (RDA) is applied for the detection of the baby's cries. The experimental results show that the proposed RDA achieved high performance when compared with the standard machine learning algorithms.

**Corresponding author*: drkswarna@kluniversity.in

R. Nidhya, D. Pavithra, Manish Kumar, A. Dinesh Kumar and S. Balamurugan (eds.) Generative Artificial Intelligence: Concepts and Applications, (19–38)

Keywords: Regularized discriminant analysis, multi-layer perceptron, recurrent neural networks and convolution neural networks, mel-frequency cepstral coefficients (MFCC), spectrogram

2.1 Introduction

Infant cry analysis is more crucial in developing countries than in developed countries because of their limited healthcare infrastructure and poor hygiene practices. Approximately 295,000 newborns die worldwide within 28 days of their birth every year due to some long-term disability [23].

It is very important to identify the cause of these difficulties. They may be genetic, infectious, and environmental. The most common and severe disabilities are heart defects, neural tube defects, and down syndrome [15].

As per Indian statistics, birth defects affect nearly 32 in 1000 infants born every year. In spite of its large population, India is neither the highest nor the lowest in infant mortality rate worldwide. It is very easy to identify structural problems in infants, but some symptoms are invisible to identify [2, 18, 24].

Crying is the first sound a child makes when he/she enters the world. It is a way of expressing different circumstances. Young parents face difficulty in caring for these newly born babies. The basis for this is not easy to identify. Experienced parents and doctors can handle the situation by predicting the reason to some extent [12, 26]. However, for first-time parents, this is a difficult circumstance in distinguishing various cry signals to provide comfort to their new-born. Based on the literature, there are mainly four reasons for cries such as pain, hunger, discomfort, and fear [7].

The detection of infant cry signals is one of most important steps in pre-processing numerous applications, which involve cry analysis. Cry signals have been used as the object of analysis and research for many years. Many researchers and scientists can detect the necessary information about the psychological and physical states of newborn babies. Sound classification is the process of hearing and analyzing sound recordings. This is also called the classification of sound, which is the important block of various modern technologies, which include artificial intelligence, such as speech and text emotion recognition. Over the decades, a number of works has been done in the field of infant cries. Infant cry sounds are due to several reasons that includes ailment, environmental factors, pain, discomfort, emotional need and hungry [8].

Therefore, developing an inexpensive automatic infant cry detection system to identify the reasons of infant cries is essential to reduce the mortality rate. It should be able to differentiate cries from various noise signals (elders voice, equipment sounds, pet animal sounds, etc.,) around the infants in real time.

2.2 Literature Survey

In literature, various feature extraction and classification algorithms are proposed by researchers on automatic infant cry detection and classification systems. Even though there are several prosodic and spectral features used, most of the works are concentrated on spectral features such as the mel-frequency cepstral coefficients (MFCC). An effective comparative study on machine learning and deep learning classification techniques has been done in literature shown in Table 2.1. But the accuracy on real time cry signals is not optimal [22, 25]. Still researchers are trying to fill the performance gap with novel neuro computing algorithms.

In 2019, Rami *et al.* proposed a chapter, which compares classical approaches and deep learning approaches in detecting cry signals. The classification algorithms like logistic regression and support vector machines (SVM) as classical approaches and convolutional neural network (CNN) and recurrent neural network (RNN) for deep learning. The accuracy of the CNN is more like 95% when compared with the traditional architecture [5, 9, 14].

In 2016, Yizhar Lavner *et al.* proposed a deep learning algorithm for detecting cries in a domestic environment. In this they have used logistic regression and a CNN algorithm for classifying baby cries including domestic sounds like parents' speech signal and door sounds. When compared with logistic regression, CNN gives the highest accuracy as it is the most suitable for a large dataset. They have used features like MFCC, pitch, and formants on an annotated dataset [4, 16].

In 2017, Lina Abou-Abbas *et al.* proposed a framework for baby cry signal segmentation. Various time domain and frequency domain features like intensity, pitch, and MFCC are used for the classification of cry signals using different algorithms like Gaussian mixture models (GMM) or Hidden Markov models (HMM). The accuracy of the system is 94.29% with GMM. In this framework, they have used the Gaussian mixture and Hidden Markov model. Various other features are also considered in this model to increase efficiency and accuracy [1].

In 2019, Sita Purnima Dewi *et al.* analyzed baby crying using MFCC and linear frequency cepstral coefficients (LPCC). They have used classification algorithms like artificial neural networks (ANN), vector quantization (VQ)

Table 2.1 A comparison of various existing cry detection techniques.

Title	Algorithms	Features	ACC
Baby Cry Detection: Deep Learning and Classical Approaches	CNN, RNN, Logistic Regression, SVM	Mel Filter Bank (MFB), Log Mel Filter Bank (LMFB), MFCC	95
Baby Cry Detection in Domestic Environment Using Deep Learning	Logistic Regression, CNN	MFCC, Short-Time Energy (STE), Zero Crossing Rate (ZCR), Harmonic Features (HF), Harmonic-to-Noise Amplitude Ratio (HAPR)	82.5
A Review of Infant Cry Analysis and Classification	SVM, K-Nearest Neighbors, GMM, Fuzzy Classifiers	MFCC, LPCC, Linear Frequency Cepstral Coefficients (LFCC)	95
Infant Cry Detection in Real World Environments	Support Vector Machine	STFT, Zero Crossing Rate, Energy, Spectral Centroid, Spectral Flux	69
A Fully Automated Approach for Baby Cry Signals Segmentation and Boundary Detection for Expiratory and Inspiratory Episodes	GMM, Hidden Markov model	Intensity, Zero Crossing Rate, Pitch, MFCC, Empirical Mode Decomposition-Based MFCC	91
Deep Learning Assisted Neonatal Cry Classification Via Support Vector Machine Models	CNN, SVM	Fast Fourier Transform, STFT	86.67
A Database of Infant Cry Sounds to Study the Likely Cause of Cry	Linear Prediction Analysis	STFT, Auto-Correlation Analysis	85
Infant Cry Analysis and Detection	K-Nearest Neighbors	Pitch, MFCC, Short-Time Energy Parameters	92

and K Nearest Neighbor (KNN). The algorithm outperforms LPCC when compared with MFCC [6, 17].

In 2021, Ashwini *et al.* proposed a method to classify infant cries into three classes such as sleepiness, hunger, and pain. They have used short-time Fourier transform (STFT) for converting audio signals into spectrograms. A CNN is used to extract the features from these spectrograms. These features are given as input to the SVM with different types of kernels like linear, polynomial, and radial basis function for classification. The accuracy of the system is 88.89% with kernel-based classification. This work combines machine learning and deep learning techniques, which produce the best results with moderate samples. By combining a CNN-based feature extraction and SVM model, the accuracy is increased when compared with other algorithms [3, 10, 16].

The most frequently used databases are the Baby Chillanto database [5]. Because of the sensitivity of the baby cry data collection, the number of available databases is limited. The National Institute of Astrophysics and Optical Electronics, CONACYT, Mexico has collected the Baby Chillanto database [6]. It has five types of cry signals, which include normal, asphyxia, deaf, pain and hungry. There are 2268 cry signals available in the Baby Chillanto database. The other database, which is used in several literatures, is the Dunstan Baby Language database. The database is named after the Priscilla Dunstan, the inventor of the Dunstan Baby Language Theory [13]. There are 315 wav files, which are sampled at 16kHz. This database consists of utterances of five "Dustan Words" like "Neh", "Eh", "Oah" "Eairh", and "Heh" viz., hungry, burp, tired, stomach pain, and discomfort.

The names of some other databases are: i) Donate A Cry, which consists of 457 cry samples; ii) CRIED, which consists of total 2838 data samples; iii) iCOPE database, which consists of 113 data samples; iv) Chatter Baby database, which consists of 1071 data samples; and v) SPLANN database, which consists of 13373 data samples. In a similar manner, there are several self-recorded databases available, which are recorded by first-time parents, recorded in the neonatal intensive care unit (NICU) of a hospital.

2.3 Methodology

In this work, an automatic baby cry detection system is developed by using the features extracted from the cry signals. Even though several classical and deep learning approaches are used in literature, the efficiency of the system is not sufficient in real time. In this work, both machine learning and neuro computing approaches are used to improve the performance.

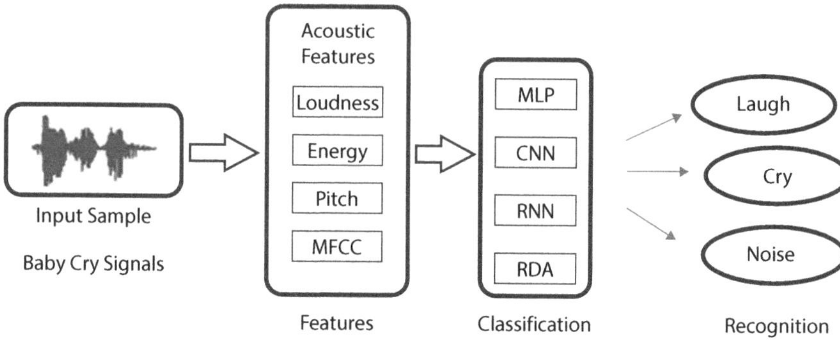

Figure 2.1 Block diagram for infant cry detection system.

The deep neural network (DNN) with several layers in end-to-end fashion is used. A regularization technique is used to reduce the singularity problem, which occurs due to high dimensionality. A selection of appropriate hyper parameters with back propagation in training the DNN will improve the performance of the automatic baby cry detection system.

The research behind the baby cry involves collecting data, pre-processing, extraction of features, optimum feature selection, and classification. It is very difficult to collect the data samples of a baby cry as the data is very sensitive. So, it is required to gather the data samples from newborn babies in hospitals. Pre-processing is applied to remove the noise from those collected samples to build the database. The proposed methodology for infant cry detection system is shown in Figure 2.1. Initially sound signals are segmented into frames and extracted short time energy, MPCC, and spectrogram features. Several classification algorithms are used to classify these extracted features and predict whether the given sound signal is infant cry, noise (human voice other than infant) or laugh (no voice signal or equipment noise). Nowadays, neuro computing algorithms are extremely prominent and well fit for most datasets with their deep architectures like DNN, CNN, and RNN. The proposed RDA is also a powerful algorithm to achieve the better performance.

2.3.1 Database

The database consists of a few seconds of soundtrack recordings made by the parents of infants. Infants' samples are recorded and pre-processed to remove the disturbances present in the signal. It includes babies' crying, laughing, sounds other than infant cries, which are considered as noise signal class of audio files.

A crying baby folder consists of crying sounds in various situations like pain, hunger, and discomfort. There are a total 283 audio files in the dataset, and each audio file consists of a minimum of 5 seconds in audio data. Among these 283 audio files, 68 audio files are from infant cry, 107 audio files are from infant laugh, and 108 audio files arc from a noisy class.

2.3.2 Feature Extraction

The extraction of discriminative features from audio files is a very important stage in feature extraction and later feeding these extracted features to the machine learning and deep learning techniques. It is a very crucial step to improve the performance of the classification techniques for infant cry detection and analysis. Short term energy-based features are one of the prosodic features, which are very useful and straightforward when detecting the cry based on the energy, but these are not robust to the background noise and variations within infant cry. To overcome this, frequency domain or spectral features are used along with the short-term energy to model the detection system. Most used spectral features are MFCC and spectrograms.

Here, the input signal is divided into frames of size 25ms with an overlap of 10ms. Instead of taking the full signal, taking 25ms width is good enough to extract the relatively stationary features to capture required information. An overlap of 10ms is useful to capture the dynamics among the frames.

2.3.2.1 Short-Term Energy

Infant cry signals differ from child to child, and the variations in the waveforms can be observed mostly in the energy. This energy represents the amplitude variations of the signal instead of taking the entire signal. Energy signal is defined as integral to the squared signal during the time. So, the short-term energy has a unit, which is the square of the unit of the original signal [11]. If an infant cries loudly, the signal itself shows the energy that the infant used. Energy is a key indicator in detecting a baby's cry, as infants often express discomfort or pain through changes in the intensity of their cries. To calculate the energy of a given audio signal, there is a need to consider sound power per area, and it needs a variable to store distance from microphone to the source. These features are important to detect the presence of cries from the other sound signals with endpoints of speech utterances since the amplitude of an audio signal varies with time. Figure 2.2 represents the detection of the cry portion from the given signal.

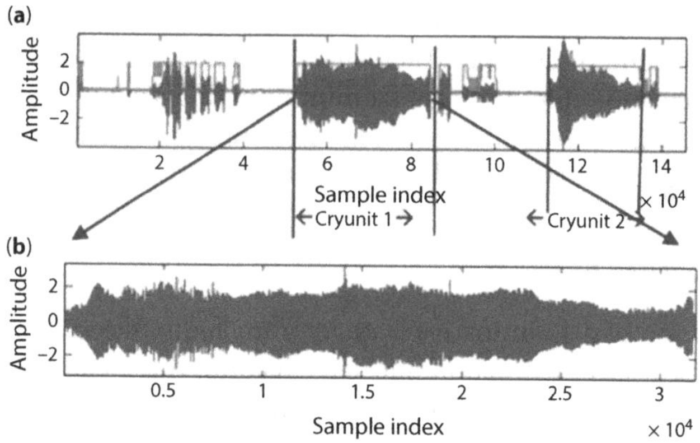

Figure 2.2 A segmentation of an audio sample into frames to extract a cry unit.

2.3.2.2 Mel-Frequency Cepstral Coefficients

The MFCC is one of the widely used feature extraction method in speech processing. Present research aims to identify performance enhancements using MFCC features. One of the most recent MFCC implementations is the Delta–Delta MFCC, which improves the performance and robustness of the application. The MFCC is a feature set that describes the shape of the short-term speech spectrum using a small vector of weights.

To calculate the MFCC features, the mel scale mimics how the human ear works. Based on literature, humans do not perceive frequencies on a linear scale. Humans are better at detecting differences at lower frequencies than at higher frequencies.

The MFCC can be obtained using the following steps.

The input signal is divided into frames for calculating the energy of each frame.

- After the framing, a hamming window is applied to remove the spectral leakages and unusual discontinuity in the signal due to framing.
- Short Term Fourier Transform (STFT) is used to convert the time domain signal into frequency domain signal, and it reflects the power of the speech at each frequency.
- A triangular-shaped, equally spaced band pass filter bank is used to get the power spectrum and then calculate the log of the filtered spectrum to reduce the non- significant acoustic variants.

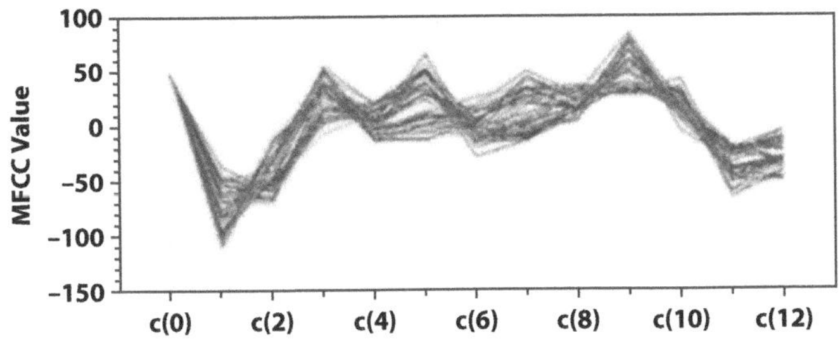

Figure 2.3 Extracted MFCC features for a given cry sample.

- Finally apply the discrete cosine transform (DCT) to find uncorrelated features.

The first DCT coefficient gives the average power of the spectrum, and the next few coefficients are useful to find the spectral shape. The higher order coefficients represent the finer spectral details of the speech signal. This work considers the first 20 feature values from each frame and discards the remaining values. Dynamic features such as delta and double delta features are calculated from these 20 MFCC features along with short-term energy feature. To improve the accuracy of the classification system, there is a need to calculate the statistical features such as the mean and the variance of the MFCC. The sample MFCC is shown in the Figure 2.3.

2.3.2.3 Spectrograms

Along with the prosody (time domain) and spectral (frequency domain) features, the time- frequency domain representation of the signal will also be useful to analyze. For that, the spectrogram is the standard technique. The magnitude square of the STFT gives a spectrogram (with change in colors based on magnitude). A spectrogram is a visual form of representing energy and the loudness of frequencies of signal as it varies with time. It is easy to analyze the energy levels in the audio file using spectrograms. It represents the distribution of frequencies present in the signal changes over time. A spectrogram is also depicted as a heat map because it shows intensity as an image with varying colors and brightness. Colors in the spectrogram indicate vertical displacement. The color on the left side indicates the color scheme used. The sample spectrograms obtained are shown in the Figures 2.4, 2.5, and 2.6.

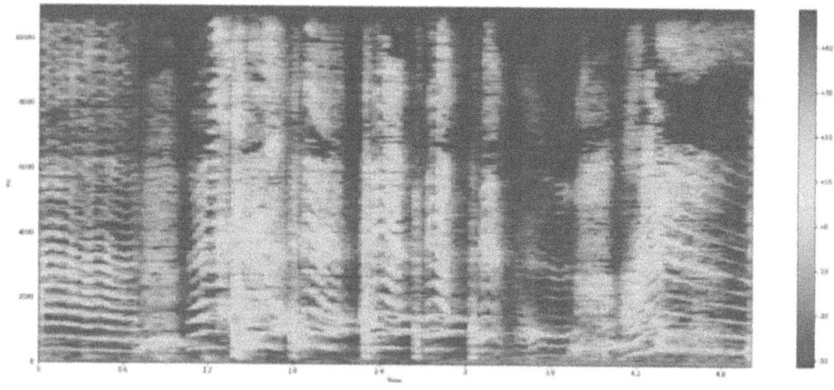

Figure 2.4 Extracting the cry feature from a data sample using a spectrogram.

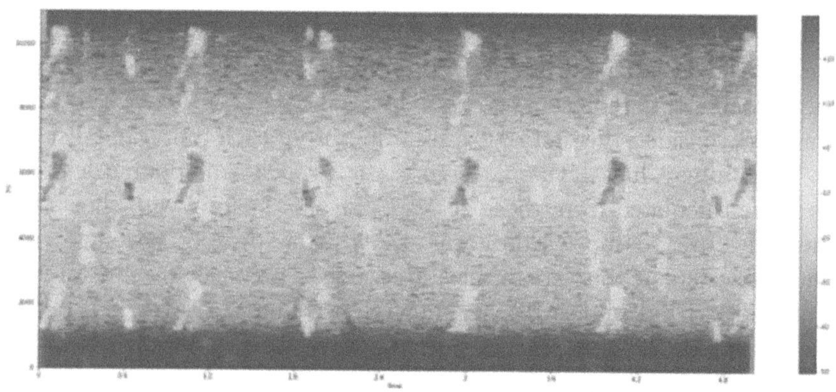

Figure 2.5 Extracting the laugh feature from a data sample using a spectrogram.

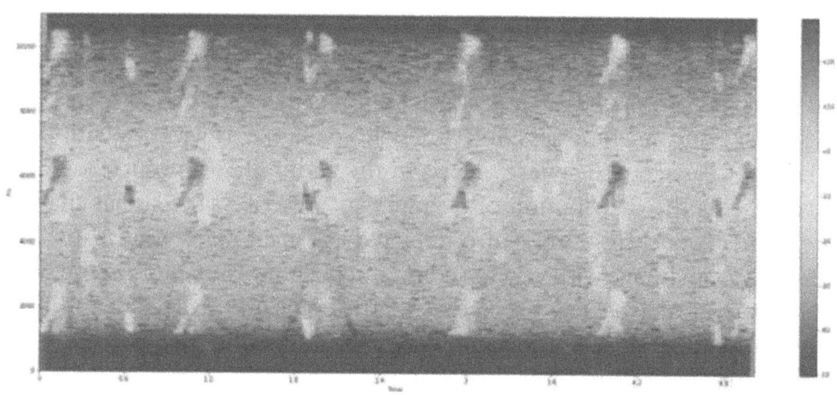

Figure 2.6 Extracting the noise feature from a data sample using a spectrogram.

Figure 2.5 represents the spectrogram of the infant laugh audio signal. A baby's laugh follows a particular pattern. During regions of silence, and at frequency regions where there is little energy, the spectrogram appears white or in a light color. During the regions of laugh or high energy signals, the spectrogram appears in dark red/orange color. Figure 2.4 shows the excitation or sudden changes in the frequency of the audio signal, when the infant is crying.

Figure 2.6 refers to the silence in the audio signal except noise. Noise is distributed uniformly. Therefore, there are no sudden variations in the spectrogram.

2.3.3 Classification

The RDA, RNN, MLP, and CNN are used as classification algorithms for the infant cry detection system. The acoustic features extracted from the frames are given as input to the classification algorithms to detect the cry. These classification algorithms are very efficient and are used in several applications like image processing and speech processing. The cry detection system requires a huge dataset with a significant number of data samples. A high dimensional dataset consists of correlated features, which are reduced by using a dimensionality reduction technique. Covariance and correlation matrices are calculated for RDA for reducing the dimensionality without losing any information. This can be done by projecting the data samples into a lower dimensional space. This reduced feature vector is used for efficient classification of the samples. Finally, it will classify whether these samples belong to cry, noise, or laugh.

2.3.4 Convolutional Neural Network (CNN)

The CNN is a type of DNN, which is most widely used for image classification, object recognition, image segmentation, etc. It consists of one or more convolutional layers, pooling layers and fully connected layers. In classical neural networks, the extracted features are given as input to the input layer, the processing will be done in the hidden layers, and then the output will be generated at the output layer. But in CNN, the feature extraction will be done automatically from the input data. The filters are used to perform the convolution operation, the extracted features are given as input to the pooling layer. In this layer, the dimensionality of the data is reduced without losing the information. The extracted information will be given as input to the nonlinear activation function like Sigmoid, Rectified Linear Unit (ReLU) and tanh for performing threshold operation. The complexity of the network will be reduced by the pooling layer. There are different types of pooling techniques available (max pooling, average pooling etc.). Max pooling will take the highest value among the existing values, and average pooling will take the average value within that filter. In this work, max pooling is used after the ReLU threshold operation.

The extracted information will be given as input to the fully connected layer where the SoftMax function is used as an activation function in order to process the data samples. Here, the SoftMax layer is used to classify the given audio signal that belongs to an infant cry, infant laugh, or noise class. As shown in Figure 2.7, the convolution layer and pooling layer are used in the extraction of features, and classification is done in a fully connected layer. Layer information is shown in Figure 2.8. In this work, keras is used to build the CNN model. To extract the features, convolutional layer and pooling layer are used. In the convolution layer, 32 filters with kernel size 3 are used. The kernel size is fixed so that the extracted images size will be reduced based on the kernel size. If more features are extracted, multiple kernels need to be added. In the pooling layer, the size of the image is

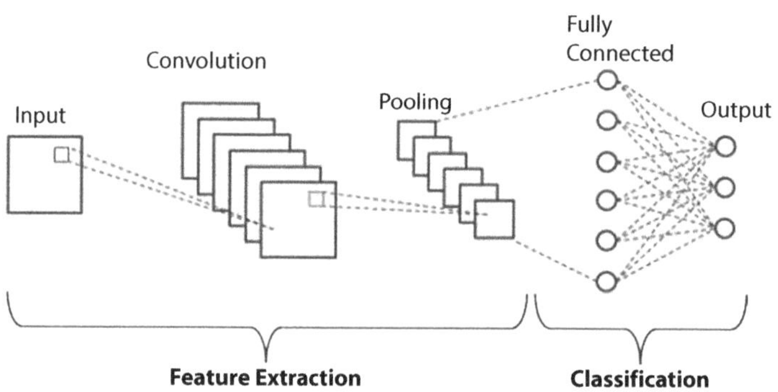

Figure 2.7 The process followed in a convolutional neural network.

Parameters	Input Layer	Output Layer
Input	[71*180]	[11*180]
Output	[11*180]	[11*180]
Activation	tanh	softmax
Batch Size	256	256
Learning rate	constant	constant
Alpha	0.01	0.01
Maxiter	1024	1024
Momentum	0.9	0.9

Figure 2.8 Input and output layer details in a convolutional neural network.

reduced using Max Pooling. After the completion of pooling, an image is converted to the column vector by using the flatten layer. A fully connected layer will combine all the outputs from the convolutional layer and pooling layer using dense with 128 units. The Soft Max activation function in the output layer combines all values into one single unit and predicts the class label of the given audio sample.

2.3.5 Recurrent Neural Network (RNN)

A recurrent neural network or RNN is a class of DNN. It can use their internal state memory to process variable length sequences of inputs. This makes them applicable to tasks connected to recognition. The term RNN is used to refer to the class of networks with an infinite impulse response.

The RNN is most suitable for any type of sequence data or time series data. The storage of information is possible with the help of hidden units. Input units, hidden units, and output units are the components of RNN, and most of the information is processed in hidden units. It has feedback connections. It can process not only single data points but also entire sequences of data such as speech or video. It will store and use previous state information to generate the next output sequence.

The proposed model consists of four long short-term memory (LSTM) layers with 50 units and a dropout of 0.2, and an output layer as a fully connected layer. To optimize the efficiency of the algorithm, the Adam optimizer is used. The mean square error is used to calculate the loss function. The model is trained with 100 epochs and a batch size of 32. Energy and MFCC features and their corresponding class labels are given as input to this model. An estimate of 70% of the data is used for training, and the remaining 30% of the data is used for testing. The training data was further divided into training and validation data, where the validation set is 20% of training set. The samples considered are crying, noise, and laughter, and the features used here are energy and MFCC. This RNN model is implemented to predict the suitable class on the dataset.

2.3.6 Regularized Discriminant Analysis (RDA)

Regularized discriminant analysis or RDA is a dimensionality reduction technique in machine learning. This technique is used as a pre-processing step to extract the appropriate features required to classify the audio sample. The procedure for the RDA is an extension of the LDA, which eliminates the drawbacks that occur in the LDA. The block diagram of the RDA is shown in Figure 2.9. Linear Discriminant Analysis (LDA) is applicable

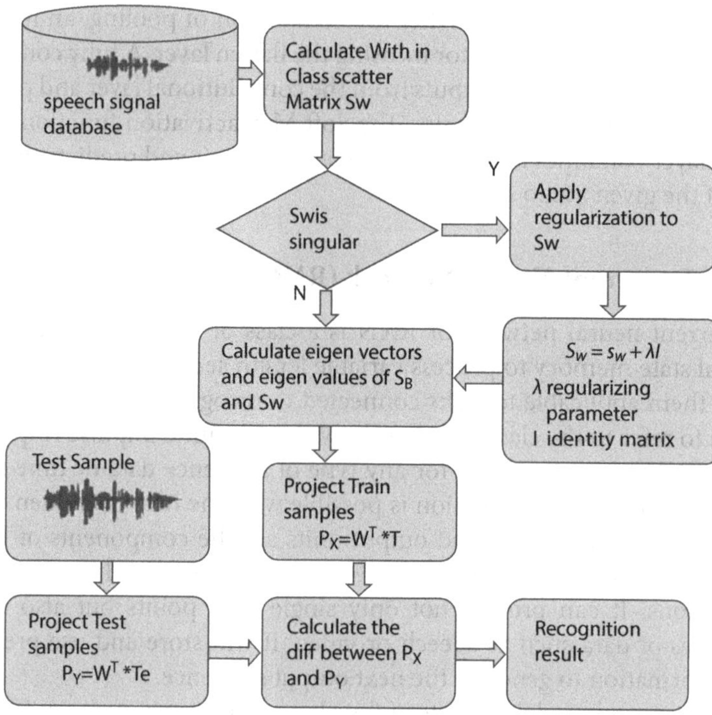

Figure 2.9 A schematic diagram of steps followed in the regularized discriminant analysis.

when the within-class covariance matrix S_w is non singular. In contrast, Regularized Discriminant Analysis (RDA) should be used if the covariance matrix S_w is singular. The main idea behind this RDA is to add a constant λ to the diagonal elements in class scatter matrix

$$S_w = S_w + \lambda I \tag{2.1}$$

where λ is the regularized parameter, which is relatively small in such a way that S_w is a positive definite. The S_w is with in class covariance matrix, and I is the Identity Matrix. The value of λ considered is 0.001. The estimation of the regularization parameter value is very difficult as lower values of λ, and they will not solve the singularity problem. For higher values of λ will disturb the information in the class scatter matrix in LDA. The transformation matrix $_W$ is computed by using within class and between class scatter matrices S_w and S_b. Once the transformation matrix W is given, the speech samples are projected onto the matrix $_W$. After the projection, the distance between each train speech sample and the test speech sample is calculated by using the Euclidian distance measure. The minimum value among them will classify the result. The RDA is a regularization technique, which is particularly used when there are many features that are potentially correlated. As shown in Figure 2.9, the audio files are taken as input, and these are processed into RDA, and then by considering the eigen value objectives, the discriminant analysis accuracy improves.

2.3.7 Multi-Layer Perceptron (MLP)

The MLP uses a back propagation technique for training the data. There are three layers of nodes in the MLP. The data is fed to the input layer, and there are many other hidden layers that provide levels of abstraction and predictions made on the output layer also known as a visible layer. Except for the input node, every other node is a neuron that uses a non-linear activation function. It can distinguish data that is not linearly separable. In MLP, there are too many parameters because it is fully connected to one another in every way resulting in redundancy and inefficiency.

2.4 Experimental Results

As several infant cry databases exist in the literature, this work concentrated to do the research by collecting the sampling in non-standard environment also gives the appropriate solution for consoling the baby immediately. The rate of pattern changes in the data sample is used to detect the baby cry signal. This work is concentrated on collecting the various patterns of babies' cries for different audio samples and, based on that a model, is being created with available samples. The classification techniques such as MLP, CNNs, RNNs and proposed RDA are used to build the model with various features. The RDA is used to reduce the intra class scatter matrix and increase the inter class scatter matrix to improve the performance of the model. The available data samples are divided into training and testing data to evaluate the algorithms. Using the performance of the deep learning techniques, hyper parameter tuning, and back propagation are used to increase the performance of the model and to reduce the error of the model. There are two important values to be measured for evaluation of confusion matrices. They are true positive and false positive rates. True positive is defined as the ratio between the total number of actual features files to the total number of predicted features files. There are 68 infant crying files, 107 noise files, and 108 laugh files out of 283 audio files from the taken dataset.

The Table 2.2 shows the confusion matrix for MLP, RNN, CNN, and the proposed RDA. The MFCC features are extracted for all audio samples, 64 audio files are predicted as crying files through MLP. A total of 101 audio files are correctly predicted as noise, and 103 audio files predicted as laughter. For RNN, energy and MFCC features are extracted for all samples. From Table 2.2, the confusion matrix of the RNN has predicted 50 crying files, 99 noise files, and 95 laughter files. The confusion matrix for CNN and RDA are shown in Table 2.2. The confusion matrix shows that the RDA with energy+ MFCC and CNN with spectrogram techniques outperforms the MLP and RNN techniques. From Table 2.3, experimental results of proposed RDA with MFCC features outperform all implemented techniques with an accuracy of 96.46%.

Figure 2.10 shows the performance comparison of various classification techniques on the given dataset.

Table 2.2 A comparison of various existing cry detection techniques.

Classifier	**MLP**			**RNN**			**CNN**			**RDA**		
Classes	C	N	L	C	N	L	C	N	L	C	N	L
C	64	2	2	50	10	8	65	1	2	66	1	1
N	4	101	2	7	99	1	1	6	101	2	103	2
L	1	2	103	9	4	95	95	1	5	1	5	104

Table 2.3 A comparison of various existing cry detection techniques.

S. no.	**Algorithm**	**Accuracy**
1	Spectrogram+ CNN	95.75%
2	Energy+MFCC+RNN	86.21%
3	MFCC+MLP	94.34%
4	MFCC+RDA	96.46%

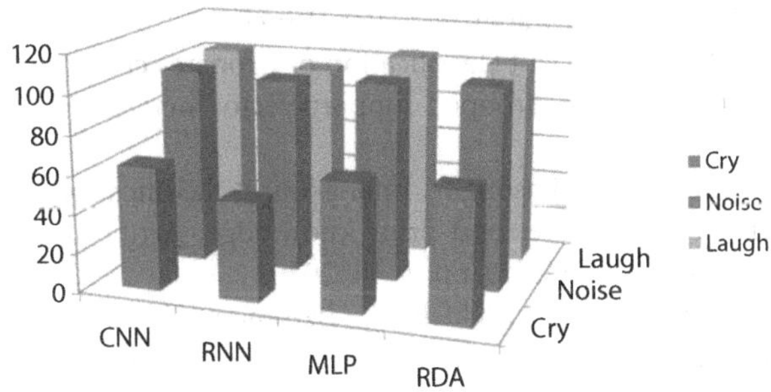

Figure 2.10 A performance comparison of various algorithms with the proposed RDA technique.

2.5 Conclusion

Experiments are conducted using machine learning and deep learning techniques. The proposed RDA is compared with existing techniques such as MLP, CNN, and RNN to calculate the accuracy of the classification on the infant cry datasets. The RDA outperforms other deep learning and machine learning methods. Here, different features are extracted to test the performance. The proposed system can classify the infant cry signal from other noisy and laughing signals in the dataset. The dynamic complex process integrated with a screening tool in the presence of appropriate medical staff inside a clinical environment is required to achieve better accuracy. Our recent study on different infant cry detection papers states that many machine learning algorithms are used, and a different set of features are extracted, which help us know different kinds of diseases are also responsible for infant cries apart from crying from normal situations like feelings of hunger, pain, fuzziness. This work mainly focused on the identification of infant cry signals instead of finding the reason behind the cries. Further research can be extended to identify the reason behind the cries.

References

1. Abou-Abbas, L., Tadj, C., Fersaie, H.A., A fully automated approach for baby cry signal segmentation and boundary detection of expiratory and inspiratory episodes. *J. Acoust. Soc. Am.*, 142, 3, 1318–1331, 2017.
2. Jean Ayres, A. and Robbins, J., *Sensory integration and the child: Understanding hidden sensory challenges*, Western psychological services, California, United States, 2005

3. Chang, C.-Y., Bhattacharya, S., Raj Vincent, P.M., Lakshmanna, K., Srinivasan, K., An efficient classification of neonates cry using extreme gradient boosting-assisted grouped-support-vector network. *J. Healthc. Eng.*, 1–14, 2021.
4. Xiao, X., Pan, Y., Ji, C., Basodi, S., Infant sound classification on multi- stage cnns with hybrid features and prior knowledge. *Artificial Intelligence and Mobile Services - AIMS 2020*, pp. 3–16, 2020.
5. Cohen, R., Ruinskiy, D., Zickfeld, J., IJzerman, H., Lavner, Y., Baby cry detection: deep learning and classical approaches, in: W. Pedrycz, S.-M. Chen (Eds.), *Development and analysis of deep learning architectures*, pp. 171–196, Springer International Publishing, Cham, 2020, 10.1007/978-3-030-31764-5_7.
6. Dewi, S.P., Prasasti, A.L., Irawan, B., The study of baby crying analysis using mfcc and lfcc in different classification methods, in: *2019 IEEE International Conference on Signals and Systems (ICSigSys)*, IEEE, pp. 18–23, 2019.
7. Dharwadkar, N.V., Dixit, A.A., Kannur, A.K., Kadampur, M.A.B., Joshi, S., Identification of reasons behind infant crying using acoustic signal processing and deep neural network for neonatal intensive care unit. *Int. J. Inf. Retr. Res. (IJIRR)*, 12, 1, 1–17, 2022.
8. Floridi, L., Ai and its new winter: from myths to realities. *Philos. Technol.*, 33, 1–3, 2020.
9. Foo, L.S., Yap, W.-S., Hum, Y.C., Kadim, Z., Hon, H.W., Tee, Y.K., Real-time baby crying detection in the noisy everyday environment, in: *2020 11th IEEE Control and System Graduate Research Colloquium (ICSGRC)*, IEEE, pp. 26–31, 2020.
10. Krishnan, S., Sharma, G., Umapathy, K., Infant cry classification using cnn – rnn. 4th International Seminar on Sensors, Instrumentation, Measurement and Metrology. *J. Phys. Conf. Ser.*, 1528, 1–6, 2020.
11. Krishnan, S., Sharma, G., Umapathy, K., Trends in audio signal feature extraction methods. *Appl. Acoust.*, 158, 1–21, 2020.
12. Hariharan, M., Saraswathy, J., Sindhu, R., Khairunizam, W., Yaacob, S., Infant cry classification to identify asphyxia using timefrequency analysis and radial basis neural networks. *Expert Syst. Appl.*, 39, 10, 9515–9523, 2012.
13. Hariharan, M., Sindhu, R., Yaacob, S., Normal and hypoacoustic infant cry signal classification using time–frequency analysis and general regression neural network. *Comput. Methods Programs Biomed.*, 108, 2, 559–569, 2012.
14. Ji, C., Infant cry signal processing, analysis, and classification with artificial neural networks, 2021.
15. Ji, C., Bamunu Mudiyanselage, T., Gao, Y., Pan, Y., A review of infant cry analysis and classification. *EURASIP J. Audio Speech Music Process.*, 2021, 1, 1–17, 2021.
16. Lavner, Y., Cohen, R., Ruinskiy, D., IJzerman, H., Baby cry detection in domestic environment using deep learning, in: *2016 IEEE international conference on the science of electrical engineering (ICSEE)*, IEEE, pp. 1–5, 2016.

17. Liang, Y.-C., Wijaya, I., Yang, M.-T., Juarez, J.R.C., Chang, H.-T., Deep learning for infant cry recognition. *Int. J. Environ. Res. Public Health*, 19, 10, 6311, 2022.
18. Priyanka, M.J. and Anjum, M., Baby motion and cry detection. *Int. J. Eng. Res. Technol. (IJERT)*, 8, 14, 2020.

3

Improved Brain Tumor Segmentation Utilizing a Layered CNN Model

Bilal Hikmat Rasheed[1*] and P. Sudhakaran[2]

[1]Department of Computer Science, Cihan University – Duhok, Duhok, Kurdistan Region, Iraq

[2]Department of Computer Science and Engineering, SRM TRP Engineering College, Trichy, India

Abstract

In medical imaging, automatic brain tumor segmentation from MR images is essential for examining and monitoring the disease development. When gliomas are benign and malignant, appropriate and effectual segmentation approaches are needed for resourceful tumor delineation into multiple classes. With the growing advancements in deep learning, various learning algorithms perform the semantic segmentation tasks more effectually in contrast to traditional context-based computer vision techniques. Generally, convolutional neural networks (CNN) is extensively utilized for a biomedical image segmentation process where it shows better prediction accuracy in brain tumor segmentation tasks. Here, the CNN model is adopted with multiple layers to attain better prediction accuracy. The models are trained separately with the online available dataset to acquire better segmentation with considerable tumor subregion segmentation. The recommended CNN model attains the finest dice score for improving the tumor core, entire tumor, and tumor enhancement on the validation set with a favorable performance while comparing prevailing architectures.

***Keywords*:** Segmentation, brain tumor, malignant, CNN

**Corresponding author*: bilal.rasheed@duhokcihan.edu.krd

R. Nidhya, D. Pavithra, Manish Kumar, A. Dinesh Kumar and S. Balamurugan (eds.) Generative Artificial Intelligence: Concepts and Applications, (39–52) © 2025 Scrivener Publishing LLC

3.1 Introduction

With rising advancements in medical imaging, tumor segmentation offers essential information for the diagnosis and analysis of tumors for mapping treatment monitoring and options of disease progression [1]. Brain tumors are among one of the most dangerous cancers considered globally and are classified based on the origin of primary and secondary tumors. The generalized form of histological regions of preliminary brain cancer is known as a glioma, which initiates from glial attributes and cells of 85% of malignant brain tumors [2]. Gliomas are a gradually progressing lower-grade tumor with a superior patient prognosis and is aggressive towards glioblastoma and higher-grade glioma that requires instant treatment [3]. These tumors are related to substantial morbidity where the median patient survival with glioblastoma is with a 10-years survival rate over nil despite maximum medical and surgical therapy [4]. The timely diagnosis is considered to be imperative for effectual patient treatment.

Magnetic resonance imaging (MRI) is a considerable approach, which extensively uses radiologists for the assessment and computation of brain tumors [5]. It offers diverse complimentary MRI modalities attained based on an excitation degree and repetitive manner that is T1-weighted, T2-weighted, and fluid attenuation inversion recovery post-contrast T1 weighted model recovery [6]. The highlighted sub-regions of the tumor over various intensities with higher sequencing orders like a complete tumor and tumor inclusive iterative oedema is extremely prominent to T2 modalities and FLAIR. However, T1 images provide tumor core with peri-tumoral oedema [7]. It facilitates the integration of scans and complementary information that are delivered from the prediction of various tumor regions.

Multi-modal tumor segmentation challenges is an essential platform to compute the enhancement of machine learning approaches for tumor segmentation process, which facilitates the volunteers with improved modelling of MRI dataset of gliomas (higher-grade glioma and lower-grade glioma) and related ground truth annotated by expert physicians [8]. The offered multi-modal scans are utilized for both the validation and training purpose over the modeling of a neural network for a certain segmentation task.

The manual detection process of brain tumor segmentation from the online available MRI scans is a subjective task [9]. Thus, it is completely prone to variability and inefficient time consumption. The automated segmentation of tumors from multi-modal MRI images can help physicians surgically enhance and improve the diagnosis rate along with an appropriate and reproducible outcome for better tumor monitoring and analysis. The traditional techniques of automatic brain tumor segmentation rely on feature engineering, which includes handcrafted feature extraction from input images by training the classifiers [10]. The unsupervised learning approaches bypass the designing complexity and choose the feature by learning the model automatically with hierarchical feature specification by excelling deep learning models. A convolutional neural network (CNN) is considered as a well-known approach to brain tumor segmentation as it learns the most appropriate and resourceful features automatically.

Moreover, the appropriate segmentation of tumor regions are considered to be challenging factors owing to heterogeneity in appearance, shape, and size of gliomas along with a fuzzy and ambiguous boundary that prevails among the brain tissue and cancer. The MRI data intensity variability is considered to be a further complexity. Hence, it is still an open issue that facilitates exploration for superior segmentation approaches and accuracy.

In this investigation, the CNN model with multiple layers is adopted for an efficient brain tumor segmentation from multi-modal MRI scans and mapping probability for appropriate predictions. Networks are completely trained with hyper-parameters of all models over the available dataset attained from brain tumor segmentation challenges. The evaluation of the available dataset is an outcome as the anticipated CNN model can attain a better dice score for improving the tumor, tumor core, and entire core region, respectively.

The remaining parts are provided as Section 3.2 is Related Works; section 3.3 is Methodology; section 3.4 is Numerical Results and Discussion; section 3.5 is Conclusion with Future Research Directions.

3.2 Related Works

Recently, an enhancement in computer performance and constant development of machine learning approaches show various automatic and semi-automatic approaches for tumor segmentation, which need to be concentrated. Generally, deep learning approaches were used automatically for learning features with higher success in natural image processing; however, it is considered as a biological image processing.

Kansas *et al.*, [11], concentrated on the weighted clustering of an MRI image with brain tumor segmentation with dimensionality reduction by various generalized principal component analysis (PCA) algorithms. Ding *et al.* [12] utilized region growing and fuzzy c-means algorithms for automatic tumor image segmentation over meningioma patients. Huang *et al.* [13] generated a multi-stage fuzzy modeling structure for an accurate and automatic prediction of brain tumor from multi-modal 3D image data. Lin *et al.* [14] adopted the completely automatic approach, which used Gabor and an un-decimated wavelet transformation for segmenting MRI images.

The convolutional network adopts pixel information to predict the objects and maintains position invariant and global information by consistent layer addition. The features are learned automatically and use pre-estimation of probability distribution among the brain tumors via deep learning. Therefore, the shape and position information of brain tumors are attained effectively.

The conventional CNN-based segmentation model generally categorizes a single pixel with the utilization of image block over pixel as input. Moreover, conventional CNN-based approaches possess various demerits and outcomes in storage overhead. For instance, if the image block size is utilized for every pixel, the essential storage space is 225 times better than the original image. Also, it causes inefficient computation as image blocks of adjacent pixels are highly similar to those outcomes in waster computer resources. Also, the block size restricts the receptive area size as the size is much lesser than the size of the complete image, and certain local features are extracted.

To deal with this issue, Vemulapalli *et al.*, [15] anticipated fully CNN for segmenting images. The network pretends to deal with every pixel from the feature abstracted with extending classification process of image-level towards the pixel level [16]. The foremost deep learning approaches utilize shallow network architecture. Thus, certain underlying texture information is acquired and deep spatial features are eliminated. Thus, deep neural networks are completely complex during training purpose [17]. Some investigation concentrates on output layers where the complexity is to enhance network feedback. Thus, the shorter connection is essential for the network to make further optimization [18].

3.3 Methodology

Here, the anticipated CNN with a multi-layer model is considered for performing brain tumor segmentation. In this work, the brain tumor segmentation challenge dataset is used for training and validating the given samples. It is composed of 259 higher-grade and lower-grade glioma with ground truth values. The validation is performed with 125 unknown grade cases [19]. The images are attained from 19 diverse volunteers (MRI multi-modal scans) known as fluid-attenuated inversion recovery, contrast-enhanced and weighted models. The regions are segmented and processed to get rid of discrepancies to fulfil anatomical template and resolution re-sampling. The manual ground truth projects the tumor regions like non-enhancing core, enhancing core, and peritumoral oedema. The access towards the given dataset is limited and compared with prevailing approaches [20].

Here, a multi-layer CNN model is adopted for performing segmentation, and it gives higher benefits in terms of performance and results. The network outputs are segmented regions with certain sub-regions. It is merged with the final prediction model [21]. The layers of the CNN model is used for feature specification with volumetric segmentation. This multi-layered CNN model gives superior outcomes over the provided challenge. The anticipated model is fine-tuned for enhancing the segmentation process. The input sample is augmented with mirroring and cropping before providing it to multiple network layers. The model training is done with 150 epochs with a patch size and loss function variation, merging the dice loss by generalization. The hyper-parameters are fine-tuned with an input size of 128*128*128, the learning rate of $1*10^{-3}$, batch size of 5, an epoch of 120 respectively. The input data is applied for zero-padding as the original image is converted to 240*240*160, which is partitioned by the multiple layers of the network [22]. The mapping process is carried out for further prediction. The images are merged for mapping segmentation to provide the outcome of the prediction model. The CNN model is trained with the available dataset samples using the training and validation set. The segmentation mapping is performed to give the final prediction for tumor tissue, indeed of averaging the values. The dice cores of a complete tumor are 0.810, weighted tumor is 0.910, and core tumor is 0.870, respectively [23].

The proposed multi-layer CNN is used for segmenting the brain tumors to attain better classification accuracy by validating the set. The anticipated model gives favorable outcomes by attaining the dice score values like 0.810, 0.910, and 0.870, respectively. Multiple layers and their combinations are decided based on the CNN model by modifying the layers provided in conventional CNN architecture. However, it shows the worst classification accuracy [24]. The method needs to give favorable core tumor and tumor classes, respectively. Similarly, the threshold process is used to measure the threshold level, which set the investigators; when the value is lesser than the threshold value, then it is said as tumorless. If the value is higher than the level, then it is set as the lower level. But, some limitations are encountered in the prevailing approaches. The betterment of this method is validated by testing the clinical MRI data, which is independent of existing challenges. Similarly, the dataset is not pre-processed, and no proper post-processing is done. The imaging data is prepared via bias correction and intensity normalization to reduce data variability and comparability [25]. The post-processing methods like random fields are provided to improve segmentation accuracy. The robustness and efficiency of the model are exhibited with tumor segmentation with multiple regions. This work is intended to include image processing to tune hyper-parameters. Figure 3.1 shows the multi-layer CNN model, and Figure 3.2 depicts the block diagram of the multi-layer CNN model.

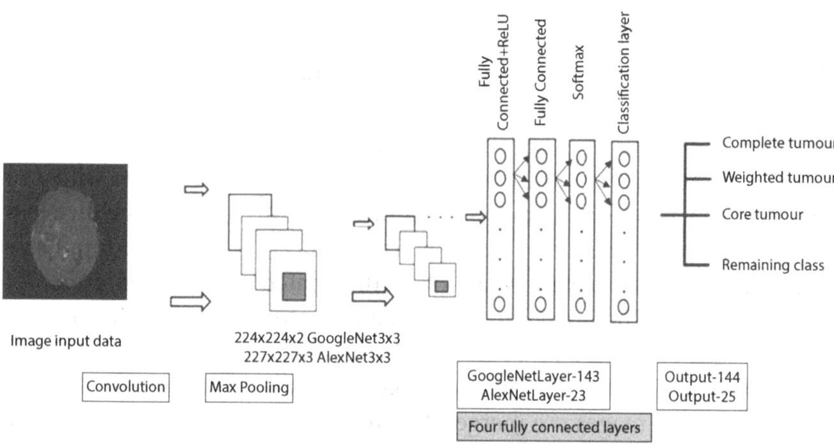

Figure 3.1 A multi-layer CNN model.

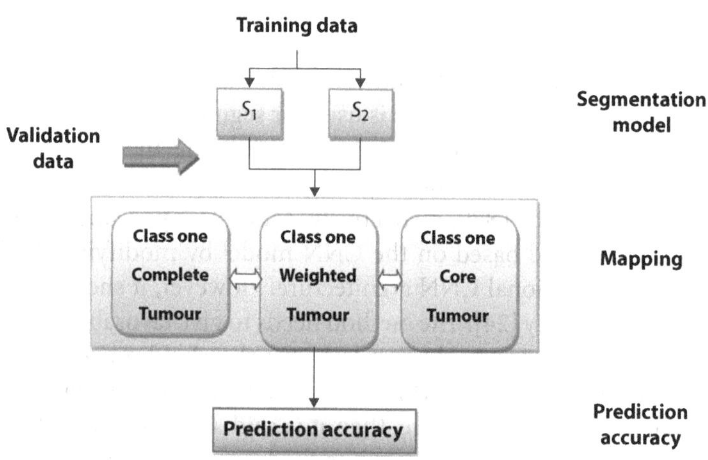

Figure 3.2 A block diagram of multi-layer CNN.

3.4 Numerical Results

The simulation is performed in MATLAB environment. Here, the proposed multi-layer CNN model is compared with fully convolutional network, residual inception dense network, U-Net, 3D multi-encoder and decoder network, CNN, and CNN-multilayer, respectively. There are three different classes known as a complete tumor, weighted tumor, and core tumor, respectively. The dice score of a complete tumor is 0.799, 0.780, 0.790, 0.76, 0.801, and 0.810. Similarly, a weighted tumor value is 0.900, 0.900, 0.898, 0.91, 0.900, and 0.910. Finally, a core tumor is 0.800, 0.790, 0.810, 0.85, 0.86, and 0.870, respectively. The dice score of an anticipated multi-layer CNN with the complete tumor is 0.810, the weighted tumor is 0.910, and core tumor is 0.870, which is higher than other models.

Table 3.1 depicts the comparison of a dice score of a multi-layer CNN with prevailing approaches. Figure 3.3 depicts five different process carried out during the segmentation process. Here, 3.3a is the original input image given for the segmentation process with an initial pre-processing step. Then, 3.3b is given into the multi-layer CNN model where the layers perform step by step process. Similarly, Figures 3.3c, 3.3d, and 3.3e show the concurrent process carried out during segmentation. The segmented regions are provided with three different classes. This process gives better segmentation accuracy.

Table 3.1 Comparison of a dice score of multi-layer CNN with prevailing approaches.

Approaches	Complete tumor	Weighted tumor	Core tumor
Fully convolutional network	0.799	0.900	0.800
Residual inception dense network	0.780	0.900	0.790
U-Net	0.790	0.898	0.810
3D multi-encoder and decoder network	0.76	0.91	0.85
CNN	0.801	0.900	0.86
CNN-multilayer	**0.810**	**0.910**	**0.870**

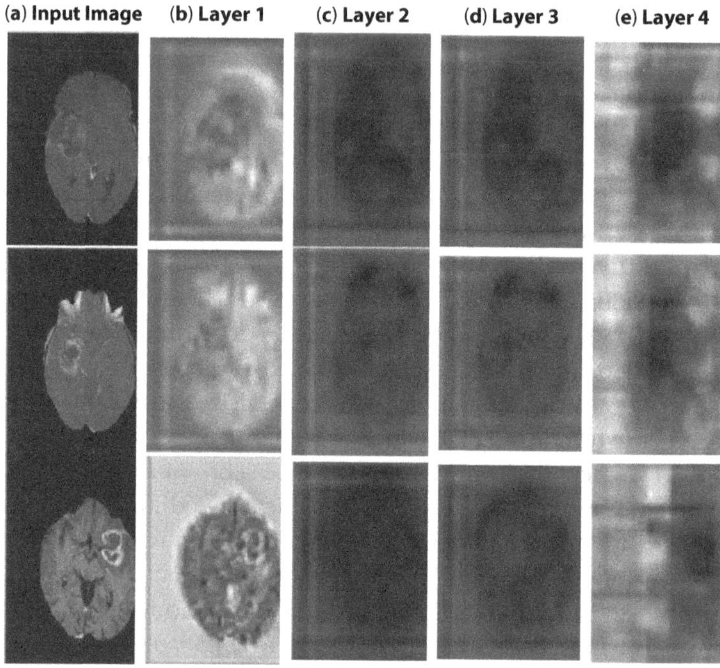

Figure 3.3 Multiple layers of brain tumor segmented images.

Figure 3.4 depicts the graphical representation of the core tumor extraction process. The evaluation is done with fully convolutional network (FCN), residual inception dense network, U-net, 3d multi-encoder and decoder network, CNN, and CNN multi-layer process. Figure 3.5 depicts the graphical representation of the weighted tumor extraction process. Figure 3.6 shows the core tumor extraction. Figure 3.7 shows the overall tumor extraction process along with the comparison. It is observed that the performance of the proposed model is higher when compared to existing approaches. It is noted in the above-given graphical representation. The segmentation process is considered as an essential part before performing classification. The modeling of an efficient segmentation process with deep learning approaches plays a crucial role in medical imaging. This process helps the physicians to find the disease in an earlier stage and provides a better decision-making process to save the lives of a human community [26].

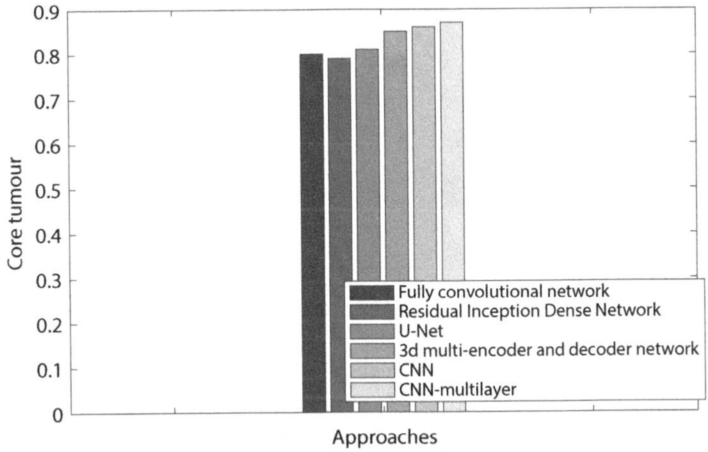

Figure 3.4 A core tumor extraction-based comparison.

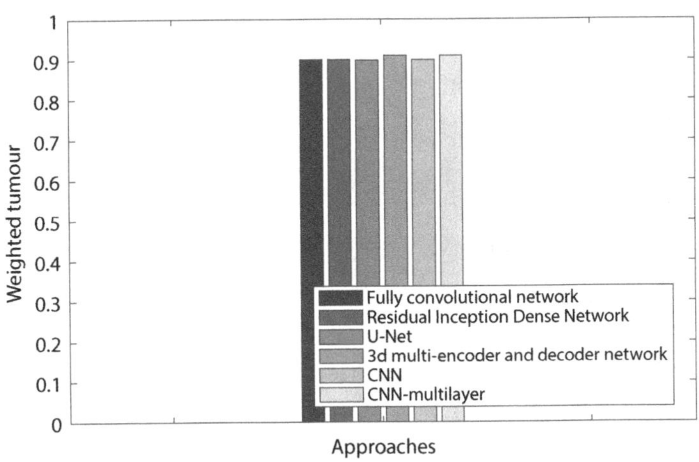

Figure 3.5 A weighted tumor extraction-based comparison.

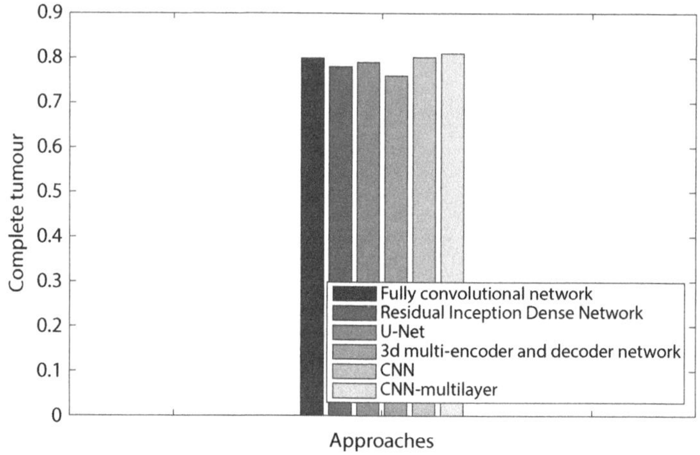

Figure 3.6 A complete tumor extraction-based comparison.

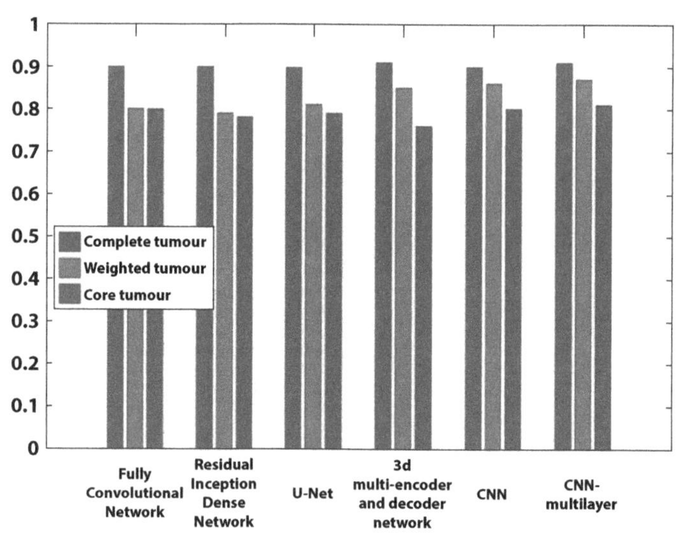

Figure 3.7 An overall comparison of the tumor extraction process.

3.5 Conclusion

In this investigation, an enhanced CNN model with a multi-layer design is proposed, which is adopted for performing a bio-medical based image segmentation process. The anticipated CNN with the multi-layer model can generate a superior segmentation process with brain tumor with online available MRI images, and the performance is evaluated and compared with various existing models. The proposed model gives superior prediction accuracy compared to prevailing approaches where the model gives superior scores. The proposed model offers the finest predictor approach and projects better segmentation task. This model helps the physicians to make appropriate patient management process and disease planning clinically.

References

1. Leece, Xu, J., Ostrom, Q.T., Chen, Y., Global incidence of malignant brain and other central nervous system tumors by histology, 2003_2007. *Neuro Oncol.*, 19, 11, 1553–1564, Oct. 2017.
2. Louis, and Perry, A., The 2016 World Health Organization classi_cation of tumours of the central nervous system: A summary. *Acta Neuropathol.*, 131, 6, 803–820, 2016.
3. Bakas, Segmentation labels and radiomic features for the pre-operative scans of the TCGA-LGG collection. *Cancer Imag. Arch.*, vol. 286, 2017.
4. Naceur, and Saouli, R., Fully automatic brain tumor segmentation using end-to-end incremental deep neural networks in MRI images. *Comput. Methods Programs Biomed.*, 166, 39–49, Nov. 2018.
5. Pereira, Pinto, A., Alves, V., Silva, C.A., Brain tumor segmentation using convolutional neural networks in MRI images. *IEEE Trans. Med. Imaging*, 35, 5, 1240–1251, May 2016.
6. Wang, Li, W., Ourselin, S., Vercauteren, T., Automatic brain tumor segmentation based on cascaded convolutional neural networks with uncertainty estimation. *Front. Comput. Neurosci.*, 13, 56, Aug. 2019.
7. Chen, Li, Y., Li, C., A visual detection method for foreign objects in power lines based on mask R-CNN. *Int. J. Ambient Comput. Intell.*, 11, 1, 34–47, Jan. 2020.
8. Raschke, T.R., Barrick, Tissue-type mapping of gliomas. *NeuroImage Clin.*, 21, 1–12, 2019.

9. Ji, Shen, Y., Ma, C., Gao, M., Scribble-based hierarchical weakly supervised learning for brain tumor segmentation, in: *Proc. Int. Conf. Med. Image Comput. Comput.-Assist. Intervent.*, pp. 175–183, 2019.
10. McKinley, Meier, R., Wiest, R., Ensembles of densely-connected CNNs with label-uncertainty for brain tumor segmentation, in: *Proc. Int. MICCAI Brainlesion Workshop*, p. 456_465, 2018.
11. Kamnitsas, and Ledig, C., Efficient multi-scale 3DCNN with fully connected CRF for accurate brain lesion segmentation. *Med. Image Anal.*, 36, 61–78, Feb. 2017.
12. Ding, Chen, F., Zhao, Y., Wu, Z., Zhang, C., Wu, D., A stacked multi-connection simple reducing net for brain tumor segmentation. *IEEE Access*, 7, 104011–104024, 2019.
13. Huang, Liu, Z., van der Maaten, L., Weinberger, K.Q., Densely connected convolutional networks, in: *Proc. IEEE Conf. Comput. Vis. Pattern Recognit.*, 2016.
14. Lin, Shen, C., Reid, I., van dan Hengel, A., Efficient piecewise training of deep structured models for semantic segmentation, in: *Proc. IEEE Conf. Comput. Vis. Pattern Recognit.*, pp. 3194–3203, 2016.
15. Vemulapalli, Tuzel, O., Liu, M.-Y., Chellappa, R., Gaussian conditional random field network for semantic segmentation, in: *Proc. IEEE Conf. Comput. Vis. Pattern Recognit.*, pp. 3224–3233, 2016.
16. Yuvaraj, D. and Hariharan, S., Content-based image retrieval based on integrating region segmentation and colour histogram. *Int. Arab J. Inf. Technol.*, 2, 11, 12, 2016.
17. Naveen Raju, D., Shanmugasundaram, H., Yuvaraj, D., Hybrid approach for melonama detection in dermoscopic images. *Mater. Today: Proc.*, 1–4, 2021.
18. Yuvaraj, D., Noori, S.F., Swaminathan, S., Multi-perspective scaling convolutional neural networks for high-resolution MRI brain image segmentation. *Mater. Today: Proc.*, 56–63, 2021.
19. Sundara Vadivel, P., Yuvaraj, D., Navaneetha Krishnan, S., Mathusudhanan, S.R., An efficient CBIR system based on colour histogram, edge, and texture features. *Concurrency Comput. Pract. Exper.*, 31, 12, e4994, 2019.
20. Yuvaraj, D., Sivaram, M., Karthikeyan, B., Abdulazeez, J., Shape, colour and texture-based CBIR system using the fuzzy logic classifier. *CMC-Comput. Mater. Continua*, 59, 3, 729–739, 2019.
21. Geetha, K. and Yuvaraj, D., A Novel Shape Feature Extraction Technique for Content-Based Image Retrieval (CBIR) Systems. *Int. J. Adv. Sci. Technol.*, 28, 2, 158–169, 2018.
22. Yuvaraj, D., Dinesh, K.R., Harirahan, S., Content-Based Image Retrieval: A Survey on the Start of Art. *Int. J. Eng. Sci. Res. Technol.*, 3, 8, 128–132, 2014.
23. Sivaram, M., Shanmugapriya, S., Yuvaraj, D., Porkodi, V., Akbari, A., Hashim, W., Huda, M., Decision Support System for Determining Academic Advisor Using Simple Additive Weighting, in: *Cognitive Informatics and Soft Computing*, pp. 149–156, Springer, Singapore, 2020.

24. Ahamed, B.B., Yuvaraj, D., Priya, S.S., Image Denoising With Linear and Non-linear Filters, in: *2019 International Conference on Computational Intelligence and Knowledge Economy (ICCIKE)*, pp. 806–810, 2019.
25. Subudhi, P. and Yuvaraj, D., A New Z-source Inverter for Application in Wind Energy Conversion System. *Turk. J. Physiother. Rehabil.*, 32, 2, 2640–2645, 20212021.
26. Yuvaraj, D., Priya, S.S., Braveen, M., Krishnan, S.N., Nachiyappan, S., Mehbodniya, A., Sivaram, M., Novel DoS Attack Detection Based on Trust Mode Authentication for IoT. *Intell. Autom. Soft Comput.*, 34, 3, 1505–1522, 2022.

4

Natural Language Processing in Generative Adversarial Network

P. Dhivya[1]*, A. Karthikeyan[2], S. Pradeep[2] and H. Umamaheswari[2]

[1]*Department of Computer Science and Engineering, Bannari Amman Institute of Technology, Sathyamangalam, Erode, Tamil Nadu, India*
[2]*Department of Electronics and Communication Engineering, SNS College of Technology, Coimbatore, Tamil Nadu, India*

Abstract
Natural language processing (NLP) has also been used in generative adversarial networks (GANs) to generate human-like text. These GANs have been used for generating realistic images, videos, and audio. Natural language processing and GAN can be combined to create innovative applications. By using NLP techniques in GANs, it is possible to improve the natural language generation and pre-process data, enhance semantic understanding, improve text-to-image generation, and increase flexibility. These NLP techniques can improve the quality of generated natural language text, making it more coherent and grammatically correct. Pre-processing text data with NLP techniques like tokenization, stemming, and POS tagging can remove noise and irrelevant information. Natural language processing can also help GANs understand the meaning of words and sentences in the text, which is useful for applications like sentiment analysis. Additionally, incorporating NLP techniques in GANs enables generating images based on textual descriptions. This is useful for generating realistic images of products based on descriptions. Moreover, NLP can help GANs be more flexible in generating text or images by allowing control over the style, tone, or topic of the generated text or images. This customization and personalization can be useful in various applications. The usage of NLP in GAN is demonstrated using three different datasets such as CLINC150, Animal dataset, and tennis_articles dataset. The performance of NLP with GAN is analyzed based on accuracy, loss respectively.

**Corresponding author*: dhivyap@bitsathy.ac.in

R. Nidhya, D. Pavithra, Manish Kumar, A. Dinesh Kumar and S. Balamurugan (eds.) Generative Artificial Intelligence: Concepts and Applications, (53–80) © 2025 Scrivener Publishing LLC

***Keywords*:** Generative adversarial transformer (GAT), natural language processing (NLP), sequence generative adversarial network (SeqGAN)

4.1 Introduction

Natural language processing (NLP) is a field of artificial intelligence (AI) that focuses on enabling computers to understand, interpret, and generate human language. It involves the application of computational techniques and algorithms to process and analyze natural language data, such as text, speech, and images.

Natural language processing is a broad and interdisciplinary field that draws upon various areas of study, including computer science, linguistics, cognitive psychology, and mathematics. Its primary goal is to bridge the gap between human language and computers, enabling machines to process and understand human language in a way that is similar to how humans do. Some of the key applications of NLP include sentiment analysis, text classification, machine translation, information extraction, question-answering systems, and chatbots. Natural language processing has been used in various industries, including healthcare, finance, marketing, and education, to improve efficiency, accuracy, and decision-making. The development of NLP has been driven by the rapid growth of data, particularly text data, and the need to automate language-related tasks. Advances in machine learning, deep learning, and neural networks have played a significant role in advancing the field of NLP and making it possible to process and analyze large volumes of text data. Overall, NLP has the potential to transform the way we interact with computers and enable machines to understand and communicate with humans in a more natural and intuitive way [1].

The architecture of NLP systems can vary depending on the specific application, but generally, NLP systems have the following components:

- Text pre-processing: This component involves cleaning and normalizing raw text data by removing stop words, punctuation, and other irrelevant information.
- Tokenization: This component involves breaking the text data into smaller units, such as words or phrases, known as tokens.
- Part-of-speech (POS) tagging: This component involves labeling each token with its corresponding part of speech, such as nouns, verbs, and adjectives.

- Named entity recognition (NER): This component involves identifying and extracting entities from the text, such as names of people, places, organizations, and other entities.
- Sentiment analysis: This component involves analyzing the sentiment or emotion expressed in the text, such as positive, negative, or neutral.
- Syntax and parsing: This component involves analyzing the structure of sentences and the relationships between words.
- Machine learning: This component involves training models on large datasets to automatically perform tasks such as classification, clustering, and prediction.
- Natural language generation (NLG): This component involves generating human-like text based on input data.

These components can be combined in various ways to build different types of NLP systems, such as chatbots, virtual assistants, and recommendation systems.

Generative adversarial networks (GANs) are a type of deep learning architecture that consists of two neural networks: a generator network and a discriminator network; these were first introduced by Ian Goodfellow and his colleagues in 2014 and have since become one of the most popular and powerful approaches to generative modeling. The generator network in a GAN is trained to generate new samples that are similar to a training dataset, such as images or text. The discriminator network is trained to distinguish between the generated samples and the real samples from the training dataset. The two networks are trained in an adversarial way, with the generator network trying to generate samples that can fool the discriminator network, and the discriminator network trying to correctly identify the real samples from the generated ones. The GAN architecture is based on game theory, where the generator network and discriminator network are playing a minimax game. The generator network tries to generate samples that can minimize the probability of the discriminator network correctly identifying the samples as generated, while the discriminator network tries to maximize its probability of correctly identifying the samples. Generative adversarial networks have been used to generate realistic images, music, and text, and they have shown impressive results in various applications, such as image and speech recognition, data augmentation, and data synthesis. They have also been used to address various problems, such as data imbalance, missing data, and data privacy [2].

Generative adversarial networks are a powerful class of machine learning models that have found numerous applications in various fields. For instance, in computer vision, GANs can be used to generate realistic images or videos, or to perform tasks such as image super-resolution or style transfer. In speech and audio processing, GANs can be applied to tasks such as speech synthesis or voice conversion. In NLP, GANs can be used for tasks such as text generation, machine translation, or text summarization.

Beyond these traditional areas, GANs have also been applied to many other domains such as finance, healthcare, or gaming. For instance, in finance, GANs can be used for tasks such as fraud detection or risk assessment. In healthcare, GANs can be applied to tasks such as medical image analysis or drug discovery. In gaming, GANs can be used to generate realistic game environments or to enhance the realism of game characters [15].

Another popular approach for NLP in GANs is the generative adversarial transformer (GAT), which is a framework that uses a transformer-based generator network and a discriminator network to generate high-quality text. The generator network takes a random noise vector as input and generates a sequence of word embeddings, which are then converted into text using a decoding algorithm. The discriminator network takes a sequence of text as input and outputs a probability that the text is real (generated by a human) or fake (generated by the generator network). In GAT, the generator network is trained to generate text that has high probabilities of being classified as real by the discriminator network. The discriminator network is trained to distinguish between real and fake text. The generator network is updated based on the feedback from the discriminator network, and the discriminator network is updated based on the feedback from both the real and fake text [8].

Natural language processing can be integrated into GAN models to generate realistic textual data such as product descriptions, news articles, and social media posts. One way to use NLP in GANs is to use a sequence-to-sequence (Seq2Seq) model.

The Seq2Seq model consists of two main components: an encoder and a decoder. The encoder takes in a sequence of words and converts it into a fixed-length vector representation. The decoder then takes this vector representation and generates a sequence of words.

In the context of GANs, the generator network can be trained to generate sequences of words using the Seq2Seq model. The discriminator network can then be trained to distinguish between the generated sequences and real sequences of words. By training the generator and discriminator networks in an adversarial manner, the generator learns to generate realistic sequences of words that can fool the discriminator. Another approach is to use a language model like the generative pre-trained transformer (GPT) in the generator network of GANs. It is a state-of-the-art language model that has been pre-trained on a large corpus of text. It can be fine-tuned on a specific task such as generating realistic text using the GANs framework. Overall, integrating NLP into GANs models can lead to exciting possibilities in generating realistic textual data for various applications [1, 2].

4.2 Literature Survey

Text generation is a key aspect of many NLP applications, including language modeling, text summarization, and machine translation. While generative adversarial networks (GANs) have achieved great success in generating high-quality images in computer vision, their application to NLP is more challenging due to the discrete nature of text. To address this challenge, we propose a method that uses knowledge distillation to effectively leverage the GAN setup for text generation. Specifically, we use autoencoders to provide a continuous representation of sentences that assigns non-zero probabilities to multiple words, resulting in a smooth representation. We then distill this representation to train the generator to produce similar smooth representations.

Through a series of experiments on various datasets, we demonstrate that our approach outperforms traditional GAN-based text generation approaches that do not utilize pre-training. We show improved performance in terms of both the BLEU score and Jensen-Shannon distance (JSD) measure [3].

This paper presents a comprehensive review of GAN methods, examining them from the perspectives of algorithms, theory, and applications. It gives the motivations, mathematical representations, and structures of the most common GAN algorithms in detail, highlighting their similarities and differences. Next, it has the theoretical aspects of GANs, analyzing the various issues related to their use. Finally, the typical applications of GANs in a variety of fields, including image processing and computer vision, NLP, music, speech and audio, the medical field, and data science [4].

Bayesian learning for natural language has wide-ranging applications from speech recognition to document summarization, text classification, image caption generation, and machine translation.

In traditional deep learning, inference and optimization are based on real-valued deterministic models, which may not accurately capture the semantic structure of words, sentences, entities, actions, and documents from a large vocabulary. Discrete or continuous latent variable models for natural language may also be difficult to decompose or estimate. This tutorial covers the basics of statistical models and neural networks and focuses on advanced Bayesian models and deep models, such as hierarchical Dirichlet process, Chinese restaurant process, Indian buffet process, GAN, and policy neural network, among others. It explains how these models are connected and how they can be used for a variety of applications on symbolic and complex patterns in natural language. It has several studies and domain applications to address various issues in deep Bayesian processing, learning, and understanding [5].

The goal of this paper is to address the issue of manipulating images using natural language descriptions. While existing methods can synthesize images with new attributes, they often fail to preserve text-irrelevant details from the original image. To tackle this problem, we propose a novel approach called the text-adaptive generative adversarial network (TAGAN), which is designed to generate semantically manipulated images while maintaining the text-irrelevant content of the original image. The key feature of our method is the text-adaptive discriminator, which creates word-level local discriminators based on the input text to classify fine-grained attributes independently. Using this discriminator, the generator can learn to modify only the regions of the image that correspond to the given text. Our experimental results demonstrate that our approach outperforms existing methods on both Caltech-UCSD birds dataset (CUB) and Oxford-102 datasets, and our results were preferred in a user study. We also provide extensive analysis showing that our method effectively disentangles visual attributes and produces visually pleasing outputs [6].

In recent years, the use of deep neural networks (DNNs) has become increasingly popular in many AI applications due to the development of high computational devices. However, it has been shown that DNNs are vulnerable to adversarial examples, which are strategically modified samples that can fool DNNs into giving false predictions. While generating adversarial examples against DNNs in computer vision (CV) has been extensively studied, research efforts on attacking DNNs for NLP applications are emerging. However, the differences between image (CV) and text (NLP) pose challenges to directly applying attacking methods in CV to NLP. Various methods have been proposed to address this difference and attack a wide range of NLP applications. This article presents a systematic survey on these works, covering all related academic works since 2017. The article summarizes, discusses, and analyzes 40 representative works comprehensively, and includes preliminary knowledge of NLP and related seminal works in CV. The survey concludes with a discussion on open issues and future directions to bridge the gap between existing progress and more robust adversarial attacks on NLP DNNs [7].

Generative adversarial networks have made remarkable progress in the field of machine learning by generating realistic synthetic data.

However, GAN's generator is limited to producing differentiable data, making it challenging to use GAN in NLP research where discrete data is prevalent. To address this limitation, we propose a novel text-to-text generative adversarial network (TT-GAN) capable of generating text based on semantic information derived from the source text. Our model can generate not only realistic text but also paraphrases and semantic summarizations of the source text, making it the first framework that can generate natural language on a semantic level. Our research provides a new perspective for applying GAN to NLP research [9].

The field of NLP has seen significant progress with the advent of deep learning approaches. However, deep neural models often face the challenge of overfitting and limited data availability, which can hinder their performance in NLP tasks. To overcome these issues, multi-task learning (MTL) has emerged as a promising solution, allowing for the utilization of useful information from related tasks to improve performance on multiple tasks simultaneously. In this article is an overview of MTL in NLP tasks. We categorize MTL architectures used in NLP tasks into four classes: parallel, hierarchical, modular, and generative adversarial architecture. We also discuss optimization techniques, including loss construction, data sampling, and task scheduling, that can be used to train multi-task models effectively. Furthermore, we present various applications of MTL in NLP tasks, and provide benchmark datasets for evaluation. Finally, we conclude with a discussion on potential research directions in this field [10].

In recent times, DNNs have become the preferred approach for speech enhancement due to their ability to produce superior speech quality and intelligibility compared to traditional methods. However, DNN-based techniques typically require a large parallel corpus containing clean speech and noise for training, limiting their application to real-world environments where clean speech and noise are not available. Additionally, noise varies with time and environment, making it difficult to obtain parallel speech and noise data. To address this issue, we propose a novel parallel-data-free speech enhancement method that employs multi-objective learning and cycle-consistent generative adversarial network (CycleGAN). During training, we use two encoders to encode the features of clean and noisy speech, respectively. Two forward generators predict the time-frequency (T-F) mask and log-power spectrum (LPS) of clean speech, while two inverse generators map the magnitude spectrum (MS) and LPS of noisy speech. We employ four discriminators to distinguish between real and generated speech features. We simultaneously train the two encoders, four generators, and four discriminators using adversarial, identity-mapping, latent similarity, and cycle-consistent loss. During testing, we use forward generators and encoders to obtain the enhanced speech. Our method not only overcomes the limitation of parallel data but also makes effective use of multi-objective learning [11].

In the paper titled "Multiple Text Style Transfer by Using Word-Level Conditional Generative Adversarial Network with Two-Phase Training", Lai *et al.* (2019) present a new approach for non-parallel text style transfer. The proposed method utilizes a word-level conditional GAN and a two-phase training procedure to alter specific attributes of a given text while preserving its remaining attributes and content.

The authors test their model on polarity sentiment transfer and multiple-attribute transfer tasks, achieving comparable evaluation scores in transfer accuracy and fluency while significantly outperforming other state-of-the-art models in content compatibility on three real-world datasets. This research was presented at the 2019 Conference on Empirical Methods in Natural Language Processing and the 9th International Joint Conference on Natural Language Processing (EMNLP-IJCNLP) [12].

This article offers a thorough survey of the latest advancements in text generation using GANs. Although GANs have shown potential in generating natural language, their original architecture was designed for continuous data, not discrete data like text, which makes text generation more challenging. To overcome this challenge, researchers have explored three main approaches: Gumbel-Softmax differentiation, reinforcement learning, and modified training objectives. Each selected study is critically analyzed and evaluated based on its objectives, methodology, and experimental results [13].

Recent transformer-based architectures, including BERT, have achieved impressive results in various NLP tasks. However, these models rely heavily on large-scale annotated datasets, which are costly and time-consuming to obtain. Conversely, unlabeled data, which is readily available, can be utilized to improve model performance through semi-supervised learning. In the field of image processing, Semi-supervised generative adversarial networks have shown promise in this regard. In this paper, we propose a new method called GAN-BERT that extends the fine-tuning of BERT-like architectures with unlabeled data in a generative adversarial setting. Our experimental results demonstrate that the need for annotated examples can be significantly reduced (as few as 50 – 100 annotated examples) while maintaining a strong performance in various sentence classification tasks [14].

Generative adversarial networks have gained significant attention in AI applications such as NLP, speech recognition, and CV. Although GANs are state-of-the-art, their high computational complexity poses a challenge.

While ReRMA-based process-in-memory has demonstrated promise in accelerating CNNs, it is difficult to run GANs on existing neural network acceleration platforms due to their unique training process that requires the simultaneous co-training of two competing networks, increasing the need for memory and computation resources. In this study, we introduce ReGAN, a novel ReRAM-based process-in-memory accelerator that reduces off-chip memory accesses and increases system throughput by pipelining layer-wise computation. We propose spatial parallelism and computation sharing techniques to further enhance GAN training efficiency. Our experimental results show that ReGAN achieves an average performance speedup of 240× and an average energy saving of 94× compared to the graphics processing unit platform [16].

The analysis of text sentiment is crucial for public opinion monitoring, service evaluation, and satisfaction analysis in network environments.

Convolutional neural networks have been shown to enhance the performance of affective analysis models by automatically learning relevant features from sentences. However, the original CNN model does not account for sentence structure, which is crucial in text sentiment analysis. It proposes a piece-wise pooling technique to capture sentence structure, enabling the extraction of key features from different sentences to analyze the emotional tendencies of the text. Additionally, user feedback typically involves various fields with limited labeled data. To address this issue, we use a GAN to extract common features associated with emotions across different fields, thereby enhancing the model's generalization ability with less training data. Experimental results on various datasets demonstrate the efficacy of our approach [17].

4.3 The Implementation of NLP in GAN for Generating Images and Summaries

4.3.1 Working of Sequence Generative Adversarial Network (SeqGAN)

Sequence generative adversarial network (SeqGAN) is a generative adversarial network that is specifically designed for generating realistic sequences of text. The SeqGAN model uses a reinforcement learning approach to train the generator network, which makes it different from the traditional GAN models. The SeqGAN model consists of two main components: a generator network and a discriminator network. The generator network generates sequences of text, and the discriminator network evaluates the generated sequences and provides feedback to the generator network. The generator network in SeqGAN is based on the recurrent neural network (RNN) architecture, which is designed to generate sequential data. The generator network receives a random noise vector as input and generates a sequence of text. The discriminator network is a binary classifier that evaluates the generated sequence and provides feedback to the generator network [18].

The SeqGAN model uses a reinforcement learning approach to train the generator network. After generating a sequence of text, the generator network receives a reward signal from a pre-trained policy network that indicates how good the generated sequence is. The generator network is then trained to maximize the expected reward signal over all possible sequences. The SeqGAN model has shown promising results in generating realistic sequences of text, such as product reviews, news articles, and social media posts. The model has the potential to be used in various applications, such as language translation, text summarization, and text generation. Overall, SeqGAN is an effective approach to generating realistic sequences of text, and its reinforcement learning approach makes it a unique and powerful model in the field of natural language processing [19].

Steps involved in creating a Sequence Generative Adversarial Network

- Data Pre-processing: Pre-process the text data to remove noise and normalize the text, including tokenization, stop word removal, and stemming.
- Generator Network: Build a generator network that can generate text sequences using recurrent neural network (RNN) architecture. The generator network should take in a random noise vector as input and output a sequence of text.
- Discriminator Network: Build a discriminator network that can differentiate between real and generated text sequences. The discriminator network should be based on a binary classification model that takes in a sequence of text and outputs a binary classification score.
- Reinforcement Learning: Use a reinforcement learning approach to train the generator network. This involves using a pre-trained policy network to provide a reward signal to the generator network after generating a sequence of text. The generator network is trained to maximize the expected reward signal over all possible sequences.
- Adversarial Training: Train the generator and discriminator networks in an adversarial manner, with the generator

network trying to generate realistic text sequences that can fool the discriminator network, and the discriminator network trying to distinguish between real and generated text sequences.

- Loss Functions: Define the loss functions for the generator and discriminator networks. The generator network should be trained to minimize the generator loss, which measures how well the generated text sequences can deceive the discriminator network. The discriminator network should be trained to minimize the discriminator loss, which measures how well it can distinguish between real and generated text sequences.
- Fine-Tuning: Fine-tune the generator network on specific tasks, such as language translation or text summarization, using transfer learning techniques.
- Evaluation: Evaluate the performance of the SeqGAN model using metrics such as perplexity, BLEU score, and human evaluation.

4.3.2 Working of Generative Adversarial Transformer (GAT)

The GAT is a deep learning model that combines two powerful models: GANs and transformers. The GAT is designed to generate realistic sequences of text, such as product descriptions, news articles, and social media posts. The GAT model comprises a generator network and a discriminator network. The generator network uses the transformer architecture to generate text sequences, while the discriminator network uses the CNN architecture to differentiate between real and fake sequences of text. To train the GAT model, the generator network generates a text sequence using a random input vector, and the discriminator network evaluates the sequence and provides feedback to the generator network. This process repeats several times until the generator network produces realistic sequences of text that can deceive the discriminator network [20].

The GAT model employs an innovative training approach called adversarial training. Here, the generator and discriminator networks are trained in an adversarial manner, with the generator network trying to generate realistic sequences that can fool the discriminator network, and the discriminator network trying to distinguish between real and fake text sequences. The GAT model is a promising solution for generating realistic sequences of text, particularly in tasks such as language translation, text summarization, and text generation. The model has the potential to transform the field of NLP by enabling the development of more advanced and realistic language models.

4.3.2.1 Steps to Incorporate NLP in GAN

There are several steps involved in integrating NLP into GANs to generate realistic textual data and described as follows and shown in Figure 4.1.

- Data Preprocessing: The first step is to preprocess the textual data. This may include tasks such as tokenization, stemming, stop word removal, and POS tagging.
- Seq2Seq Model: A Seq2Seq model is used to generate text sequences. The Seq2Seq model consists of an encoder that encodes the input sequence into a fixed-length vector representation, and a decoder that generates the output sequence based on the encoded vector.
- Generator Network: The generator network generates realistic text sequences using the Seq2Seq model.
- Discriminator Network: The discriminator network distinguishes between real and fake text sequences. It is trained to differentiate between real text sequences from the training data and fake text sequences generated by the generator network.
- Adversarial Training: The generator and discriminator networks are trained in an adversarial manner. The generator network learns to generate more realistic text sequences by trying to deceive the discriminator network, while the discriminator network learns to distinguish between real and fake text sequences.

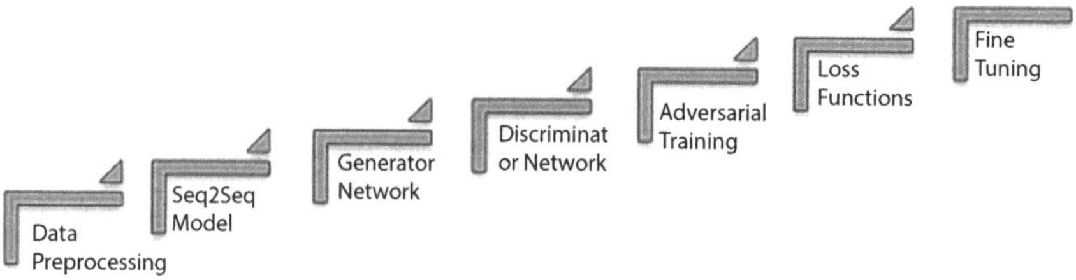

Figure 4.1 Working of natural language processing in GAN.

- Loss Functions: The loss functions are used to evaluate the performance of the generator and discriminator networks. The generator network is trained to minimize the generator loss, which measures how well the generated text sequences can deceive the discriminator network.
- The discriminator network is trained to minimize the discriminator loss, which measures how well it can distinguish between real and fake text sequences.
- Fine-Tuning: The generator network can be fine-tuned on specific tasks such as language translation or text summarization by using transfer learning techniques.

Overall, integrating NLP into GANs models involves several steps, from pre-processing the data to training the generator and discriminator networks in an adversarial manner. The result is a model that can generate realistic textual data for various applications [21].

4.3.3 Implementation of NLP in GAN

Intent classification is a widely studied NLP problem that involves feeding written text or audio input into a model to predict the user's goal or intent. This problem is particularly relevant when building chatbots, where correctly identifying the intent behind a user's message is crucial to generating an appropriate response. By leveraging intent classification, chatbots can better understand the needs and goals of their users, resulting in more effective and accurate responses.

Utilizing BERT embeddings is a viable approach to generate text representations that are context-aware, given that we are dealing with textual data. However, while transformer models like BERT are highly effective, exploiting their full potential requires a significant amount of labeled data, which may not always be feasible. One possible solution to this challenge is to merge labeled and unlabeled data to form a comprehensive training dataset, known as "semi-supervised classification." This strategy can be further enhanced by combining BERT's capabilities with GANs, allowing for the best of both worlds to be utilized in this project [22].

The dataset for this project is CLINC150, consisting of 150 "in-scope" intent classes, each containing 100 training samples, 20 validation samples, and 30 test samples. This presents a promising opportunity to leverage the power of BERT and GANs to develop a robust and effective model for this task. GAN-BERT is a model that uses GANs to enable semi-supervised learning for NLP tasks. It extends the fine-tuning of BERT-like architectures with unlabeled data in a generative adversarial setting. By doing so, the model reduces the need for annotated examples while still obtaining good performances in several sentence classification tasks. GAN-BERT has been applied to the CLINC150 dataset, which contains 150 different classes of text-based commands. The experimental results show that GAN-BERT achieves state-of-the-art performance on the CLINC150 dataset, with an accuracy of 98.4%. This suggests that GAN-BERT has great potential for improving text classification models and reducing the amount of labeled data required for training as shown in Table 4.1.

The length of the training data is shown in Figure 4.2.

Table 4.1 Summary of the GAN-BERT model.

Layer	Output shape	Parameter
Keras layer	(None, 50)	48190600
Dense layer	(None, 256)	13056
Dropout	(None, 256)	0
Dense layer	(None, 150)	38550

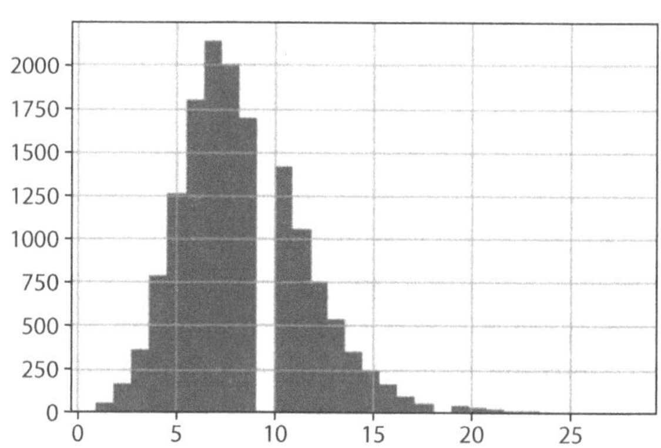

Figure 4.2 Show the length of all the text in the train data.

The GAN-BERT model gives the accuracy of 92% during training and 89% during validation as shown in Figure 4.3. The loss of the model is 0.3% and 0.2 % as shown in Figure 4.4. From the analysis, the GAN-BERT model for CLINC150 dataset gives a better performance than other traditional machine learning models [23].

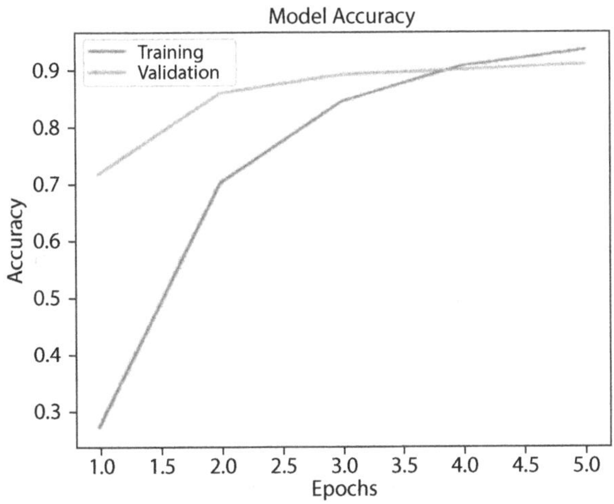

Figure 4.3 Accuracy of the GAN-BERT model for CLINC150.

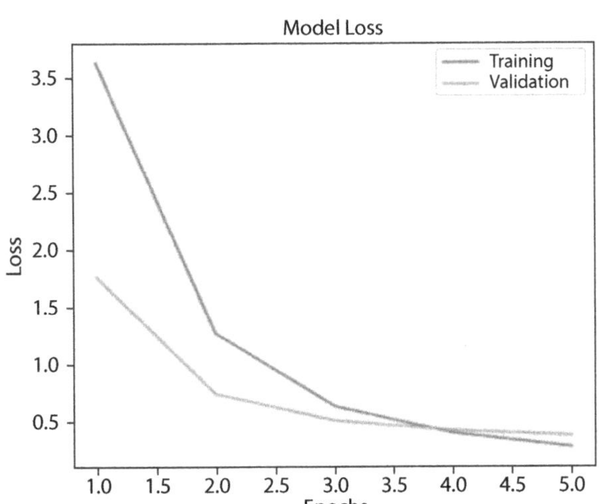

Figure 4.4 Loss of the GAN-BERT model for CLINC150.

4.3.4 Generate the Image Using Textual Description

Generating photorealistic images based on textual descriptions is an intriguing yet extremely difficult problem. These GANs have faced challenges in creating photorealistic images when using other images as input.

In this case, the only input provided is a text description of the image, where numerous details regarding the expected image can be unclear, and the model is expected to make its own assumptions. The animal dataset is collected from the Kaggle repository using OpenAI Glide. The generation of image from the text information is given in Figure 4.5.

In scenarios where high-resolution images are required, capturing all the necessary details and finesse becomes a significant challenge. Additionally, generalizing the images for different text descriptions can pose further difficulties. To overcome these challenges, researchers have employed StackGANs or ST-GANs. This architecture comprises two GANs that are stacked on top of each other, providing a solution to generating photorealistic images from text descriptions. This process involves utilizing both NLP and GAN to convert text into an image. The first step is to encode the textual description into a vector, which is then fed into the GAN for processing. The GAN is made up of two key components - a generator and discriminator, which work in tandem to create an image that matches the textual description. To refine the image, the GAN goes through several feedback loops until it closely resembles the textual description. Although generating an image from text is a challenging and complex task, advances in NLP and GAN technology have made it increasingly possible [24].

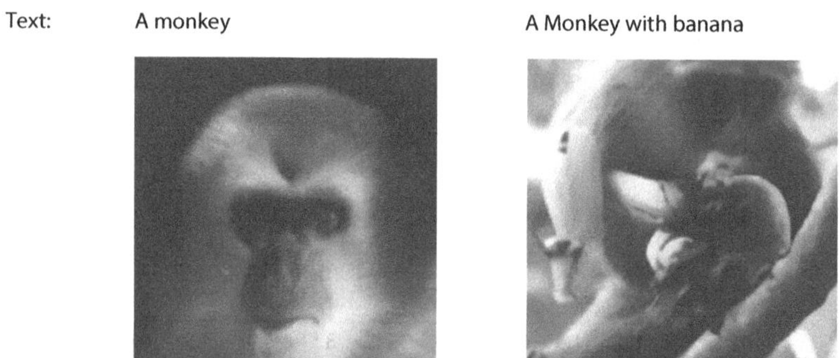

Figure 4.5 Generation of image using text information.

4.3.5 Text Summarization

Text summarization is the process of creating a concise version of a text that captures its essential information. While humans can easily comprehend the primary points of a text by reading it, machines can also perform this task through the use of NLP. There are two primary techniques for summarizing text:

1. Extractive summarization involves identifying and extracting the most significant sentences from the original text. This technique is relatively easy to implement and can be performed quickly using an unsupervised approach that does not require prior training.
2. Abstractive summarization involves comprehending the main concepts of the text and generating a new, summarized version based on that understanding. Abstractive summarization has the advantage of being able to generate new text, but it is more complex to implement and requires language generation capabilities [25].

Generating an image using textual description involves the following steps:

1. Data Preparation: The first step is to prepare the textual data for processing. This involves cleaning the text data, extracting relevant information, and encoding it into a numerical format that can be used as input to the GAN.
2. GAN Architecture Design: The next step is to design the GAN architecture. This involves deciding on the number of layers, neurons, and other parameters for both the generator and discriminator models.
3. Training the GAN: Once the GAN architecture is designed, the next step is to train the model. This involves optimizing the generator and discriminator models to create an accurate image that matches the textual description.
4. Generating Images: After the GAN is trained, the next step is to generate images from textual descriptions. This involves feeding the encoded textual description into the generator model and generating the corresponding image.

5. Image Refinement: The final step is to refine the generated image to improve its accuracy and quality. This is done through several feedback loops between the generator and discriminator, where the discriminator evaluates the generated image and provides feedback to the generator for further refinement.
6. Overall, generating an image using textual description is a complex process that involves several steps, including data preparation, GAN architecture design, training the GAN, generating images, and refining the image through feedback loops. Advances in NLP and GAN technology have made this process increasingly feasible and effective.

Extractive text summarization methods aim to select informative sentences from a document to form a summary based on specific criteria. The main challenge is determining which sentences from the input document are significant and likely to be included in the summary. Sentence scoring is employed based on features of sentences, with the highest-scoring sentences being included in the final summary. There are various techniques for extractive text summarization, including Term Frequency-Inverse Document Frequency (TF-IDF), cluster-based, neural network-based, fuzzy logic-based, graph-based, latent semantic analysis-based, machine learning-based and query-based methods. TF-IDF uses numerical statistics to determine the importance of a word in a given document, and sentences are scored according to product. Cluster-based methods group sentences based on their themes, and summary sentences are selected based on their relationship to the theme of the cluster [26].

Neural network-based methods use a processing system modeled on the human brain to capture the type of sentences that should be included in the summary, while fuzzy logic-based methods use a way of reasoning that resembles human reasoning based on degrees of truth.

Graph-based methods use a graph-based ranking algorithm to decide the importance of a sentence within a graph, and latent semantic analysis-based methods extract meaning and resemblance of a sentence by the information about words in a particular environment. Machine learning-based methods model summarization as a classification problem, and query-based summarization scores sentences based on a search query given by the user. While each method has its strengths and weaknesses, they all aim to provide an accurate summary of a document while avoiding the inclusion of irrelevant information [27].

4.3.5.1 Graph-Based Summarization

The main concept of this approach involves identifying similarities between sentences and selecting those with the highest similarity scores. The similarity matrix is created using Cosine Similarity, while the TextRank algorithm is used to rank the sentences based on their significance.

To comprehend the TextRank algorithm, it is essential to briefly discuss the PageRank algorithm, which served as the inspiration for TextRank. Google employs the PageRank algorithm to rank web pages based on their search results. The algorithm constructs a graph with pages serving as the vertices and links between pages serving as edges. The PageRank score is determined for each page, representing the likelihood of a user visiting that particular page. This paper provides a detailed explanation of the PageRank algorithm for tennis_articles dataset. The detailed text summarization is represented in Figures 4.6 and 4.7.

Abstractive text summarization is a process that involves generating a shorter, more concise summary of a longer piece of text. This is done using NLP techniques, which enable computers to understand and interpret human language. The process involves analyzing the text and identifying the key ideas and concepts. Then, using advanced algorithms and machine learning techniques, the computer generates a summary that captures the essence of the original text. Abstractive text summarization is a complex and challenging task, but recent advancements in NLP and machine learning technology have made it increasingly effective. This technique has many potential applications, including news summarization, legal document summarization, and automated report generation [28].

Text summarization using GAN can be accomplished by following a set of key steps. These steps include preparing the text data for summarization, designing the GAN architecture, training the GAN, generating summaries, and evaluating the quality of the summaries. To begin, the text data must be cleaned, stop words and non-relevant information should be removed,

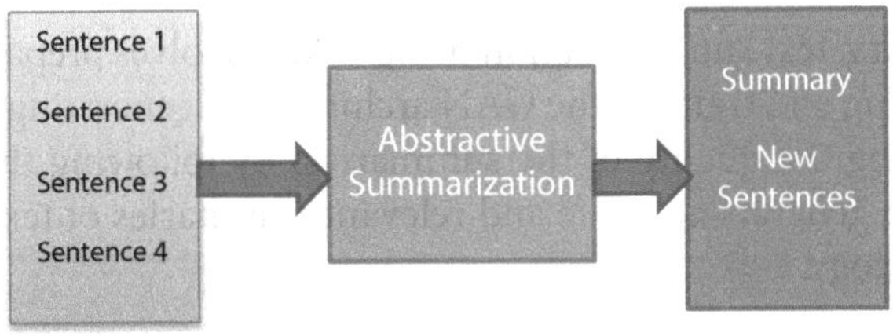

Figure 4.6 Text summarization.

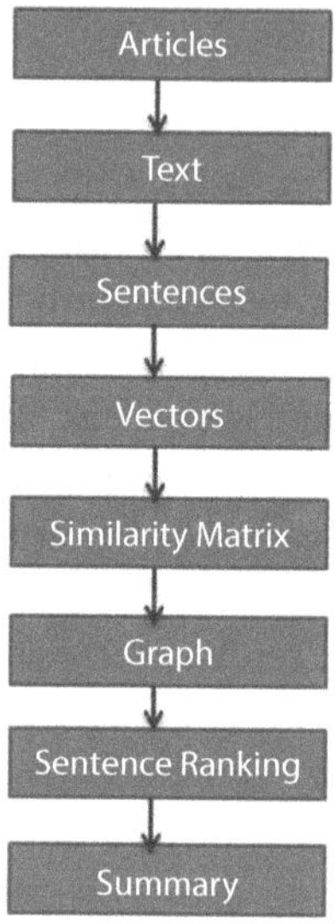

Figure 4.7 Steps involved in text summarization.

and the text should be converted into a numerical format that can be processed by the GAN. Next, the architecture of the GAN must be designed, which includes a generator and discriminator. The generator takes in the input text and generates a summary, while the discriminator evaluates the summary and provides feedback to the generator. Once the GAN architecture is designed, the next step is to train the model using the prepared text data. This involves optimizing the generator and discriminator models to improve the quality of the generated summaries. Once the GAN is trained, the generator model can be used to generate summaries of new text data by feeding the text data into the model. The final step is to evaluate the quality of the generated summaries. This involves comparing the generated summary to the actual summary of the text data and using metrics such as ROUGE and BLEU to evaluate the accuracy and relevance of the summaries.

In summary, text summarization using GAN involves preparing the text data, designing and training the GAN architecture, generating summaries, and evaluating the quality of the summaries. By following these steps, it is possible to generate accurate and relevant summaries of text data using GAN technology.

The steps involved in text summarization are given in Figure 4.7. The distribution of number of articles in each category is shown in Figure 4.8.

Distribution of category and its values are given in Figures 4.9 and 4.10. Figure 4.11 represents the coverage ratio of each category. The graphical representation of Similar Sentences in 2D space using bokeh.models is given in Figure 4.12.

The graphical representation of similar sentences in 2D space using bokehmodels involves creating a scatter plot where each point represents a sentence. The final summary from the original text is shown in Figure 4.13.

The position of each point in the plot is determined by the similarity between the corresponding sentence and a reference sentence. To create such a plot, we first need to compute the similarity between each sentence and the reference sentence using a text similarity metric. In the example above, we use TF-IDF to compute the similarity between the sentences. This results in a matrix of similarity scores between all pairs of sentences. Next, we use the principal component analysis to reduce the dimensionality of the similarity matrix from n to 2, where n is the number of sentences.

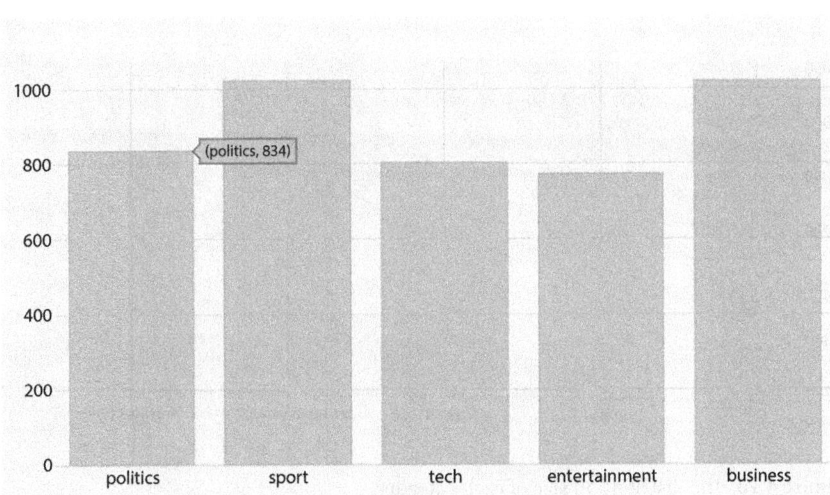

Figure 4.8 The distribution of a number of articles in each category.

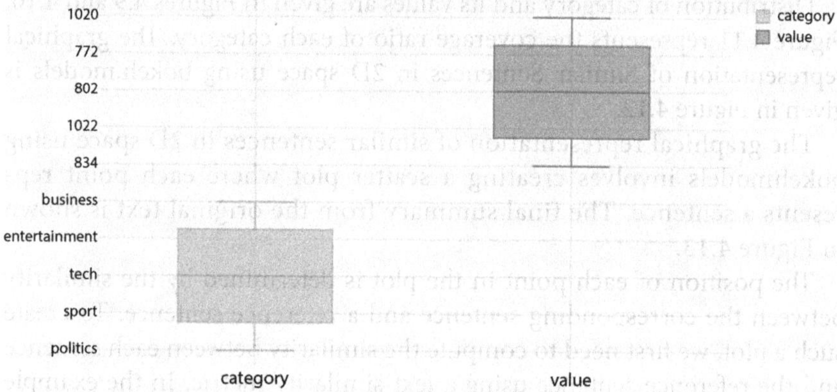

Figure 4.9 The distribution of a category and its values.

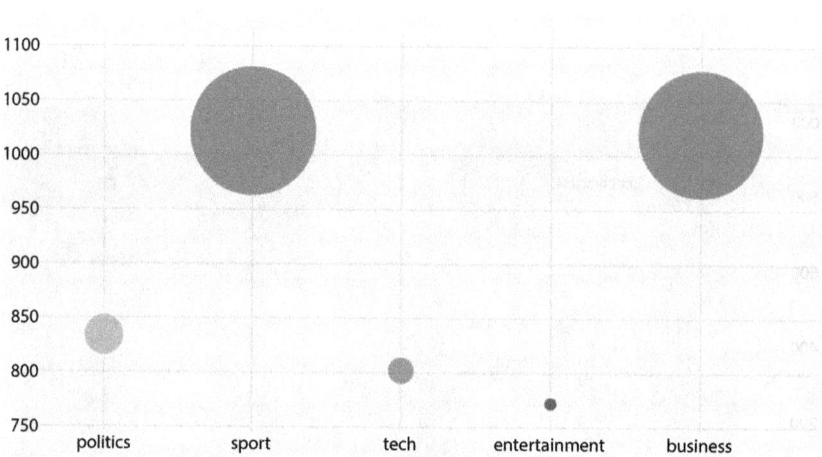

Figure 4.10 The distribution size of each category.

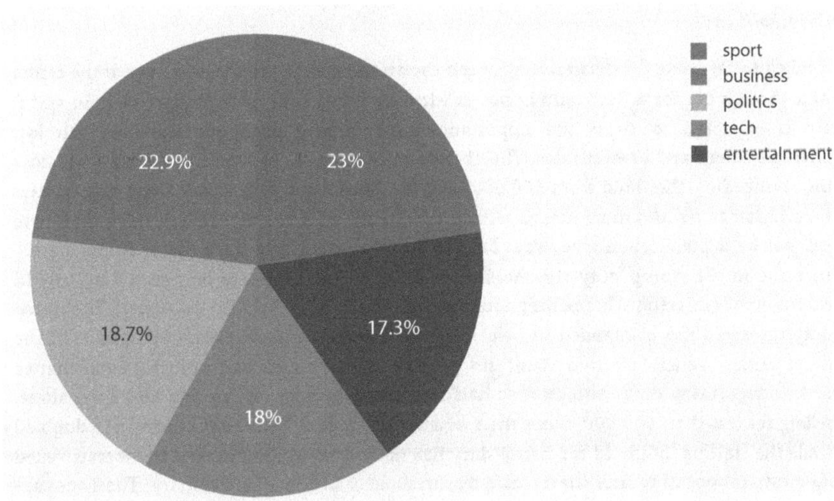

Figure 4.11 The coverage ratio of each category.

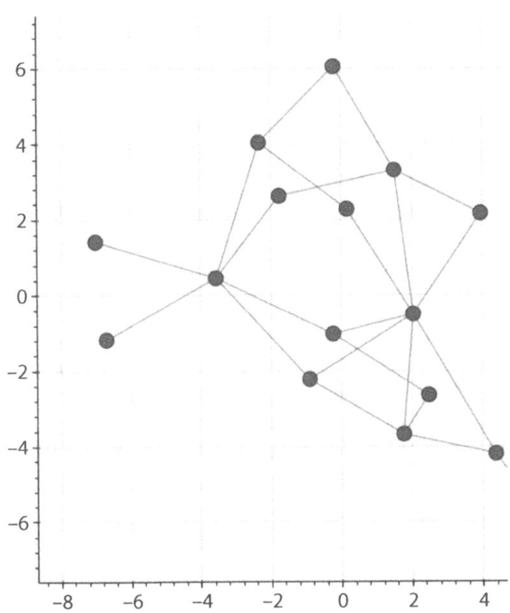

Figure 4.12 A graphical representation of similar sentences in 2D space using bokeh. models.

Original Text

'Budget to set scene for election\n\nGordon Grown will seek to put the economy at the centre of Labour\\'s bid for a third term in power when he delivers his ninth Budget at 1230 GMT. He is expected to stress the importance of continued economic stability, with low unemployment and interest rates. The chancellor is expected to freeze petrol duty and raise the stamp duty threshold from £60,000. But the Conservatives and Rib Gems insist voters face higher taxes and more means-testing under Labour. Treasury officials have said there will not be a pre-election giveaway, but Or Grown is thought to have about £in to spare. - Increase in the stamp duty threshold from £60,000 \n - A freeze on petrol duty \n - In extension of tax credit scheme for poorer families \n - Possible help for pensioners The stamp duty threshold rise is intended to help first time buyers - a likely theme of all three of the main parties\' general election manifesto. Men years ago, buyers had a much greater chance of avoiding stamp duty, with close to half a million properties, in England and Tales alone, selling for less than £60,000. Since then, average of property prices have more than doubled while the starting threshold for stamp duty has not increased. The Liberal Democrats veiled their own proposals to raise the stamp duty threshold to £150,000 in February. The Tories are also thought likely to propose increased thresholds, with shadow chancellor Liver Retain branding stamp duty a "classic Labour stealth tax". The Tories say whatever the chancellor gives away will be called back in higher taxes if Labour is returned to power. "Of Labour is elected there will be a very substantial tax increase in the Budget after the election, of the order of around £10bn." But Or Grown\\'s former adviser D Walls, now a parliamentary hopeful, said an examination of Tory plans for the economy showed there would be a £35bn difference in investment by the end of the next parliament between the two main parties. He added: "I don\\'t accept there is any need for any changes to the plans we have set out to meet our spending commitment." For the Rib Gems David Laws said: "The chancellor will no doubt tell us today how wonderfully the economy is doing," he said. "But a lot of that is built on an increase in personal and consumer debt over the last few years - that makes the economy quite vulnerable potentially if interest rates ever do have to go up in a significant way." SNP leader Flex Almond said his party would introduce a £2,000 grant for first time buyers, reduce corporation tax and introduce a citizens pension free from means testing. Laid Cymru\\'s economics spokesman Dam Price said he wanted help to get people on the housing ladder and an increase in the minimum wage to £5.60 an hour.'

Summary Text after graph based summarization:

"I don\\'t accept there is any need for any changes to the plans we have set out to meet our spending commitment." He is expected to stress the importance of continued economic stability, with low unemployment and interest rates. "But a lot of that is built on an increase in personal and consumer debt over the last few years - that makes the economy quite vulnerable potentially if interest rates ever do have to go up in a significant way." Treasury officials have said there will not be a pre-election giveaway, but Or Grown is thought to have about £in to spare. Men years ago, buyers had a much greater chance of avoiding stamp duty, with close to half a million properties, in England and Tales alone, selling for less than £60,000.'

Figure 4.13 The final summary from the original text.

This allows us to represent each sentence in a 2D space while preserving the relative similarities between the sentences. Finally, we use bokeh.models to create a scatter plot where each point represents a sentence. We use similarity scores to set the position of each point in the 2D space. We also add tooltips using the HoverTool, which displays the text of the corresponding sentence when the user hovers over a point. In addition, we can use LabelSet to add labels to each point, making it easier to identify the corresponding sentences. The resulting plot provides a visual representation of the similarity between the sentences, allowing us to easily identify clusters of similar sentences.

4.4 Conclusion

The integration of NLP and GAN has opened up new possibilities for generating images, text summaries from textual descriptions. By encoding text into vectors and utilizing GANs to generate images, it is possible to create images that accurately match the textual descriptions using OpenAI Glide. This technology has many potential applications, including creating realistic images for video games and virtual reality, generating images for e-commerce product listings, and even assisting with medical imaging. However, there are still limitations to this technology, such as the challenge of generating high-quality images from complex textual descriptions. Nonetheless, with continued advancements in NLP and GAN technology, we can expect to see more impressive results in the future.

References

1. Kang, Y., Cai, Z., Tan, C.W., Huang, Q., Liu, H., Natural language processing (NLP) in management research: A literature review. *J. Manage. Anal.*, *7*, 2, 139–172, 2020.
2. Creswell, A., White, T., Dumoulin, V., Arulkumaran, K., Sengupta, B., Bharath, A.A., Generative adversarial networks: An overview. *IEEE Signal Process Mag.*, *35*, 1, 53–65, 2018.
3. Haidar, M.A. and Rezagholizadeh, M., Textkd-gan: Text generation using knowledge distillation and generative adversarial networks, in: *Advances in Artificial Intelligence: 32nd Canadian Conference on Artificial Intelligence, Canadian AI 2019, Kingston, ON, Canada, May 28–31, 2019, Proceedings 32*, Springer International Publishing, pp. 107–118, 2019.

4. Gui, J., Sun, Z., Wen, Y., Tao, D., Ye, J., A review on generative adversarial networks: Algorithms, theory, and applications. *IEEE Trans. Knowl. Data Eng.*, 35, 4, 3313–3332, 2021.
5. Nam, S., Kim, Y., Kim, S.J., Text-adaptive generative adversarial networks: manipulating images with natural language. *Adv. Neural Inf. Process. Syst.*, *31*, 1–10, 2018.
6. Zhang, W.E., Sheng, Q.Z., Alhazmi, A., Li, C., Adversarial attacks on deep-learning models in natural language processing: A survey. *ACM Trans. Intell. Syst. Technol. (TIST)*, *11*, 3, 1–41, 2020.
7. Li, C., Su, Y., Liu, W., Text-to-text generative adversarial networks, in: *2018 International Joint Conference on Neural Networks (IJCNN)*, pp. 1–7, IEEE, 2018, July.
8. Xu, J., Ren, X., Lin, J., Sun, X., Diversity-promoting GAN: A cross-entropy based generative adversarial network for diversified text generation, in: *Proceedings of the 2018 conference on empirical methods in natural language processing*, pp. 3940–3949, 2018.
9. Chen, S., Zhang, Y., Yang, Q., Multi-task learning in natural language processing: An overview. *Artif. Intell.*, 2021, Url: https://arxiv.org/abs/2109.09138.
10. Xiang, Y. and Bao, C., A parallel-data-free speech enhancement method using multi-objective learning cycle-consistent generative adversarial network. *IEEE/ACM Trans. Audio Speech Lang. Process.*, *28*, 1826–1838, 2020.
11. Lai, C.T., Hong, Y.T., Chen, H.Y., Lu, C.J., Lin, S.D., Multiple text style transfer by using word-level conditional generative adversarial network with two-phase training, in: *Proceedings of the 2019 Conference on Empirical Methods in Natural Language Processing and the 9th International Joint Conference on Natural Language Processing (EMNLP-IJCNLP)*, pp. 3579–3584, 2019, November.
12. Rosa, G.H. and Papa, J.P., A survey on text generation using generative adversarial networks. *Pattern Recognit.*, 119, 108098, 2021.
13. Croce, D., Castellucci, G., Basili, R., GAN-BERT: Generative adversarial learning for robust text classification with a bunch of labeled examples, in: *Proceedings of the 58th annual meeting of the association for computational linguistics*, pp. 2114–2119, 2020, July.
14. Ren, Y., Lin, J., Tang, S., Zhou, J., Yang, S., Qi, Y., Ren, X., Generating natural language adversarial examples on a large scale with generative models, 2020, arXiv preprint arXiv:2003.10388.
15. Chen, F., Song, L., Chen, Y., ReGAN: A pipelined ReRAM-based accelerator for generative adversarial networks, in: *2018 23rd Asia and South Pacific Design Automation Conference (ASP-DAC)*, pp.178–183, IEEE, 2018, January.
16. Du, C. and Huang, L., Sentiment analysis method based on piecewise convolutional neural network and generative adversarial network. *Int. J. Comput. Commun. Control*, 14, 1, 7–20, 2019.

17. Pan, Z., Yu, W., Yi, X., Khan, A., Yuan, F., Zheng, Y., Recent progress on generative adversarial networks (GANs): A survey. *IEEE Access*, *7*, 36322–36333, 2019.
18. Tu, Y., Mak, M.W., Chien, J.T., Variational domain adversarial learning with mutual information maximization for speaker verification. *IEEE/ACM Trans. Audio Speech Lang. Process.*, *28*, 2013–2024, 2020.
19. Kameoka, H., Tanaka, K., Kwaśny, D., Kaneko, T., Hojo, N., ConvS2S-VC: Fully convolutional sequence-to-sequence voice conversion. *IEEE/ACM Trans. Audio Speech Lang. Process.*, *28*, 1849–1863, 2020.
20. Breazzano, C., Croce, D., Basili, R., MT-GAN-BERT: Multi-Task and Generative Adversarial Learning for Sustainable Language Processing, in: *NL4AI@ AI* IA*, 2021, November.
21. Wang, L., Yan, X., You, Z.H., Zhou, X., Li, H.Y., Huang, Y.A., SGANRDA: semi-supervised generative adversarial networks for predicting circRNA–disease associations. *Briefings Bioinf.*, *22*, 5, bbab028, 2021.
22. Wu, Y.C., Hayashi, T., Okamoto, T., Kawai, H., Toda, T., Quasi-periodic parallel WaveGAN: a non-autoregressive raw waveform generative model with pitch-dependent dilated convolution neural network. *IEEE/ACM Trans. Audio Speech Lang. Process.*, *29*, 792–806, 2021.
23. Li, T., Liu, X., Su, S., Semi-supervised text regression with conditional generative adversarial networks, in: *2018 IEEE International Conference on Big Data (Big Data)*, pp. 5375–5377, IEEE, 2018, December.
24. Philip, P. and Minhas, S., A Brief Survey on Natural Language Processing Based Text Generation and Evaluation Techniques. *VFAST Trans. Softw. Eng.*, 2022, URL: https://vfast.org/journals/index.php/VTSE/article/view/1104.
25. Zhou, H., Jiao, L., Zheng, S., Yang, L., Shen, W., Yang, X., Generative adversarial network-based electromagnetic signal classification: A semi-supervised learning framework. *China Commun.*, *17*, 10, 157–169, 2020.
26. Sun, S., Guo, P., Xie, L., Hwang, M.Y., Adversarial regularization for attention based end-to-end robust speech recognition. *IEEE/ACM Trans. Audio Speech Lang. Process.*, *27*, 11, 1826–1838, 2019.
27. Evholt D. and Larsson, O., Generative Adversarial Networks and Natural Language Processing for Macroeconomic Forecasting. Digitala Vetenskapliga Arkivet, 2020, url: https://www.diva portal.org/smash/record.jsf?pid=diva2%3A1431649&dswid=-7516.
28. Yan, S., Wu, F., Smith, J.S., Lu, W., Zhang, B., Image captioning using adversarial networks and reinforcement learning, in: *2018 24th International Conference on Pattern Recognition (ICPR)*, pp. 248–253, IEEE, 2018, August.

5

Modeling A Deep Learning Network Model for Medical Image Panoptic Segmentation

Jyothsna Devi Koppagiri and Gouranga Mandal*

School of Computer Science and Engineering, VIT-AP University, Andhra Pradesh, India

Abstract
Panoptic segmentation has garnered significant interest in recent years, which has sped up the creation of several related algorithms. The notable success of deep learning techniques on other tasks has encouraged the adoption of a wider range of deep neural networks for panoptic segmentation. With an emphasis on the interpretation and analysis of RGB picture data, this paper offers a thorough investigation of panoptic segmentation. This work begins by outlining the history of panoptic segmentation, which includes panoptic segmentation and deep learning algorithms. The work moves into detail on a wide range of panoptic segmentation-related subjects using deep masking convolutional model (DMCM), which include evaluation metrics, panoptic segmentation models, datasets linked to the field, and derived sub-fields based on panoptic segmentation. Lastly, the writers assess the challenges and opportunities in this field and suggest directions for the future.

Keywords: Panoptic segmentation, deep learning, prediction, accuracy, learning model

5.1 Introduction

It is believed that scene understanding is essential to real vision frameworks, such as expanded realism or autonomous driving. The most common techniques used to address the problem of scene understanding

**Corresponding author*: gourangamandal@yahoo.com

R. Nidhya, D. Pavithra, Manish Kumar, A. Dinesh Kumar and S. Balamurugan (eds.) Generative Artificial Intelligence: Concepts and Applications, (81–92) © 2025 Scrivener Publishing LLC

are object detection and picture segmentation. Parts of a scene are often divided into "thing" and "stuff" items [1]. "Things" are countable items, such as pedestrians, cars, and riders, whereas "stuff" is uncountable, formless spaces like the sky, streets, and walkways. The goal of object detection, which includes classes and bounding boxes, is to provide what is perhaps the most important piece of "things" information [2]. Another method for comprehending a picture is image segmentation, which may be constructed as an instance segmentation problem or as a grouping problem of pixels with semantic labels [3]. For every input pixel, semantic segmentation applies pixel-level tagging using "stuff" or "things." By identifying and representing "things" in inputs, instance segmentation broadens the scope of semantic segmentation even more [4].

The history of object identification has historically been dominated by deep learning-based and traditional object detection techniques. The bulk of classic models (histogram of oriented gradient detector, deformable part model, etc.) were built using manually created features since efficient picture representation was deficient [5]. These features were then fed through classifiers to identify objects using sliding-window techniques. With the use of convolutional neural networks (CNNs), a deep learning architecture, deep learning-based models developed robust and high-level feature representations of an image as contrasted to handmade features. Deep learning-based object detection models usually consist of two parts (encoder and decoder) [6]. When an encoder is given an image to work with, it passes the image through several layers and blocks to extract statistical characteristics that may be used to find and identify objects. After receiving the encoder's outputs, a decoder identifies each item's bounding boxes and labels [7]. Similar to object identification, the evolution of picture segmentation has also gone through two stages: classical models and deep-learning-based models. Early methods of picture segmentation were based on digital image processing and optimization algorithms. The models used region growth and snakes' techniques to compare pixel values and gain an understanding of the segment map. To represent the characteristics in an image from a local perspective, the older models concentrated on pixel gradients and local differences [8]. Eventually, approaches like Otsu's algorithm, clustering algorithms, and adaptive thresholding were developed and added to the repertoire of common image-processing techniques [9]. These algorithms viewed the supplied image from a worldwide viewpoint. The fast development of deep learning technology has led to the rapid growth in the popularity of the deep learning-based picture segmentation approach [10]. The deep learning-based image segmentation technique's basic idea is to extract the input picture's high-level semantic information by utilizing the deep neural network's powerful feature extraction capabilities. To be more precise, the deep learning-based picture segmentation model is structured as follows:

1) **Deep Masking Convolutional Model (DMCM):** The underlying architecture of DMCM is the key idea behind deep learning-based picture segmentation. To hierarchical information from input photos, these networks are painstakingly created. The DMCM effectively captures local patterns while gradually accumulating increasingly abstract representations thanks to the use of convolutional layers.
2) **Convolutional architecture:** A popular design used by image segmentation networks is the encoder-decoder architecture. The encoder component is made up of many convolutional layers that increase the number of feature channels while progressively decreasing the input image's spatial resolution. In contrast, the decoder part restores the spatial resolution by using trans-posed convolutions or upsampling operations, which makes it easier to create precise segmentation maps.
3) **Segmentation:** In image segmentation networks, skip connections are commonly used to combine information from different resolutions. The model may simultaneously use low-level and high-level characteristics throughout the segmentation phase because of these links. The network improves its overall segmentation performance by incorporating multi-scale information, which makes it more skilled at managing fine details and gathering larger contextual information. Incorporating both semantic and instance segmentation, panoptic segmentation offers a consistent framework for examining scenes, which may be advantageous in practical scenarios. Subsequently, several significant research projects were put out, contributing to the advancement of panoramic segmentation. This article explores the problems and obstacles in deep learning-based panoptic segmentation with a focus on the development trends and prospects of all-encompassing segmentation.

The work is structured as follows: Section 5.2 provides a broader analysis of various prevailing approaches. The proposed methodology is discussed in Section 5.3, with numerical outcomes in Section 5.4. The summary is provided in Section 5.5.

5.2 Related Works

A significant advancement in computer vision is panoptic segmentation, which allows for a combinatorial view of "things" and "stuff." As a result, it signifies a novel approach to picture segmentation [11]. This section presents and thoroughly discusses the panoptic segmentation studies that have been offered in the literature to enlighten the state-of-the-art performance. Certain panoptic segmentation methods utilize instance and semantic segmentation independently, then merge or aggregate the outcomes to provide panoptic segmentation. Consequently, as shown in Figure 5.3, the shared backbone is utilized by utilizing the characteristics produced by the backbone in other areas of the network. Similar techniques have been employed by other frameworks, but they make an explicit relationship between instance and semantic networks [12]. The majority of the panoptic segmentation frameworks that were put out employed RGB photos, but some also used LIDAR data and medical imaging. We go over current frameworks in this area according to the kind of data that is used.

But Panoptic-DeepLab, a straightforward approach that only needs three loss functions for training, is presented in [13]. With its state-of-the-art performance on publicly available benchmarks, developed from the ground up, the Panoptic-DeepLab is the first panoptic segmentation method that achieves end-to-end inference speed. Dual decoder segmentation, for example, and semantic segmentation using dual atrous spatial pyramid pooling have been implemented [14]. Furthermore, the semantic segmentation design is a conventional model, whereas the instance segmentation branch that is employed is class-neutral and uses a straightforward instance centre regression. In [15], an end-to-end single-shot approach is used to get the object instances (things) and background information from panoptic segmentation. This results in non-overlapping segmentation at a video frame rate. Thus, without requiring instance segmentation, combining subnetwork outputs with instance-aware panoptic logits is taken into consideration.

5.3 Methodology

The Cancer Genome Atlas (TCGA): This dataset, which includes thirty 1000*1000 histopathology pictures, was gathered from TCGA and magnified by 40. The liver, stomach, kidney, colon, prostate, and breast are seven organs represented by each picture. We have separated the same data so that we may compare it with state-of-the-art techniques. Twelve photographs total—three from each organ—are utilized in the training process. During training from photos, 20 patches with 256*256 are selected. Next, fundamental augmentation methods, including 180-, 270-, and 90-degree rotations in both directions, are used. Next, to ensure robustness against Gaussian noise, Gaussian noise with median blur, and noise and color fluctuation in histology pictures, complicated augmentation is employed. Four pictures of the prostate, kidneys, liver, and breasts make up the validation set. The unseen testing set consists of the next 14 photos, which are six pictures of the remaining three organs that were left out. On the other hand, the eight images in the visible testing set are taken from the same four organs as those in the practice set. Nucleus instances are segmented directly from each 1000x1000 picture utilized in testing.

5.3.1 Deep Masking Convolutional Model (DMCM)

A dataset was used to train the DMCM model. The collection consists of images of 353 (graphene), 569 (MoS2), 862 (graphene), and 318 (WTe2). 456 (hBN), 4805 (graphene), 839 (MoS2), and 1053 (WTe2) were the annotated components. Our proprietary Python scripts were used to transform the annotations to a JSON format that is suitable for the COCO dataset from Microsoft. Ultimately, an $8:2$ random partition was used to divide the annotated dataset into training and test datasets. The provided multitask loss function was used to train the model on the annotated dataset. $L_{cls}, L_{box}, and\ L_{mask}$, respectively, indicate the segmentation mask losses, localization mask losses, and classification mask losses; the control parameter $\alpha - \gamma$ is used to tune the equilibrium of the loss sets, where $(\alpha, \beta, \gamma) = (0.6, 1.0, 1.0)$. The interest region for which the categorization outcome is u is represented by the probability distribution $p = (p_0, ..., p_k)$, which indicates the loss in the class. The description of the bounding box L_{box} loss is as follows:

$$L_{cls} = -\log p_u \tag{5.1}$$

Where, $smooth_{L_1}(x) = \begin{cases} 0.5x^2 & |x| < 1 \\ |x| - 0.5 & else \end{cases}$. The disappearance of the mask L_{mask} was found to be the mean loss on binary cross-entropy.

$$L_{mask} = -\frac{1}{m^2}[y_{ij}.\log \hat{y}_{ij}^k + (1 - y_{ij})\log(1 - \hat{y}_{ij}^k)] \quad (5.2)$$

Where, $\hat{y}_{ij}^k$ is the projected class label of the same cell and y_{ij} is the binary mask at (i, j) from an ROI of $(m \times m)$ size on the ground truth mask of class k. Instead of starting from scratch while training the model, the MS-COCO dataset is a sizable dataset for object segmentation in broad circumstances and was used to initialize the model weights, except for the network heads. Random values were used to initialize the remaining weights in the network. The optimization process employed a weight decay of 0.0001 and a velocity of 0.9 for a stochastic gradient descent. There were 500 iterations in every training phase. Each of the four training phases lasted for 30 epochs. The initial two training phases had a fixed learning rate of 10^{-3}. For the remaining two phases, the learning rate was lowered to 10^{-4} and 10^{-5}. In the initial step, training was solely given to the network heads.

Subsequently, the backbone's layer 4 components were optimized. The complete model, including the heads and backbone, was trained in phases three and four. A total of four GPUs (NVIDIA Tesla V100 with 32 GB RAM) were employed during the 12-hour training session. We employed data augmentation techniques, such as rotation, color channel multiplication, flips and shifts, horizontally and vertically, to enhance the number of training datasets. To minimize storage use, Figure 5.1 offers instances of the upgraded data. These activities were carried out online on training data at random frequencies. Before each image was supplied, it was enlarged to 1024×1024 pixels to the DMCM model while maintaining the aspect ratio, and any extra space was zero-padded.

To enhance the network's capacity for generalization, we divided the DMCM model's training process into two stages. Initially, a variety of 2D materials, including graphene, hBN, MoS2, and WTe2, were used to train the model. By now, the material and layer thickness had been identified, and the model had been trained to do segmentation and classification. Next, we classified layer thickness by performing transfer learning on each material subset using the taught weights as a source. Through the use of this technique, the feature values underlying the network heads that are

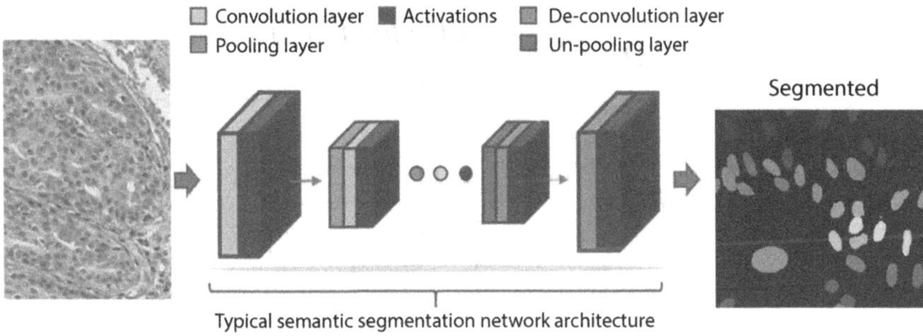

Figure 5.1 Architecture model.

shared by 2D materials were optimized and dispersed across the various materials. The backbone network sharing resulted in a decreased test loss and quicker network weight convergence, as seen below. The loss function's value as a function of the epoch count is displayed in Figure 5.3. The test (training) loss is shown by the solid (dotted) curves. Either data augmentation or none was used during training. In the absence of augmentation, the test loss rose while the training loss dropped to zero. Training resulted in a considerable rise in the difference between training and test losses, which shows that the training data is overfitted by the model and that the generalization error increased. When data augmentation was used, there was no disparity between the validation and training losses and both types of losses declined monotonically with training. These findings suggest that it is possible to train the DMCM model without overfitting in 2D materials if 2000 optical microscope pictures are generated.

5.4 Numerical Results and Discussion

As the main measure for assessing the panoptic segmentation task, the panoptic quality (PQ) is defined as follows: where g is the ground truth and DL predicts p. It is the COCO panoptic task challenge's current measure. The aforementioned equation is the result of multiplying two measures, namely the recognition quality (RQ) and segmentation quality (SQ) as follows:

$$PQ = \frac{\Sigma_{(p,g)\in TP} IoU(pred, GT)}{|TP| + \frac{1}{2}|FP| + \frac{1}{2}|FN|} \tag{5.3}$$

$$SQ = \frac{\Sigma_{(p,g)\in TP} IoU\,(pred, GT)}{|TP|} \tag{5.4}$$

$$RQ = \frac{TP}{|TP| + \frac{1}{2}|FP| + \frac{1}{2}|FN|} \tag{5.5}$$

The main metrics utilized to evaluate this study are the measurements of panoptic segmentation (PQ, SQ, and RQ). The results for these measures are shown in Table 5.1. Except for the RQ$stffb*$ the DMCM model backbone is used both in the test set and the SQ_{thighs} in the validation set provided the better metrics in the most of situations when compared to the prior "stuff" and "thing" findings. In general, there was over 2% variation in the primary analysis measure (PQ) between the backbones. The slight differences between the various topologies imply that using a lighter backbone can nevertheless produce results that are quite close in scenarios requiring less processing power. The panoptic segmentation problem introduces novel difficulties in the design of database structures and algorithms that address the specifics of semantic and object segmentation. As a result, panoptic segmentation creates a unified method for picture segmentation, altering digital image processing and necessitating the use of large, customized datasets along with new annotation tools. By creating a panoptic remote sensing dataset, creating a panoptic data annotation tool, and conducting one of the first assessments of the application of panoptic segmentation in medical imaging (See Figures 5.2 and 5.3), this research innovates in this regard. Figure 5.4 is the final outcome of the model.

Panoptic segmentation is frequently used in medical field photos, particularly for images that don't need to be processed in real-time. Since most photos are taken at least a few days apart, several often-researched metrics, including inference time, become substantially less meaningful. The more information we can obtain at the same time in medical imaging, the better. On the other hand, panoptic segmentation introduces certain non-trivial procedures for data production, requiring information for semantic, as well as instance segmentation. Furthermore, the "stuff" classes are not completely embraced by the panoptic segmentation research that is now underway and that provides unique remote sensing datasets. By overcoming some of the challenges associated with semantic and instance

Table 5.1 A comparison of an existing vs. proposed method.

Backbone	Type	PQ	SQ	RQ
Testing set				
R50	All	65	85	76
	Thing	59	82	71
	Segmentation	85	93	91
DMCM	All	63	84	74
	Thing	57	82	69
	Segmentation	85	92	92
Difference	All	1.5	0.2	1.6
	Thing	1.8	0.09	2.2
	Segmentation	0.15	0.65	-0.5
Training set				
R50	All	64	85	75
	Thing	58	83	69
	Segmentation	89	93	95
DMCM	All	62	85	72
	Thing	55	83	65
	Segmentation	87	92	94
Difference	All	2.7	0.06	3.2
	Thing	3.1	-0.17	4.04
	Segmentation	1.4	0.92	0.5

segmentation, panoptic segmentation may mark a breakthrough in the medical industry by enabling the collection of countable items and background components using a single framework. However, compared to other approaches, the data-gathering process and model construction are far more complicated, underscoring the need to close this gap.

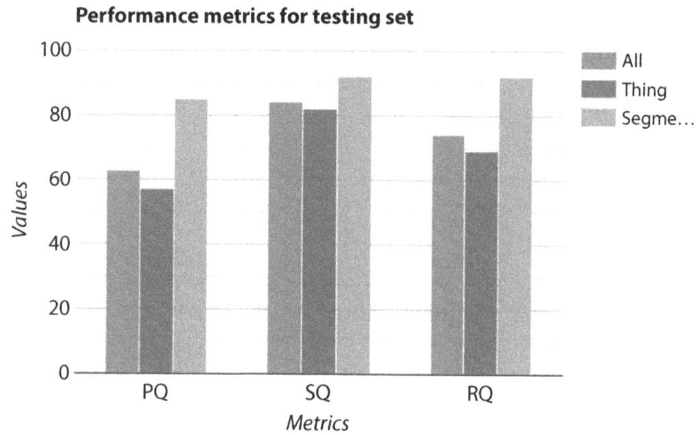

Figure 5.2 Performance metrics comparison with a testing set.

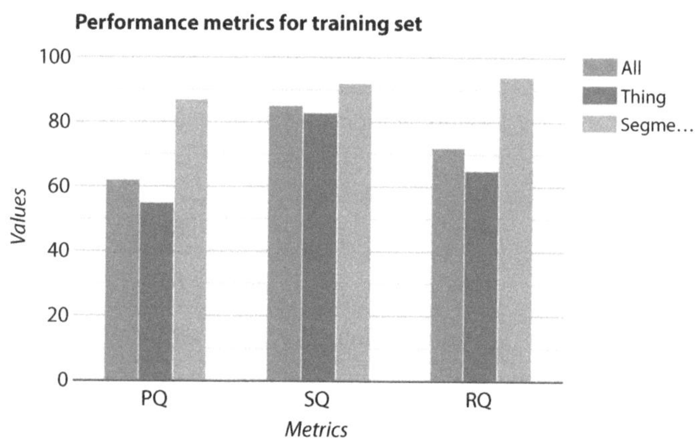

Figure 5.3 Performance metrics for training set.

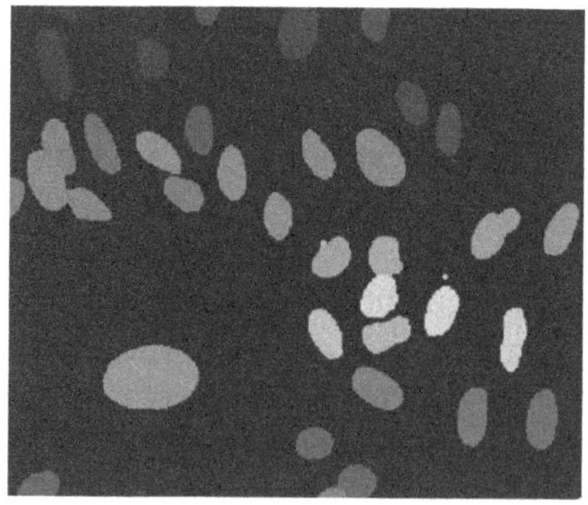

Figure 5.4 Segmented outcomes.

5.5 Conclusion

In this work, we address a panoptic segmentation problem for 2D images and classify the panoptic segmentation using DMCM model, taking into account the datasets, categories, and assessment techniques of panoptic segmentation. Two-branch, multi-subnetwork, and classifier-based models are the three categories into which panoptic segmentation methods may be separated from the standpoint of network structure. We go over the main principle behind each model, the network's performance, the data set that was utilized, etc. Additionally, we go over a few related panoptic segmentation-based subtasks and panoptic part segmentation. We also talk about the challenges that the research problem of panoptic segmentation faces, such as item sizes, conflicts, and complicated scenes. These issues are the most pressing ones that need to be resolved in the present panoptic segmentation. We also spoke about the panoptic segmentation development trend for the future in response to the existing issues. It should be noted that the work of panoptic segmentation cannot and does not fit into one article. Additionally, we believe that this study will facilitate a rapid understanding of one of the panoptic segmentation research topics for academics, particularly those who are unfamiliar with the subject.

References

1. Xing, and Yang, L., Robust nucleus/cell detection and segmentation in digital pathology and microscopy images: A comprehensive review. *IEEE Rev. Biomed. Eng.*, 9, 234–263, 2016.
2. Song, Xiao, L., Lian, Z., Contour-seed pairs learning-based framework for simultaneously detecting and segmenting various overlapping cells/nuclei in microscopy images. *IEEE Trans. Image Process.*, 27, 12, 5759–5774, Dec. 2018.
3. Payer, Štern, D., Feiner, M., Bischof, H., Urschler, M., Segmenting and tracking cell instances with cosine embeddings and recurrent hourglass networks. *Med. Image Anal.*, 57, 106–119, Oct. 2019.
4. De Brabandere, Neven, D., Van Gool, L., Semantic instance segmentation with a discriminative loss function, 2017, arXiv:1708.02551. [Online]. Available: http://arxiv.org/abs/1708.02551.
5. Zhang, Y., Liu, S., Feng, D., Wang, Y., Cai, W., Nuclei instance segmentation with the dual contour-enhanced adversarial network, in: *Proc. IEEE 15th Int. Symp. Biomed. Imag. (ISBI)*, pp. 409–412, Apr. 2018.

6. Zhang, *et al.*, Panoptic segmentation with an end-to-end cell R-CNN for pathology image analysis, in: *Proc. Int. Conf. Med. Image Comput. Comput.-Assist. Intervent.*, pp. 237–244, Springer, Cham, Switzerland, 2018.
7. Liu, *et al.*, Nuclei segmentation via a deep panoptic model with semantic feature integration, in: *Proc. 28th Int. Joint Conf. Artif. Intell.*, AAAI Press, pp. 861–868, Aug. 2019.
8. Chen, Hermans, A., Papandreou, G., Schroff, F., Wang, P., Adam, H., MaskLab: Instance segmentation by refining object detection with semantic and direction features, in: *Proc. IEEE/CVF Conf. Comput. Vis. Pattern Recognit.*, pp. 4013–4022, Jun. 2018.
9. Saleh, Aliakbarian, M.S., Salzmann, M., Petersson, L., Alvarez, J.M., Effective use of synthetic data for urban scene semantic segmentation, in: *Proc. Eur. Conf. Comput. Vis.*, pp. 86–103, Springer, Cham, Switzerland, 2018.
10. Li, Y. *et al.*, Attention-guided unified network for panoptic segmentation, in: *Proc. IEEE/CVF Conf. Comput. Vis. Pattern Recognit. (CVPR)*, pp. 7026–7035, Jun. 2019.
11. Chen, *et al.*, Hybrid task cascade for instance segmentation, in: *Proc. IEEE/CVF Conf. Comput. Vis. Pattern Recognit. (CVPR)*, pp. 4974–4983, Jun. 2019.
12. He, Zhang, X., Ren, S., Sun, J., Deep residual learning for image recognition, in: *Proc. IEEE Conf. Comput. Vis. Pattern Recognit. (CVPR)*, pp. 770–778, Jun. 2016.
13. Lin, Dollar, P., Girshick, R., He, K., Hariharan, B., Belongie, S., Feature pyramid networks for object detection, in: *Proc. IEEE Conf. Comput. Vis. Pattern Recognit. (CVPR)*, pp. 2117–2125, Jul. 2017.
14. Chen, Li, W., Sakaridis, C., Dai, D., Van Gool, L., Domain adaptive faster R-CNN for object detection in the wild, in: *Proc. IEEE/CVF Conf. Comput. Vis. Pattern Recognit.*, pp. 3339–3348, Jun. 2018.
15. Salvador, *et al.*, Recurrent neural networks for semantic instance segmentation, 2017, arXiv:1712.00617. [Online]. Available: http://arxiv.org/abs/1712.00617.

6

A Hybrid DenseNet Model for Dental Image Segmentation Using Modern Learning Approaches

Pulipati Nagaraju[1] and S. V. Sudha[2]*

[1]*School of Computer Science and Engineering, VIT-AP University, Andhra Pradesh, India*
[2]*Department of Artificial Intelligence and Data Science, KPR Institute of Engineering and Technology, Coimbatore, Tamil Nadu, India*

Abstract
Dental X-ray image segmentation is a powerful tool that helps physicians identify dental diseases and evaluate tooth status. There is a growing necessity for swift and efficient segmentation algorithms that do not rely on other computing methods but can seamlessly integrate into X-ray imaging. This work targets to explore effective deep-learning techniques for dental image segmentation, specifically designed for dental image segmentation. This study presents a unique neural network design known as a hybrid DenseNet transformer (HDNT) that makes use of knowledge distillation. This proposed technique was trained using the dataset of panoramic dental X-ray pictures, as were other deep learning algorithms now in use. Afterwards, several accuracy indicators were used to assess and contrast the effectiveness of these simple techniques. Notably, with an Intersection over Union (IoU) of 0.75 and Dice coefficient of 0.85, the suggested hybrid technique outperforms existing methods with huge network parameters for the trained model. This study demonstrates the memory-efficient and comparable performance of the anticipated method for segmenting dental images. Because of its modest memory requirements, it may be suitable for deployment, which might help physicians improve the accuracy of their analysis and streamline their daily routine.

***Keywords*:** Segmentation, deep learning, prediction, hybrid model, accuracy

**Corresponding author*: svsudha.mvenki@gmail.com

R. Nidhya, D. Pavithra, Manish Kumar, A. Dinesh Kumar and S. Balamurugan (eds.) Generative Artificial Intelligence: Concepts and Applications, (93–106) © 2025 Scrivener Publishing LLC

6.1 Introduction

By accurately defining the borders of teeth, correct tooth segmentation aids in surgical planning and is crucial for the clinical diagnosis of dental disorders [1]. In orthodontics, it is essential to have instant access to real-time data on tooth movement and root depths to swiftly align a patient's teeth and finish the orthodontic treatment cycle faster [2]. Accurate tooth division in dental panoramic radiography pictures is essential to achieve this, with further applications in age estimate, quickly straightening a patient's teeth and expediting the completion of the orthodontic treatment cycle [3]. Precise tooth segmentation in oral panoramic radiography provides a thorough depiction of the interior structure of the mouth, dentistry heavily depends on them for diagnosis [4]. Extra-oral radiographs, such as the cephalometric and panoramic pictures, provide vital information about a patient's dental health by capturing the complete dentition and its surrounding regions. On the other hand, manual and semi-automated techniques for segmenting the tissues and teeth in these radiographs are frequently tedious, subjective, and time-consuming, and they mostly depend on the dentist's experience [5]. Furthermore, segmenting in contexts with low-quality images poses further difficulties. It is still essential to build an automated, precise, and effective teeth segmentation approach in light of these limitations.

Developing an automated tooth segmentation method with excellent accuracy has been the focus of several attempts [6]. But teeth segmentation is still a difficult process, mainly because of blurry borders from noisy and poor contrast dental panoramic X-ray pictures. The availability of dental tools like as metal racks and implants, together with the variation in tooth health across patients, provides significant barriers to precise tooth segmentation. This work offers a unique panoptic segmentation-based technique in consideration of these difficulties [7]. Semantic segmentation, which recognizes and categorizes objects in a picture, and instance segmentation, which distinguishes different instances of each item, are often independent jobs—and are combined in panoptic segmentation. A more thorough and precise method of segmenting teeth and oral tissues is offered by this amalgamation. Panoptic segmentation has been shown in several studies to be effective in improving the deep learning models' performance.

We introduce an innovative architecture designed for effective training and inference utilizing the mask transformer. Unlike traditional designs [8] that position the transformer on a convolutional neural network (CNN), the method employs path design that smoothly blends transformers [9]. Including self-attention, pixel-to-memory, memory attention, and memory-to-pixel, this integration makes it easier for CNN layers to interact with global memory. Thus, the transformer might be introduced dynamically at any CNN layer allowing for different phases of connection with global memory. Moreover, A decoder akin to a stacked hourglass [10] is incorporated into the existing design to aggregate multi-scale information and provide an output with a high resolution. The transformer model is then predicted by combining this output with information from global memory. We achieve significant improvements in segmentation performance with our system, which may have applications in tooth numbering. The UFBA-UESC dental imaging dataset is used to rigorously test our model, and the outcomes demonstrate that it performs noticeably superior to prevailing methods currently in segmentation accuracy and resilience.

The following is how this paper is organized: The backdrop and relevant work are covered in detail in Section 6.2. Section 6.3 offers a thorough explanation of the dataset and network design. In Section 6.4, the experimental setup is described in great depth. Section 6.4 presents the findings, and a thorough examination of these outcomes is conducted. Section 6.5 summarizes the findings and suggests possible topics for future research.

6.2 Related Works

Experimental evidence has showcased the superior performance of deep learning algorithms in tasks related to image segmentation, particularly in domains like dental image segmentation, compared to conventional methods. Semantic segmentation in dental X-ray imaging has been accomplished through the use of many conventional procedures encompassing approaches such as the level set technique, fuzzy method, region growth, splitting and merging, and global thresholding. For instance, a comparison utilizing dental X-ray images was presented in the work by [11], highlighting the efficacy of employing diverse techniques.

Studies have elucidated that methods utilizing deep learning for segmenting panoramic X-ray images outperform standard methodologies, marking the initial research to illustrate these advantages. Recent investigations, notably explored, thoroughly examined modern deep learning-based segmentation techniques in stomatological images. Notable methodologies encompass the creation of instance segmentation for dental X-ray images via mask R-CNN (MRCNN), as well as the utilization of U-Net, a prominent technique employed to develop semantic segmentation for dental X-ray pictures for image classification assignments. According to these studies, U-Net demonstrated enhanced performance, particularly when augmented with data augmentation techniques like horizontal flipping and an ensemble approach [12]. Nonetheless, challenges arise concerning image variables, such as poor contrast between the base and border of a tooth, impacting the efficacy of MRCNN and U-Net. Strategies focused on enhancing the image focus have been proposed to mitigate this issue.

Dental image segmentation offers the potential to develop a streamlined model through alternative strategies like knowledge distillation methods and compression approaches [13]. Knowledge distillation typically involves transferring knowledge from sophisticated, larger teaching models to train a compact student model capable of replicating the exemplary performance of its teacher. Initially, employing a soft probability output was the primary technique in knowledge distillation to attain teacher-like performance in a student model. However, a more advanced method involves training an intermediate student network using feature maps, contributing to a refined approach to knowledge distillation. Manipulating intermediate feature maps has shown promise in enhancing the performance of tasks such as image segmentation [14]. In addressing challenges specific to semantic segmentation, novel knowledge distillation techniques have recently emerged. For instance, an effective and adaptable technique utilizing knowledge distillation has been introduced for the segmentation of medical images like CT scans [15]. Moreover, semantic segmentation can also benefit from alternative knowledge distillation methods, including transformer-based knowledge distillation and structured knowledge distillation. An unconventional approach for segmenting dental X-rays involves transformer-based knowledge distillation, which entails distilling extensive teacher transformations utilizing feature maps and patch embedding to facilitate the learning process of compact student transformers.

6.3 Methodology

6.3.1 Dataset

In this experimental evaluation, our algorithms were tested using a dataset comprising 1500 dental panoramic X-ray pictures. The dataset originally consisted of 10 categories; however, in alignment with recommendations, categories 5 and 6, containing images featuring implants and deciduous teeth, were excluded from our experiments. Therefore, a total of 1321 panoramic dental X-ray images were employed in our study. These pictures were divided into 432 training, 111 validation, and 778 testing images. As part of the picture preparation process, the photos were resized and normalized. In particular, the pictures were scaled down from their original dimensions of $1991*1127$ to a standardized size of $256*256$ as part of our preprocessing protocol.

6.3.2 Dense Transformer Model

The transformer architecture, initially introduced and aimed to address the constraints on parallel computing in natural language understanding. Some authors extended this concept by proposing the transformer model for image classification tasks in computer vision, operating across various domains. Figure 6.1 shows the structural representation of the transformer inside the dense network. An important part of the transformer is an enhancement of the attention system is the self-attention mechanism. It assigns various weights to distinct pixel information and mostly depends on the internal relationships among picture feature information. The incoming picture data is converted into three different matrices using the self-attention mechanism. The similarity matrix, QK^T, is then obtained by multiplying matrix Q by the transpose of matrix K reflecting

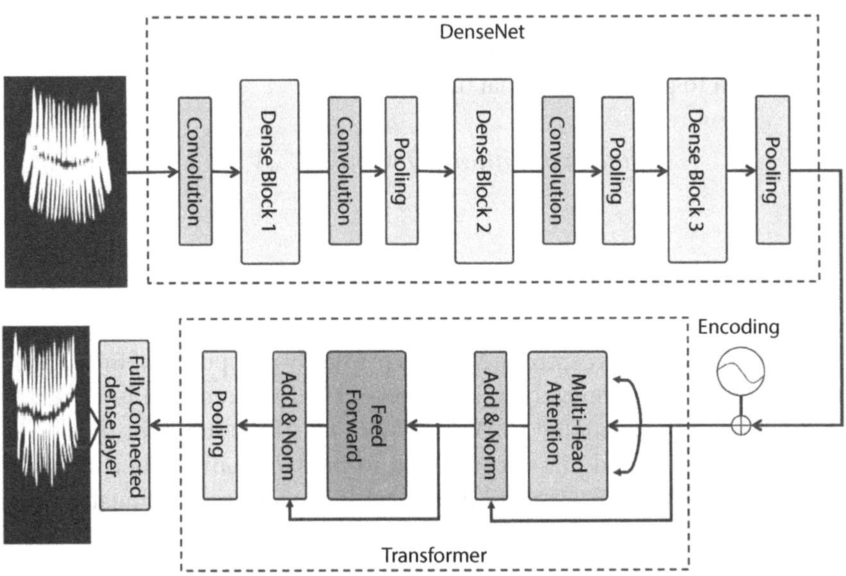

Figure 6.1 Hybrid DenseNet transformer.

the correlations between them. A higher value in this matrix signifies a stronger correlation. By using the softmax function to similarity matrix normalization and ensure match probabilities, the weight matrix is produced. Ultimately, the input matrix's attention mechanism is attained by multiplying the weight matrix by value matrix. This process is succinctly expressed in Equation 6.1, yielding the final result.

$$Attention\,(V,K,Q) = softmax\,\frac{QK^T}{\sqrt{d_k}}V \tag{6.1}$$

The matrices $Q, K, and\ V$ are derived from the same input but processed using different parameters. A moderating factor, $\sqrt{d_k}$ is employed to smoothen the impact of dimensions ($k\ dimensions$) in the key matrix, preventing the resultant multiplication from becoming excessively large. Following this, the resultant vector undergoes normalization via a softmax activation function, ensuring all values are positive and conform to a probability distribution. The self-attentive process is the central element of the transformer design. It comprises n self-attentive modules, each consisting of distinct linear transformation matrices: $W_i^Q, W_i^K, and\ W_i^V$, illustrating the transformation matrices with self-attentiveness.

The input vectors X_i, are subjected to these matrices. projecting them into different spaces to augment the model's representational capacity and generate corresponding $Q, K, and\ V$ matrices. These output matrices are multiplied and combined with the linear matrix W^0 from self-attentive mechanism to generate the final output matrix.

$$head_1 = attention\,(QW_i^Q, KW_i^K, VW_i^V) \tag{6.2}$$

$$Multi\,(Q,K,V) = concat\,(head_i, \ldots, head_h)W^0 \tag{6.3}$$

The multi-layer perceptron (MLP) is primarily composed of linear activation layer, two completely linked layers called the rectified linear units (ReLU), which are denoted as $W_1, b_1, W_2, and\ b_2$. They stand for the corresponding weights and biases connected to the two completely connected layers. The calculation involved in the MLP is expressed in Equation 6.3. This calculation typically entails a linear combination of inputs via the weights and biases, followed by the application of the ReLU activation function. This process contributes to the nonlinear mapping of the input data through the MLP layers.

$$MLP\,(X) = (0, XW_1, b_1)W_2 + b_2 \tag{6.4}$$

Position embedding plays a crucial role in enabling self-attentiveness within an image, unlike in natural language processing where multiple sequences of words are present. To achieve this within image data, first, the CNN is employed to split the picture into tiny, fixed-sized segments. Next, an embedding matrix of positions that can be learned is concatenated to assimilate positional information relevant to the image segments. Following this step, layer normalization (LN) and multilayer perceptron (MLP) operations are applied. Ultimately, each layer of the transformer can be represented using Equations 6.5 and 6.6.

$$O_l' = MLP\,(LN(O_{l-1})) + O_l \tag{6.5}$$

$$O_l = MLP\,(LN(O_l')) + O_l') \tag{6.6}$$

This process enables the transformer architecture to harness self-attention within the segmented image, enhancing its ability to capture relationships and dependencies among different segments. The equation provided indicates the transformation process within the transformer architecture. In the context of medical imaging, before inputting the medical image data into the transform layer, the image undergoes segmentation. This segmentation operation partitions an input image X, which belongs to the space of three-dimensional real numbers $X \in R^{3*H*W}$, into $N = (H/P) \times (W/P)$ blocks for labeling. Here, $H \times W$ represents the resolution of the image, P represents each image segmentation size, and N represents total picture segmentation blocks. The two-dimensional picture is segmented and then converted into a one-dimensional embedded image sequence X_e in the real number space $X_e \in R^{(N \times C_e)}$ via a projection function., where C_e represents the dimensionality of each block. The resultant sequence of one-dimensional images is then sent to the transform layer for additional processing.

6.3.3 DenseNet Model

The DenseNet model is an enhancement of the dense network structure that aims to diminish overall parameters and boost network running speed. To support integer divisions of k, where $n \geq 0$ *and* $k - 2^n \geq 0$, The sparse connection pattern used by a dense network connects layer k to layers $k - 2^n$ and 2^n. This connection schema enables the clearing of memory from layer 1 to layer 2^{n-1} upon processing 2^n, reducing the computational load for model parameter calculations. In this case, a CNN feature extraction network built with dense network receives $x \in R^{\left(\frac{H}{16}\right)*(W/16)} \times C \times n$, as image data. Here, n is the total number of photographs and C for the image channels. This setup enables the conversion of high-resolution photos into low-resolution ones and completes the initial feature extraction of photographs. The segmentation network simultaneously feeds the upsampling process with low-dimensional feature information from the picture. During the encoding and staging stages, this method helps to reduce the size of the picture features potentially leading to some information loss.

6.4 Numerical Results and Discussion

Within our experiments, as depicted in the Figures 6.2, 6.3 and 6.4 for the sake of comparison, five different error measures were used to assess these algorithms' performance. These measures include volumetric overlap error (VOE), Hausdorff distance (HD), Dice coefficient (DC), IoU and relative volume difference (RVD). Each metric serves a specific purpose and is described as follows:

Intersection over Union (IoU): IoU serves as a metric to assess the precision of object detection within an image. It measures how much of the ground truth bounding box, which contains the items of interest, and the anticipated bounding box overlap.

$$IOU = \frac{A_{PB} \cap A_{TB}}{A_{PB} \cup A_{TB}} \tag{6.7}$$

Hausdorff Distance (HD): The metric space distance between two sets is measured using the Hausdorff distance. The greatest value among the shortest paths between each location in one set and the nearest point in the other set is quantified. This distance metric provides an interpretation of the furthest proximity or dissimilarity between two sets.

$$d_H\ (X,Y) = (superior\ d(x,Y),\ superior\ (X,y))\} \tag{6.8}$$

Dice Coefficient (DC): One metric for comparing two sets' similarity is the dice coefficient. Specifically, in the context of image segmentation, it assesses how closely the segmented region (predicted) and the ground truth region resemble one other. In terms of math, it is defined as:

$$Dice = \frac{2(O_{pred} \cap O_{truth})}{O_{pred} + O_{truth}} \tag{6.9}$$

The predicted set is denoted by O_{pred}, the ground truth set by O_{truth}, the intersection (common elements) between the ground truth and projected sets, the cardinality of the predicted set and the cardinality of the ground truth set by O_{truth}.

Volumetric Overlap Error (VOE): The VOE is a metric utilized to quantify the error rate in segmentation tasks. It assesses how much the anticipated segmentation volume and the ground truth volume diverge or mismatch. An entirely accurate overlap or similarity between ground truth and segmented volumes is indicated by a VOE value of '0'. The VOE has a range of 0 to 1. As the value moves towards '1', it indicates an increasing level of discrepancy or error between the volumes, signifying poorer accuracy of segmentation.

$$VOE = \frac{2 * (O_{pred} - O_{truth})}{O_{pred} + O_{truth}} \tag{6.10}$$

Relative Volume Difference (RVD): The RVD serves as a metric to quantify the dissimilarity or variance in volume between the anticipated segmentation and the segmentation based on ground truth. The value of this statistic falls between 0 and 1. Here, '0' value denotes that the model's segmentation prediction perfectly matches the ground truth volume. As the RVD value increases towards '1', it shows that the volume difference or disparity between the projected and actual segmentations is growing. In essence, RVD provides insight into how closely or disparately the segmented volumes align with each other.

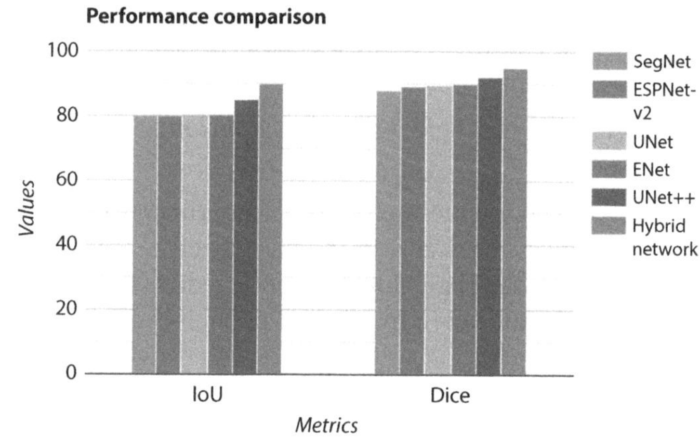

Figure 6.2 Performance comparison based on IoU and Dice.

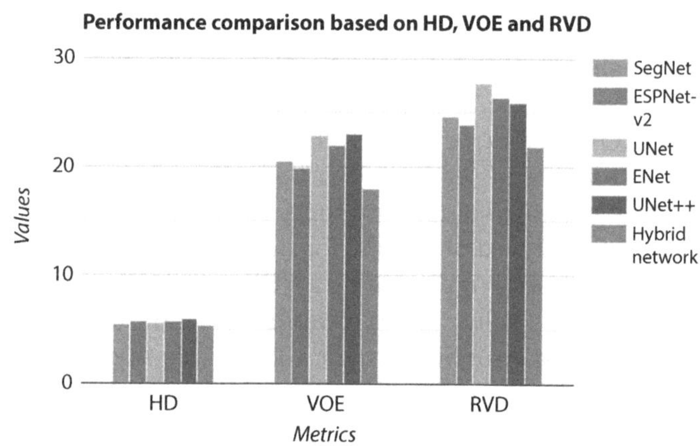

Figure 6.3 Performance comparison based on HD, VOE, and RVD.

6.4.1 Discussion

The comparison between our algorithm and other approaches is shown in Table 6.1, along with the sizes of the trained models and their corresponding Floating Point Operations (FLOPs). Interestingly, our model matches ESPNet-v2 in terms of model size and FLOPs, indicating that our approach requires the fewest parameters. Concerning FLOPs, our model aligns comparably with ENet, renowned for having the smallest FLOPs among the compared methods. An analysis using IoU, Dice, and HD metrics shows that the UNet approach performed better than any of the other evaluated methods. On the other hand, our strategy performed exceptionally well,

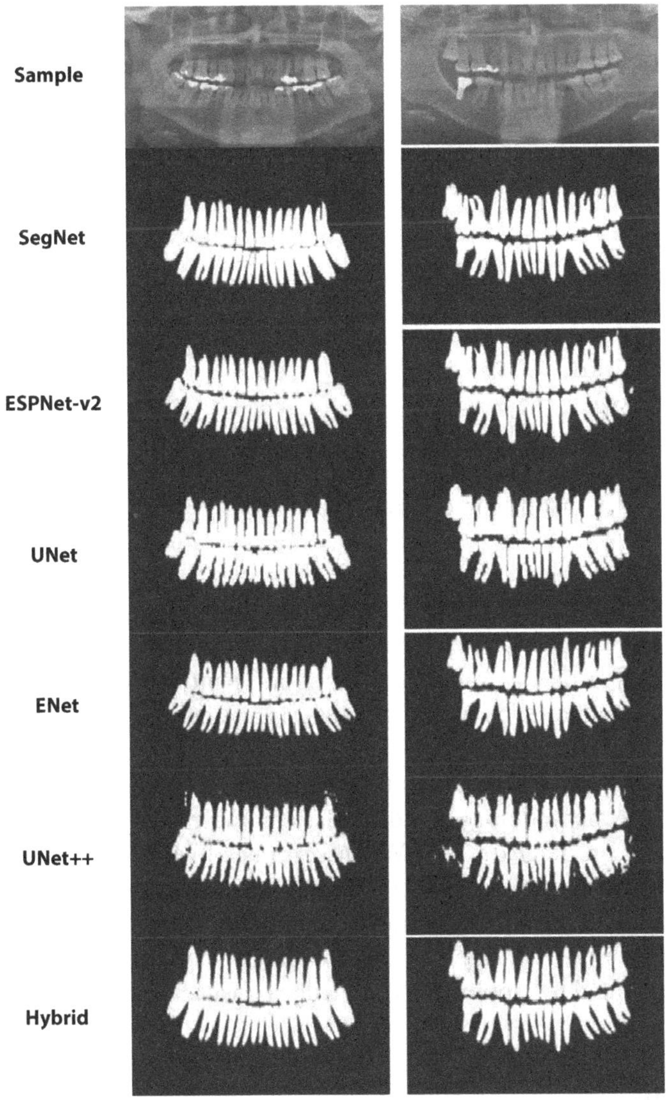

Figure 6.4 Segmented output.

showing the highest VOE and RVD indicators. Additionally, all assessment measures showed that our model beat ESPNet-v2, indicating that the knowledge consistency network efficiently promoted the transfer of information from the instructor network to the student network. Furthermore, our technique was compared with other approaches of knowledge distillation like attention, FitNet, and UNet approaches. These comparisons

Table 6.1 Performance metrics comparison.

Methods	IoU	Dice	HD	VOE	RVD
SegNet	80	88	5.5	20.5	24.6
ESPNet-v2	80.0	89	5.8	19.9	23.9
UNet	80.5	89.5	5.6	22.9	27.7
Enet	80.6	90	5.7	22	26.4
UNet++	85	92	6	23	25.9
Hybrid network (proposed)	**90**	**95**	**5.4**	**18**	**21.9**

provide a comprehensive assessment of our method's efficacy against existing knowledge distillation approaches.

6.5 Conclusion

In this study, a new method for segmenting panoramic dental X-ray pictures is presented. A comparative analysis against several other methods demonstrates that our hybrid DenseNet transformer excels in certain performance metrics and maintains comparable performance in others. Notably, our methodology stands out as a notable solution appropriate for deployment on other devices. When contrasted with other methods, our hybrid approach outperforms other approaches in five evaluation metrics. In our forthcoming research endeavors, we aim to delve deeper into interpreting our model's insights and comprehensively investigate the knowledge assimilated by employing knowledge consistency networks.

References

1. Terlemez, A., Tassoker, M., Kizilcakaya, M., Gulec, M., Comparison of cone-beam computed tomography and panoramic radiography in the evaluation of maxillary sinus pathology related to maxillary posterior teeth: Do apical lesions increase the risk of maxillary sinus pathology? *Imaging Sci. Dent.*, 49, 115–122, 2019.
2. Milletari, F., Ahmadi, S.-A., Kroll, C., Plate, A., Rozanski, V., Maiostre, J. *et al.*, Hough-CNN: Deep Learning for Segmentation of Deep Brain Regions in MRI and Ultrasound. *Comput. Vis. Image Underst.*, 164, 92–102, 2017.

3. Alsmadi, M.K., A hybrid Fuzzy C-Means and Neutrosophic for jaw lesions segmentation. *Ain Shams Eng. J.*, 9, 697–706, 2018.
4. Senthilkumaran, N., Genetic algorithm approach to edge detection for dental X-ray image segmentation. *Int. J. Adv. Res. Comput. Sci. Electron. Eng.*, 1, 5236–5238, 2012.
5. Esteva, A., Kuprel, B., Novoa, R.A., Ko, J., Swetter, S.M., Blau, H.M. *et al.*, Dermatologist-level classification of skin cancer with deep neural networks. *Nature*, 542, 115, 2017.
6. Couteaux, V., Si-Mohamed, S., Nempont, O., Lefevre, T., Popoff, A., Pizaine, G. *et al.*, Automatic knee meniscus tear detection and orientation classification with Mask-RCNN. *Diagn. Interv. Imaging*, 100, 235–242, 2019.
7. Lin, N.-H., Lin, T.-L., Wang, X., Kao, W.-T., Tseng, H.-W., Chen, S.L. *et al.*, Teeth Detection Algorithm and Teeth Condition Classification Based on Convolutional Neural Networks for Dental Panoramic Radiographs. *J. Med. Imaging Health Inf.*, 8, 507–515, 2018.
8. Fu, X., Liu, T., Xiong, Z., Smaill, B.H., Stiles, M.K., Zhao, J., Segmentation of histological images and fibrosis identification with a convolutional neural network. *Comput. Biol. Med.*, 98, 147–158, 2018.
9. Chen, L., Zhang, H., Xiao, J., SCA-CNN: Spatial and Channel-wise attention in convolutional networks for image captioning, in: *IEEE Conference on Computer Vision and Pattern Recognition, CVPR*, 2017.
10. Li, Y., Baciu, G., Han, Y., Li, C., Indoor localization with occlusion removal, in: *International Conference on Cognitive Informatics & Cognitive Computing, ICCI*CC*, pp. 191–198, 2017.
11. Liu, G., Reda, F.A., Shih, K.J., Wang, T., Tao, A., Catanzaro, B., Image Inpainting for irregular holes using partial convolutions, in: *European Conference on Computer Vision, ECCV*, pp. 85–100, 2018.
12. Pathak, D., Krahenbuhl, P., Donahue, J., Context Encoders: Feature learning by inpainting, in: *IEEE Conference on Computer Vision and Pattern Recognition, CVPR*, pp. 2536–2544, 2016.
13. Rakhshanfar, M. and Amer, M.A., Low-frequency image noise removal using white noise filter, in: *IEEE International Conference on Image Processing, ICIP*, pp. 3948–3952, 2018.
14. Yang, C., Lu, X., Lin, Z., Shechtman, E., Wang, O., Li, H., High-Resolution image inpainting using multi-scale neural patch synthesis, in: *IEEE Conference on Computer Vision and Pattern Recognition, CVPR*, pp. 6721–6729, 2017.
15. Kudo, K. and Okada, Y., Development of training system for dental treatment using webar and leap motion controller, in: *Conference on complex, intelligent, and software intensive systems*, Springer, Berlin, pp. 579–587, 2020.

7

Modeling A Two-Tier Network Model for Unconstraint Video Analysis Using Deep Learning

P. Naga Bhushanam and Selva Kumar S.*

School of Computer Science and Engineering, VIT-AP University, Andhra Pradesh, India

Abstract

Presently, deep learning achievements in video generation remain restricted, with only initial advancements in video prediction and an absence of noteworthy developments in video completion. These limitations stem from the fundamental inherent challenges in three problems, which are considerably ill-posed. A comprehensive two-tier convolutional neural network (2T-CNN) deep framework that can produce videos with different constraints or no constraints at all is presented in this research, which focuses on the production of human action videos. This framework effectively addresses three primary challenges: generating videos in the absence of input frames, predicting videos with only a limited number of initial frames, and completing videos when both the initial and final frames are available. Our 2T-CNN approach in addressing this complex problem involves two distinct steps. Initially, we construct a 2T-CNN model specifically tailored to produce a sequence of images depicting human postures from random noise. Subsequently, we developed the 2T-CNN network. This network leverages the previously generated complete human pose sequence and generates a human action video. This two-tier strategy allows us to circumvent the inherent ill-posed nature of the original problems. This approach makes it easier to generate, predict, and complete high-quality video results over much longer time spans than previous attempts. Our 2T-CNN approach outperforms current techniques in video generation, prediction, and completion, as evidenced by quantitative and qualitative evaluations that confirm the effectiveness of our strategy.

**Corresponding author*: selvakumar.s@vitap.ac.in

R. Nidhya, D. Pavithra, Manish Kumar, A. Dinesh Kumar and S. Balamurugan (eds.) Generative Artificial Intelligence: Concepts and Applications, (107–120) © 2025 Scrivener Publishing LLC

***Keywords*:** Unconstraint video, deep learning, prediction, frames, noise

7.1 Introduction

To address the previously overlooked concerns, this paper presents a two-tier deep framework for unconstraint video generation, prediction, and completion, aiming to provide a comprehensive approach to these issues [1]. Previous video generation attempts with the most advanced deep convolutional neural networks (CNNs) like [2] have shown how difficult this task is, with early results falling short of photorealism. Present day endeavors to predict the future [3], particularly through video prediction, have produced short films that forecast future events in a very limited domain. Even though image completion has been studied [4], representative deep learning research on video completion is clearly not available. It is critical to comprehend the pixel changes required to produce a full temporal object action in order to address the more general problem of general video synthesis. It is more difficult to determine with certainty how moving objects will move from one frame to the next, as [5] demonstrates. In our case, the underlying structure of moving objects (human poses) can be used to model the uncertainty, which simplifies the problem [6]. It is believed that videos of human actions are some of the most captivating and useful videos for various computer vision purposes. As a result, we limit our focus in this study to videos of people acting [7]. Two phases comprise the task: first, we generate human pose sequences (pose space); second, we generate images (pixel space) that are derived from the human pose sequences they generate [8]. There are two phases in our overall deep framework for creating videos. First of all, we present a new type of conditional generative adversarial network (GAN) designed to produce a plausible series of poses corresponding to particular action classes [9]. Next, we utilize a supervised reconstruction network that has been enhanced with loss due to feature matching. With the help of this network, a complete video output is produced by translating the generated pose sequence into the pixel space.

By developing on the latent space, the general framework for video generation can be extended to accomplish both video completion and video prediction, producing video outputs that nearly match predetermined input constraints [10]. As a result, our 2T-CNN approach can complete or predict videos using any number of input frames, and also generate videos from scratch based on the provided action class. We intend to conduct both quantitative and qualitative experiments to illustrate the efficacy of our model, highlighting its ability to produce and finish realistic human motion videos while respecting the constraints imposed by the input frames.

The work is organized as: Section 7.2 provides an extensive analysis on various prevailing approaches. The methodology is explained in Section 7.3 with outcomes discussed in Section 7.4. The conclusion is provided in Section 7.5.

7.2 Related Works

Dependable video representations have been developed through extensive research, such as the versions of the Bag of Visual Words (BoVW) model, which use low-level features such as dense trajectories (DTs) and space-time interest points (STIPs) [11]. Five crucial stages make up the BoVW pipeline and are involved in video-based action recognition: feature encoding, codebook generation, low-level feature extraction, feature pre-processing, normalization, and pooling. These low-level features mostly represent foreground elements and depict actions. They exhibit resilience when faced with recording interferences such as occlusion and clutter. Several low-level features, including 3D-HOG, MBH, HOG and HOF [12] have demonstrated potential for action recognition. These features are typically computed within local cuboids, often in conjunction with dense sampling methods STIP detectors. Dense trajectory features, in particular, have displayed notable performance compared to cutting-edge feature selections utilizing these local features. Within the BoVW framework, recognition performance is highly influenced by the selection of an appropriate encoding method. For action recognition, more complex encoding techniques have been developed, such as Fisher coding, soft-assignment, and vector of locally aggregated descriptors (VLAD). Studies demonstrate how successful these encoding techniques are for action recognition, with Fisher encoding surpassing other popular approaches. Furthermore, as mentioned in [12], improved dense trajectory features have been effectively combined with the Fisher encoding method to produce positive results on challenging action datasets.

There is a significant difference in quality between action elements and low-level video features. Mid-level representations have been suggested as a way to extract discriminative action parts in order to close this gap. Diverse methodologies have been implemented to extract these discriminative action segments. For example, techniques such as multiple instances learning frameworks and discriminative cuboids by exemplar-SVM, described concentrate on recognizing these action components. Furthermore, the literature discusses the utilization of clustering and ranking algorithms to generate 3D components, as exemplified in references [13], as a means of producing representative and discriminative results. These techniques usually involve training a classifier for each kind of part and then using max pooling to display the classifiers' outputs as video representations. A portion of the effectiveness of mid-level representations is lost when the contribution is expressed as a single value for all representations, even though the mined parts contain rich semantic information about action categories within large sub-volumes.

Hussain *et al.* [14] expanded on these concepts by introducing a mid-level approach that uses Fisher encoding to encode sample sub-volumes densely. However, this approach requires a lot of resources because a large number of spatiotemporal sub-volumes need to be considered in the second layer, and each feature sample needs to be encoded in the first layer. A different representation in terms of atoms and phrases is provided for. Although the framework seems to have potential advantages, the first stage of the framework, clustering, increases the cost of implementation. Building hierarchical feature learning pipelines with deep networks has proven to be remarkably successful. Because deep neural networks are effective at representing and classifying images, they have an influence on deep network video processing [15]. Deep features, on the other hand, generate a lot of action-unrelated video because they extract foreground and background information from image sequences. Camera rotation, tilting, and zooming are examples of factors that can introduce unnecessary characteristics into deep neural networks. As a result, using deep networks directly for action recognition is difficult due to the variety and uneven distribution of features.

7.3 Methodology

Utilizing deep structures and efficient learning strategies, 2T-CNNs have made significant advancements across CNNs and have significantly improved on a variety of computer vision tasks by utilizing deep structures and effective learning strategies. Through layered evolution, they gradually convert primary features, or raw materials, into higher-level features, allowing for more complex mappings. By leveraging transfer learning and latent information from relevant domains, CNNs trained using pretraining and fine-tuning methodologies can produce more efficient mappings for the target domain. Exploiting the benefits of deep networks, CNNs make substantial contributions to this research in two key aspects. Initially, the

CNN enhances the original features by extracting them comprehensively from a common feature space, known as DACs, resulting in deeper and more indicative features. In this process, both temporal and spatial regularities in the domain are analyzed in detail. Second, CNN makes use of the natural association between the labels and features that the face recognition (FR) metric predicts. As a result, the CNN can translate the FR metric into the ability to evaluate quality. To explain, image blocks are utilized in the proposed framework's first phase to pre-train the CNN and in the second phase, the video blocks are used to fine-tune the CNN. The CNN architecture, which is based on AlexNet has six layers, as shown in Figure 7.1. It is composed of a fully connected layer that is followed by two consecutive convolutional-max pooling groups. The output layer uses the mean squared error (MSE) to predict the video block quality scores. In the testing stage, block-level quality scores are produced by the trained CNN processing both the reference and distorted video blocks. These block-level scores are then converted into the overall quality scores for the distorted videos using a pooling stage.

More specifically, the distorted video (v_d) and the reference video (v_r) were split up into blocks with the dimensions $vb_r(x,y,z)_{M_1*M_2*M_3}$ and $vd_d(x,y,z)_{M_1*M_2*M_3}$, respectively, and designated as $vb_r\,(x,y,z)\,and\,vb_d\,(x,y,z)$. In this case, total blocks in the distorted and reference unconstraint videos are denoted by $M_1 * M_2 * M_3$. Using the following formula, the quality score matrix $(SQ(x,y,z))_{M1\times M2\times M3}$ for the distorted video is determined as:

$$Score\ quality\,(x,y,z) = (fc(vb_r(x,y,z)) - fc(vd_d(x,y,z) * \omega(x,y,z)) \tag{7.1}$$

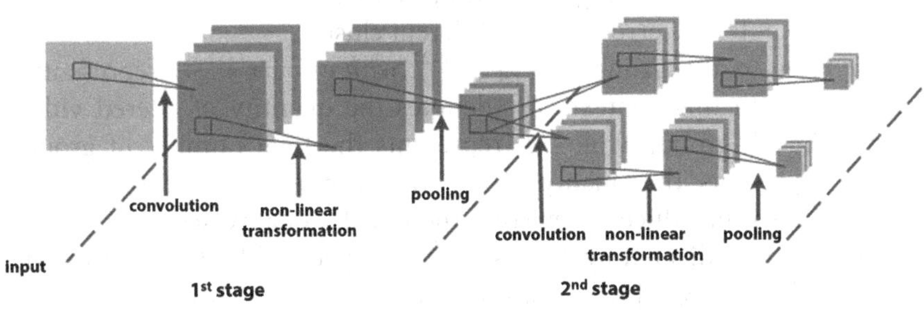

Figure 7.1 2T-CNN.

Here, "$w(x, y, z)$" stands for a weighting factor, and "$fc(.)$" indicates a function applied to the block. The mapping function that the trained CNN used is indicated by the notation $fc(vb_r(x, y, z))$. The quality score predicted by 2T+CNN for the reference block is thus represented by $fc(vd_d(x, y, z)$ and the quality score predicted by 2T+CNN for the corresponding distorted block is represented by $fc(vd_d(x, y, z)$. Furthermore, the block at $x, y, and\ z$ weighting coefficient is indicated by the symbol $\omega(x, y, z)$:

$$S = \frac{1}{M_1 * M_2 * M_3} \sum_{x=1}^{M_1} \sum_{y=1}^{M_2} \sum_{z=1}^{M_3} score\ quality\,(x, y, z) \tag{7.2}$$

As a result, the block-level quality scores are used to calculate the overall quality score S for v_d. Using visual attention during the pooling stage of quality assessment has long been standard practice. To that end, we compute the weighting coefficients using saliency maps, which quantify attention to detail. The modified video's saliency maps fall into the *smb* category. Employing a similar block strategy as that used for the distorted video, we generate saliency map blocks $smb_d(x, y, z)_{M_1 * M_2 * M_3}$ with dimensions. Thus, the definition of the weighting coefficient $\omega(x, y, z)$ is as follows:

$$\omega(x, y, z) = entropy\ (smb_d(x, y, z) \tag{7.3}$$

In this case, the entropy function used to estimate the average information quantity is denoted by $en(\cdot)$. This portion employs the operator "$en(.)$" to compute the saliency level attributed to each block within the saliency map. The preprocessing phase encompasses the filtration and grouping of the training videos. Each cluster comprises a reference video and distorted videos with different levels of distortion that belong to the same category of distortion. As a result, training video block labeling is restricted to each cluster, i.e., within an intragroup setting. We suggest a postprocessing step to mitigate potential errors across different clusters.

We refer to the groups as $\{g^i\}_{i=1}^{i=M}, with\ g_i = \{rv_j^i\}_{j=1}^{j=M_i}$ representing each group. In this context, M_i denotes the quantity of altered videos within the ith group, while M represents the total number of groups. $\{s_i^i\}_{j=1}^{j=M_i}$ represents the quality scores at the pooling stage for the ith group, g_i. To introduce an existing metric, the quality scores of the ith group, g_i, are indicated by $S^i = \{s_j^i\}_{j=1}^{j=M_i}$, as specified by the final metric. $S_i = \{s_j^i\}_{j=1}^{j=M_i}\ and\ OS_i = \{os_j^i\}_{j=1}^{j=M_i}$ are the results of standardizing these two sets of quality scores, $S_i = \{s^i_j\}_{j=1}^{j=M_i}$ and $OS_i = \{os^i_j\}_{j=1}^{j=M_i}$, respectively. Thus, for the distorted videos in the ith group, the final quality scores are as follows (represented as $final\ S_i = \{s^i_j\}_{j=1}^{j=M_i}$:

$$final\ s^i_j = s^i_j + \frac{1}{M_i}\sum_{i=1}^{i=M_i} os^i_j - s^i_j \tag{7.4}$$

In summary, the preprocessing procedure confines the training video block labels within each group, correcting the inaccuracies in predictions made by the existing metric. Simultaneously, the postprocessing stage is aimed at counterbalancing any biases introduced by errors in label predictions across different groups.

7.4 Numerical Results and Discussion

Short film clips (between one and three seconds) from classic movies were used as data sets for training and validation in the AFEW 2016 dataset [16–18]. However, the testing data encompassed not only clips from movies but also excerpts from reality TV shows, adding a level of realism and complexity compared to purposefully created and recorded facial expressions. The dataset consisted of a total of 653 testing samples, 773 training samples, and 383 validation samples. One of the following seven emotional states was assigned to each video segment in the training and validation sets: disgust, anger, happiness, fear, surprise, neutral, and sadness. Interestingly, the test clips lacked labels corresponding to different emotional states. Consequently, for this study, our evaluation of the proposed models was conducted using the AFEW 2016 validation set.

Our models underwent training using data from CEV and the designated training data from AFEW. To mitigate overfitting during the training process, we employed four distinct data augmentation strategies: horizontal flips, left and right rotations, and the introduction of Gaussian noise. The training phase encompassed the utilization of over ten thousand movies. For model evaluation, we utilized 383 samples allocated for validation within the AFEW dataset. Tables 7.1 to 7.4 present a comparative analysis of each model's recognition accuracy against the baseline approach. The EmotiW challenge's baseline performance, determined by the classification of the support vector regression (SVR) using the LBP-TOP descriptor

Table 7.1 Prediction accuracy comparison.

Model	Accuracy
CNN	39%
CNN+VGG16	50%
LSTM+VGG16	45%
Xception14	40%
SegNet+ConvNet	95%
2T CNN	97%

Table 7.2 Performance analysis based on a provided dataset.

Emotions	Prediction accuracy
Angry	88%
Disgust	30%
Fear	55%
Happy	80%
Neutral	60%
Sad	50%
Surprise	20%

Table 7.3 Prediction accuracy comparison based on subject independent model.

Model	Accuracy
CNN	65%
CNN+VGG16	85%
LSTM+VGG16	83%
Xception14	85%
SegNet+ConvNet	94.5%
2T-CNN	96%

Table 7.4 Performance analysis based on facial expression recognition (FER) for subject independent performance.

Emotions	Prediction accuracy
Angry	93%
Disgust	88%
Fear	85%
Happy	89%
Neutral	96%
Sad	95%
Surprise	96%

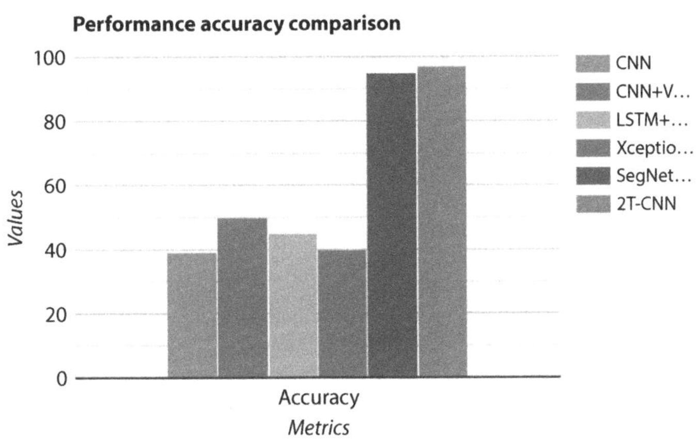

Figure 7.2 Accuracy comparison.

calculation, serves as the benchmark. Notably, the SegNet combined with ConvNet [19] emerged as the most impactful individual model, achieving an increase in accuracy of over 10% compared to the initial findings. Moreover, both the combined CNN+VGG16 and LSTM+VGG16 [20] models, along with the Xception14 model, exhibited slightly higher accuracies when contrasted with the baseline results. However, the proposed 2T-CNN model shows better performance compared to other approaches, i.e. 97% shown in the Figure 7.2.

To extract high-level features from facial expressions, we proposed three distinct 2T-CNN-based networks in our research. By combining these networks, we were able to make predictions across a range of emotional categories. Because our proposed system integrates multiple 2T-CNN-based architectures through a sequential model, it can potentially improve FER performance in real-world scenarios, according to the competitive evaluation results, especially on unconstrained scenario data like AFEW 2016 shown in Figures 7.3 and 7.4. The ConvNet with SegNet models, utilizing CEV data, allowed for a broader comprehension of emotional data, thereby expanding the scope of our training dataset. Our effort to expand and balance the training

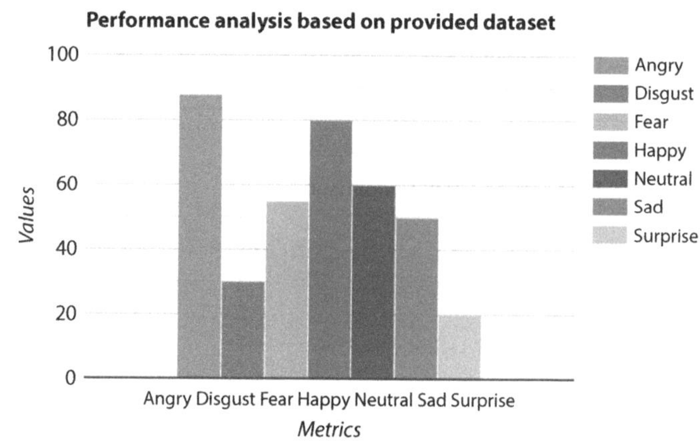

Figure 7.3 Performance analysis based on a provided dataset.

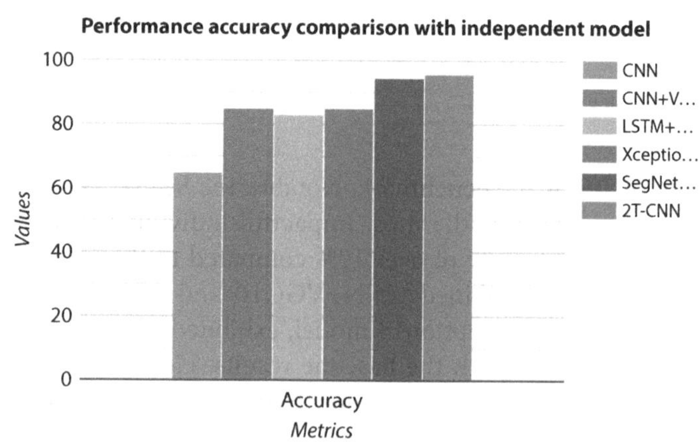

Figure 7.4 Performance analysis with an independent model.

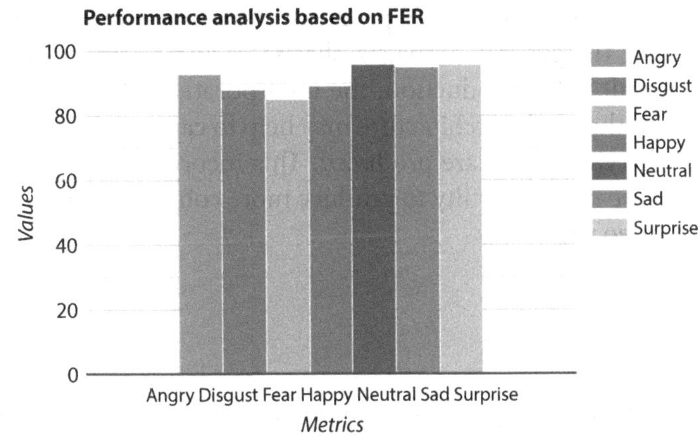

Figure 7.5 Performance analysis based on FER.

data, encompassing a diverse range of "ambiguous" emotional expressions like surprise, disdain, and terror, has been fruitful. However, the results indicate significant room for further development, especially considering the moderate accuracy levels observed using AFEW 2016 data shown in the Figure 7.5. Although the focus of our proposed method is on unconstrained scenario data, it showed promising results in a controlled environment such as the SAVEE dataset. This suggests that the proposed technology holds potential for refinement and application in real-world scenarios, such as human-robot interactions, driver monitoring systems, and similar contexts.

7.5 Conclusion

We introduce a flexible 2T-CNN model that tackles all problems related to video completion, generation, and prediction. With our novel two-tier generation process, we leverage human poses as intermediate representations to produce long-form human motion videos from scratch. Furthermore, we effectively tackle video completion and prediction tasks by employing constrained generation techniques through our model. Our findings indicate that our model excels in generating credible human action videos both with and without constraints, surpassing current methods in both quantitative and visual assessments. In future, several avenues for improvement are identified. Better training datasets for the skeleton-to-image transformer and motion generator can be added to improve the model's performance. This step is meant to support our model's robustness and universality.

Furthermore, adding multi-scale progressive training to the second stage could improve the generated images' sharpness and clarity even more. In terms of overall video production, the incorporation of recurrent neural networks into the model architecture may help to capture temporal dependencies in the videos that are produced. This incorporation could potentially enrich the model's ability to produce more coherent and contextually consistent video sequences.

References

1. Amin-Naji, M., Aghagolzadeh, A., Ezoji, M., Ensemble of CNN for multi-focus image fusion. *Inf. Fusion*, 51, 201–214, 2019.
2. Yang, B., Xiang, X., Xu, D., Wang, X., Yang, X., 3d palm print recognition using shape index representation and fragile bits. *Multimed. Tools Appl.*, 76, 14, 15357–15375, 2017.
3. Kumar, N. and Bhargava, D., A scheme of features fusion for facial expression analysis: A facial action recognition. *J. Stat. Manage. Syst.*, 20, 4, 693–701, 2017.
4. Zhao, X., Liang, X., Liu, L., Li, T., Han, Y., Vasconcelos, N., Yan, S., Peak-piloted deep network for facial expression recognition, in: *European Conference on Computer Vision*, pp. 425–442, Springer, 2016.
5. Niu, H. *et al.*, Deep feature learnt by conventional deep neural network. *Comput. Electr. Eng.*, 84, 106656, 2020.
6. Gan, Y., Facial expression recognition using convolutional neural network, in: *Proceedings of the 2nd International Conference on Vision, Image and Signal Processing*, pp. 1–5, 2018.
7. Mollahosseini, A., Chan, D., Mahoor, M.H., Going deeper in facial expression recognition using deep neural networks, in: *2016 IEEE Winter Conference on Applications of Computer Vision (WACV)*, pp. 1–10, IEEE, 2016.
8. Patil, M.N., Iyer, B., Arya, R., Performance evaluation of PCA and ICA algorithm for facial expression recognition application, in: *Proceedings of Fifh International Conference on Sof Computing for Problem Solving*, Springer, pp. 965–976, 2016.
9. Niu, B., Gao, Z., Guo, B., Facial expression recognition with LBP and ORB features. *Comput. Intell. Neurosci.*, 2021, 1–10, 2021.
10. Wang, F. *et al.*, Emotion recognition with convolutional neural network and eeg-based efdms. *Neuropsychologia*, 146, 107506, 2020.
11. Canedo, D. and Neves, A.J., Facial expression recognition using computer vision: A systematic review. *Appl. Sci.*, 9, 21, 4678, 2019.
12. Nonis, F., Dagnes, N., Marcolin, F., Vezzetti, E., 3d approaches and challenges in facial expression recognition algorithms—A literature review. *Appl. Sci.*, 9, 18, 3904, 2019.

13. Hans, A.S.A. and Smitha, R., A CNN-LSTM based deep neural networks for facial emotion detection in videos. *Int. J. Adv. Signal Image Sci.*, 7, 1, 11–20, 2021.
14. Hussain, S.A. and Ahlam, S.A.A.B., A real time face emotion classifcation and recognition using deep learning model. *J. Phys. Conf. Ser.*, 1432, 1, 012087, 2020.
15. Yang, B., Cao, J., Ni, R., Zhang, Y., Facial expression recognition using weighted mixture deep neural network based on double channel facial images. *IEEE Access*, 6, 4630–4640, 2017.
16. Li, Qiu, Z., Yao, T., Mei, T., Rui, Y., Luo, J., Action recognition by learning deep multi-granular spatio-temporal video representation, in: *ICMR*, ACM, pp. 159–166, 2016.
17. Xu, Yang, Y., Hauptmann, A.G., A discriminative CNN video representation for event detection, in: *CVPR*, 2015.
18. Szegedy, Liu, W., Jia, Y., Sermanet, P., Reed, S., Anguelov, D., Erhan, D., Vanhoucke, V., Rabinovich, A., Going deeper with convolutions, in: *CVPR*, 2015.
19. He, Zhang, X., Ren, S., Sun, J., Deep residual learning for image recognition. *CoRR*, abs/1512.03385, 770–778, 2015.
20. Jiang, Liu, J., Roshan Zamir, A., Toderici, G., Laptev, I., Shah, M., Sukthankar, R., *Thumos challenge: Action recognition with a large number of classes*, 2014, http://crcv.ucf.edu/THUMOS14.

8

Detection of Peripheral Blood Smear Malarial Parasitic Microscopic Images Utilizing Convolutional Neural Network

Tamal Kumar Kundu[1]*, Smritilekha Das[1] and R. Nidhya[2]

[1]*Department of Computer Science and Engineering, Koneru Lakshmaiah Education Foundation, Guntur, India*

[2]*Department of Computer Science and Engineering, Madanapalle Institute of Technology & Science, Madanapalle, Andhra Pradesh, India*

Abstract

In the intricate world of medical diagnostics, the battle against malaria, caused by the insidious plasmodium parasite, rages on. This microscopic foe, transmitted through the stealthy bite of mosquitoes, inflicts upon its victims a spectrum of debilitating symptoms including headaches, fatigue, convulsions, and the ominous specter of coma. Traditionally, the efficacy of a malaria diagnosis has been tethered to the discerning eye of laboratory technicians, relying on their innate skills to classify blood smears under the microscope. However, the fallibility of human observation introduces the specter of inaccuracies into reports, particularly when wielded by less experienced or novice technicians. Recognizing the imperative for enhanced precision, this study harnesses the power of a convolutional neural network (CNN), a formidable subclass of deep learning (DL), to craft a sophisticated malaria parasite detection system. the structured system analysis and development methodology guides the trajectory of this research endeavor. This robust framework ensures a systematic approach, from conceptualization to implementation, maximizing the potential for success in the realm of automated malaria diagnosis. Through the lens of a CNN, the system transcends the limitations of human observation, offering a reliable and accurate means of malaria detection. Deep learning algorithms, adept at learning intricate patterns and nuances, empower the system to discern the subtlest manifestations of the plasmodium parasite within blood smears. By automating the diagnostic process, this CNN-based system not only

**Corresponding author*: kundutamal007@gmail.com

R. Nidhya, D. Pavithra, Manish Kumar, A. Dinesh Kumar and S. Balamurugan (eds.) Generative Artificial Intelligence: Concepts and Applications, (121–142) © 2025 Scrivener Publishing LLC

mitigates the risk of human error but also enhances classification accuracy, even in the hands of less seasoned laboratory technicians. The fusion of cutting-edge technology and systematic development methodologies heralds a new era in malaria diagnosis, where precision is paramount, and technology becomes the ally in the relentless fight against this pervasive and potentially deadly disease. In the ever-evolving landscape of medical technology, the marriage of DL, structured methodologies, and a relentless commitment to accuracy stands poised to revolutionize malaria diagnosis. As this innovative system takes center stage, it holds the promise of delivering not just accurate results but also expediting the diagnosis process, potentially saving lives in the ongoing battle against malaria.

***Keywords*:** Malaria, types of parasites, blood smear with its type, machine and deep learning, convolution neural network

8.1 Introduction

In the global landscape of well-being, malaria stands as a pervasive and perilous challenge. This parasitic infection, transmitted by mosquitoes, gives rise to a formidable global health threat. The plasmodium parasite, with its intricate multistage lifecycle, induces recurring fevers, leading to severe conditions such as cerebral malaria, severe malarial anemia, coma, or even fatality if left untreated. The conventional means of diagnosing malaria involves microscopic examination of thick and thin blood smears, a process that enables the identification of parasitemia against a background of light-stained red blood cells.

However, disruptions caused by the COVID-19 pandemic in 2020 saw a surge in malaria-related deaths, as illustrated in Figure 8.1. The gold standard for malaria diagnosis still relies on micro-blood smear evaluation, providing crucial information such as parasite intensity, parasite type identification, and assessment of anti-malarial medication effectiveness. Sadly, professional training costs have limited the availability of skilled staff in malaria-affected regions, hindering accurate diagnosis. Figure 8.1(a) illustrates the documented malaria case counts per WHO region spanning 1990 to 2017. The primary global focus is on reducing cases in countries with high prevalence, leading to a decline in the overall fatality count. In 2017, global malaria-related deaths decreased to 435,000, a significant drop from the 607,000 deaths recorded in 2010.

Amid challenges, there is a growing demand for alternative diagnostic methods that are rapid, highly sensitive, and user-friendly, not reliant solely on blood tests. Early diagnosis and effective treatment become pivotal in averting the high mortality rates associated with malaria.

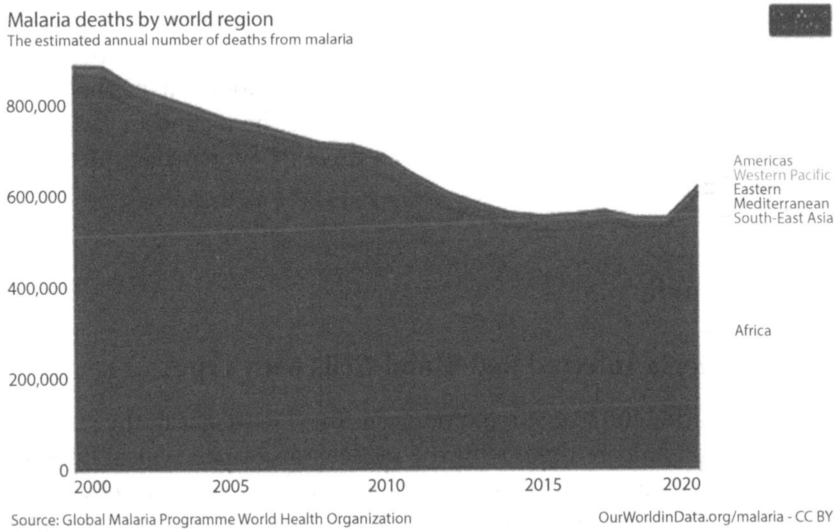

Figure 8.1 Malaria deaths worldwide (2000 – 2020).

Plasmodium protozoan parasites, responsible for this life-threatening disease, prompt the utilization of computer-aided diagnosis, leveraging technological advancements in medical imaging. Machine learning, particularly the convolutional neural network (CNN) within the realm of deep learning (DL), emerges as a transformative force in bolstering diagnostic accuracy through clinical imaging informatics. Microscopic examination reveals four distinct stages of malaria infection in the blood ring, trophozoite, schizont, and gametocyte. Early diagnosis becomes a linchpin in reducing mortality rates associated with malaria. This article introduces

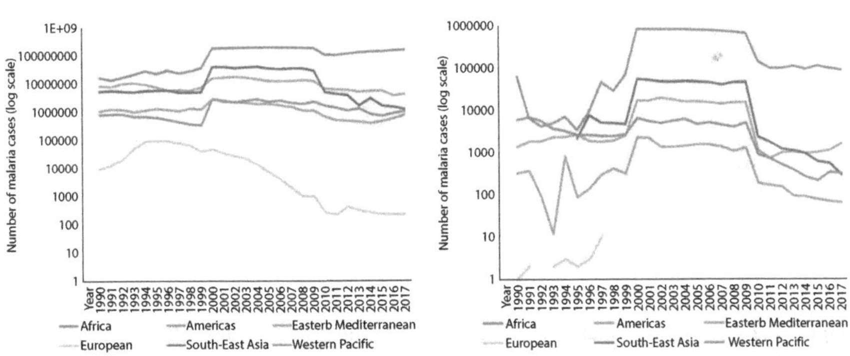

Figure 8.1 (a) Reported cases of malaria infections (1990 – 2017) reported malaria death (1990 – 2017).

a novel approach to malaria diagnosis – a mobile malaria parasite detection system utilizing CNN for end-to-end feature extraction and classification. The structured system analysis and development methodology underpins the research, aiming to revolutionize the diagnostic landscape by providing a rapid, accurate, and accessible tool for malaria detection and classification.

8.2 Malaria

8.2.1 Malaria-Infected Red Blood Cells with Types

When evaluating the size of red blood cells in a blood smear, the standard practice is to compare them with the nucleus of a small typical lymphocyte, which has an approximate width of 8 microns. Red blood cells exhibit a characteristic pink appearance due to their high hemoglobin content. The central pale area within each red blood cell is a result of their concave circular shape. In cases where abnormal parasites are present within red blood cells, or when there is distortion in shape, the presence of plasmodium is identified. Furthermore, Figure 8.2 provides a determination of the density of red blood cells infected by the plasmodium parasite.

Four strains of Plasmodium have the potential to infect and be transmitted by humans: P. falciparum, P. vivax, P. ovale, and P. malariae. Among these, the prevalence of P. falciparum infection is higher than that of other strains. P. falciparum is the most dangerous member of the Plasmodium family, responsible for significant mortality, and is the most common species in tropical regions worldwide. In India, on average, 40% – 50% of cases are attributed to P. falciparum. On the contrary, P. vivax is the most

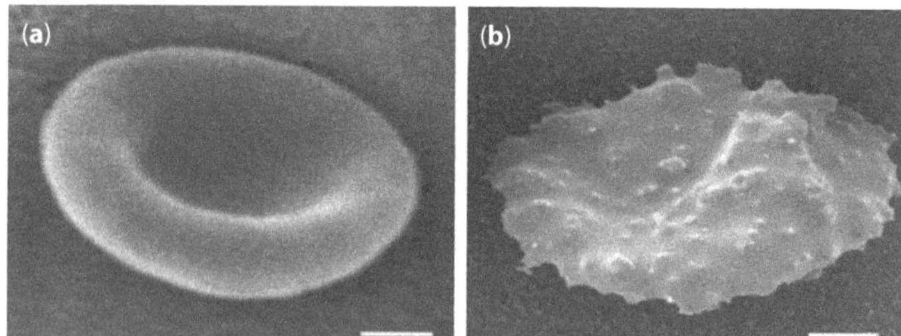

Figure 8.2 Illustrates human erythrocytes in both non-parasitized and P. falciparum-infected states; (a) non-parasitized erythrocytes exhibit a smooth surface topography; (b) In contrast, a P. falciparum-infected human erythrocyte membrane is depicted for comparison (Hayakawa *et al.*, 2016).

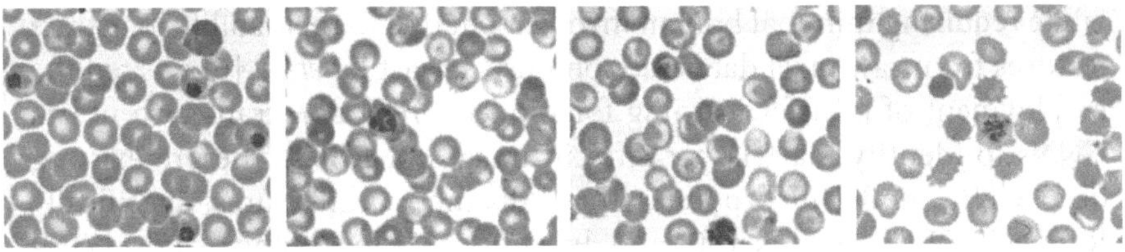

Figure 8.3 Malaria-infected blood; (a) P. falciparum; (b) P. vivax; (c) P. malariae; (d) P. ovale.

prevalent species in larger portions of the tropical zone. P. malariae is found globally and causes persistent infections that can last for extended periods. P. ovale, though rare, is relatively common in Africa. Due to morphological similarities, P. ovale is sometimes confused with P. vivax, particularly by less experienced microscopists. These species are responsible for severe cases of malaria and fatalities in West Africa. Here depicts different types of malaria parasite blood smear images shows in above in Figure 8.3.

8.3 Literature Survey

The CNN architectures are employed for the diagnostic evaluation of malaria, specifically in discerning human red blood cells (RBCs) as either normal or infected with malaria. Additionally, the classification extends to identifying the types of Plasmodium responsible for infecting human RBCs. In the field of image classification, identification, and localization, CNNs, a subset of DL models, have exhibited promising outcomes [1]. This success is attributed to the availability of extensive annotated data. In cases where data is limited, such as medical imaging, transfer learning methods are employed. Var *et al.* [2] and [3] designed computer-aided diagnostic techniques for detecting malaria parasites, utilizing pre-trained CNNs as feature extractors. To pre-train CNN models, large datasets like ImageNet are utilized [4], enabling the transfer of general image characteristics to target tasks. Pre-trained weights offer improved performance and serve as effective model initializations compared to starting from scratch with randomly initialized weights. The challenge of identifying malaria parasites in thin-blood smear images has been tackled using both traditional ML and data-driven DL techniques, as per literature reviews. Dong *et al.* [5] explored the capabilities of CNN and support vector machine (SVM) to classify infected and healthy cells. The CNNs significantly outperformed the SVM classifier, achieving more than 95% higher classification accuracy, while requiring minimal human involvement due to their ability to extract features from raw pixel data autonomously. Swastika *et al.* [6] posited the employment of transfer learning for models previously trained to utilize CNNs to identify malaria parasites in images of RBCs. The pre-existing deep CNN model incorporates three distinct architectures, specifically ResNet50V2, EfficientNetB0, and InceptionV3. In another study [7], a shallow deep belief network exhibited favorable parasite detection abilities compared to SVM-based classification. Additionally, researchers have examined the performance of custom CNN models against SVM classifiers [8]. While the results are promising, patient-level cross-validation studies using substantial clinical datasets are necessary to confirm their applicability.

Using a sizable annotated clinical image dataset, Rajaraman [9] assessed the effectiveness of pre-trained CNNs in distinguishing parasitized and uninfected cells at both cellular and patient levels. Suriya *et al.* [10] undertook an endeavor to employ a sophisticated deep convolutional neural network (DCNN) to discern malarial parasites within smear blood cell imagery. Rahman *et al.* [11] improved malaria detection using patches from segmented microscopic images. Pan *et al.* [12] expound upon specific advancements in our recent undertakings concerning the meticulous classification of malaria-infected cells through the utilization of sophisticated DCNN. Initially, the authors elaborate on the intricacies of image processing techniques employed for the segmentation of RBCs from extensive whole-slide images. Subsequently, they delve into the complexities of assembling an assiduously curated image dataset by pathologists for the explicit purpose of training the deep neural network (DNN). Furthermore, the researchers investigate methods of data augmentation strategically applied to substantially amplify the dataset's scale, taking into consideration the inherent overfitting predicament associated with the training of DCNNs.

Various DL approaches in different medical domains were discussed by Litjens *et al.* [13]. Fuhad *et al.* [14] proposed a customized CNN architecture with eight layers for utilization in smartphones, while Szegedy *et al.* [15] presented the Inception architecture. Hung *et al.* [16] applied object identification to distinguish cells in blood samples with malaria infection. Deng *et al.* [17] introduced ImageNet, and Bibin *et al.* [18] proposed a deep belief network for detecting malaria parasites. The utilization of CNN in malaria classification manifests through two principal methodologies. Initially, CNN operates as a feature extractor, extracting salient features from the input image. In this capacity, the CNN is designated as a feature extractor and is typically pre-trained on extensive datasets like ImageNet [19, 20]. Fuhad *et al.* [21] proffered a fully automated model predicated upon CNNs for the diagnostic elucidation of malaria via microscopic blood smear images. Diverse methodologies, encompassing knowledge distillation, data augmentation, Autoencoder, feature extraction via a CNN model, and subsequent classification employing SVM or K-Nearest Neighbors (KNN), are executed across three training paradigms denominated as general training, distillation training, and autoencoder training, thereby refining and enhancing the model's precision and inferential efficacy.

When CNN functions as a feature extractor, subsequent classification procedures can be delegated to other classifiers such as KNN and SVM [22]. Furthermore, Pattaniak *et al.* [23] posited an efficacious multi-magnification deep residual neural network (MM-ResNet), wherein the automated classification of microscopic blood smear images into infected or non-infected categories is accomplished seamlessly across diverse magnifications. Kundu *et al.* [24] proffered a proposed architecture facilitating the creation of a wholly automated framework dedicated to the characterization of erythrocytes in pre-processed images afflicted by the malaria parasite. The dual SVM classifier has yielded discernible and diverse features within the blood smears containing malaria-infected erythrocytes. Alternatively, CNN can be deployed in an end-to-end learning model, wherein the CNN comprehends the intricate relationship between the raw input image and its corresponding class label. The structure of the end-to-end learning model comprises both feature extraction and classification components, seamlessly integrated into a cohesive whole. The application of end-to-end learning can be delineated into two distinct approaches, namely transfer learning and learning from scratch.

The implementation of transfer learning encompasses two distinct approaches [25]. The first approach entails fine-tuning all layers, involving the retraining of every layer using the initial weights derived from the pre-trained CNN model. This approach proves apt when confronted with a substantial dataset to be trained. Conversely, the second approach involves the freezing of some initial layers while retraining the remaining layers of the network. This strategy is deemed suitable when the dataset is exceedingly limited to prevent overfitting. The rationale behind this lies in the notion that the initial layers of a pre-trained CNN encapsulate more generic features, while the subsequent layers encapsulate more specialized features following the original datasets. Transfer learning involves the utilization of established CNN models, such as VGG [26], GoogLeNet [27], or ResNet [28], which have undergone extensive training on an expansive ImageNet database. The pre-trained CNNs come equipped with intrinsic parameters that serve as valuable starting points for training the model for a particular task, especially in scenarios such as medical cases where available medical images are scarce. Liang *et al.* [29] introduced an innovative and resilient ML model founded on a CNN, designed for the automatic categorization of individual cells within slender blood smears on conventional microscope slides, distinguishing them as either infected or uninfected. Rajaraman *et al.* [30] proposed customized CNN architecture for the detection and classification of malarial parasites, which are infected and uninfected under the malaria scanner. The objective is to juxtapose the models employed in the identification of tumors from cerebral MRI images, encompassing the domain of DL methodologies. Consequently, an examination of the quintet of frequently utilized CNNs designed for the classification of brain tumors is undertaken, namely VGG19, DenseNet169, AlexNet, InceptionV3, and ResNet101, all constituting architectures of CNN [31]. Kundu *et al.* [32] introduced a distinctive method for identifying and classifying malaria through a unique hyperparameter tuning detection technique. This approach involves combining the Adagrad optimizer with a recommended pre-trained DNN using the contrastive divergence method for pre-training. Within this proposed system, features are extracted from images to train the DNN and initialize visible variables. The smear images then exhibit a concatenated feature, serving as the feature vector in the proposed system. Juliet *et al.* [33] direct their attention toward the implementation of a classification system utilizing transfer learning for malarial infected cells, aiming to enhance diagnostic accuracy. Empirical findings substantiate the efficacy of transfer learning particularly in the realm of microscopic cell images. Peñas *et al.* [34] posit an intelligent system designed for the identification of malaria parasites within images of thin blood smears. Employing a CNN in this inquiry yielded a noteworthy accuracy of 92.4% and a sensitivity of 95.2% for detecting malaria parasites. Furthermore, the system demonstrated an accuracy of 87.9% in distinguishing between the two Plasmodium species, namely P. falciparum and P. vivax. Kundu *et al.* [35] present an advanced ML-driven automated model for the detection and classification of malaria parasites in blood smear images. The proposed optimal ML-based automated malaria parasite detection and classification technique undergoes a dual-stage pre-processing, involving adaptive filtering for noise removal and contrast enhancement using the contrast level adaptive histogram equalization (CLAHE) technique. Additionally, the feature extraction process employs local derivative radial patterns. Subsequently, a Random Forest classifier is employed to assign appropriate class labels to the blood smear images. The integration of the PSO algorithm contributes to enhancing the classification performance of the RF method. Suriya *et al.* [36] have postulated a DCNN designed for discerning malaria parasites within human bladder cell images. The primary emphasis of this endeavor lies in meticulously adjusting hyperparameters to facilitate the classification of images into parasitized and uninfected cells, with a principal focus on scrutinizing validation and precision metrics. The precision in identifying parasitized and non-parasitized cells, along with the quality of the smear, assumes a pivotal role in determining the accuracy of the system.

The realm of malaria diagnostics has witnessed a significant evolution with the advent of CNN architectures. Specifically, CNNs are instrumental in distinguishing between normal and malaria-infected human RBCs, extending their classification prowess to identify various types of Plasmodium responsible for infecting RBCs. Within the domain of image classification, identification, and localization, CNNs, a subset of DL models, have demonstrated remarkable outcomes, largely attributed to the availability of extensive annotated data [1].

In cases where medical imaging data is limited, transfer learning methods have proven invaluable. Var *et al.* [2] and [3] pioneered computer-aided diagnostic techniques for malaria parasite detection, utilizing pre-trained CNNs as feature extractors. The use of large datasets like ImageNet for pre-training enhances model performance, providing improved initializations compared to starting from scratch [4].

In the pursuit of identifying malaria parasites in thin-blood smear images, both traditional ML and data-driven DL techniques have been explored. Dong *et al.* [5] showcased the superiority of CNNs over SVMs in classifying infected and healthy cells, achieving over 95% higher accuracy. Transfer learning, as proposed by Swastika *et al.* [6], further leveraged pre-existing deep CNN models, demonstrating the effectiveness of architectures like ResNet50V2, EfficientNetB0, and InceptionV3.

Studies, such as the one conducted by Rajaraman [9], utilizing sizable annotated clinical image datasets, reaffirmed the effectiveness of pre-trained CNNs in distinguishing parasitized and uninfected cells. Additionally, sophisticated deep CNNs, as explored by Suriya *et al.* [10], offer advanced capabilities in discerning malarial parasites within smear blood cell imagery.

Specific advancements in image processing techniques and dataset curation were elucidated by Pan *et al.* [12]. These researchers addressed challenges in malaria-infected cell classification using carefully curated image datasets and strategic data augmentation to mitigate overfitting during deep CNN training.

Various DL approaches in different medical domains have been comprehensively reviewed by Litjens *et al.* [13], showcasing the versatility of CNNs. Customized CNN architectures, as proposed by Fuhad *et al.* [14]

and Szegedy *et al.* [15], demonstrate tailored solutions for smartphones and present the Inception architecture, respectively. Object identification techniques applied by Hung *et al.* [16] distinguish cells in blood samples with malaria infection.

Transfer learning serves as a pivotal strategy in CNN utilization, allowing the model to leverage pre-existing knowledge from extensive datasets. Liang *et al.* [29] and Rajaraman *et al.* [30] showcase the application of pre-trained CNNs for medical image classification, while Kundu *et al.* [32] propose a hybrid model combining Adagrad optimizer and DNNs for malaria detection.

Furthermore, the implementation of transfer learning can be approached in two ways [25]. Fine-tuning all layers or freezing some initial layers while retraining the remaining layers accommodates different dataset sizes, preventing overfitting in limited datasets. Various studies, such as those by Kundu *et al.* [24], Juliet *et al.* [33], and Peñas *et al.* [34], exemplify the efficacy of transfer learning in improving diagnostic accuracy for malaria-infected cells. Table 8.1 elucidates the comparative analysis of divergent methodologies employed by various researchers, delineating the disparities in their approaches.

In conclusion, the integration of CNNs in malaria diagnosis showcases a robust and versatile approach, from feature extraction to end-to-end learning models, leveraging transfer learning for enhanced diagnostic accuracy. The ever-evolving landscape of DL methodologies continue to propel advancements in the fight against malaria, promising more accurate and efficient diagnostic tools.

8.4 Proposed Methodology and Algorithm

This scholarly article employs the Structured System Assessment and Design Technique in a systematic endeavor to construct a coherent system geared toward the attainment of predefined objectives. The method encompasses various phases, encompassing the delineation of requirements, scrutiny of design intricacies, coding implementation, rigorous testing, and sustained maintenance. Figure 8.4 offers an architectural exposition delineating the CNN employed in this scholarly inquiry.

The principal aim of neural networks, constituting an amalgamation of algorithms, resides in the discernment of latent correlations ingrained within a dataset, mirroring the cognitive intricacies observed in the human brain. Neural networks, be they of organic or synthetic origin, possess the intrinsic capability to dynamically adapt to input variations without necessitating modifications to the output criterion, thereby showcasing their inherent potential to yield optimal results. This operational modality closely

Table 8.1 Analyzing the differences in the approaches taken by various authors in comparison.

Author with year	Method utilization	Image acquisition	Classification	Classification type	Performance statistics (%)
Rajaraman *et al.*, 2019 [9]	Ensemble model with Squeeze Net and VGG-19	27,558 cellular images, comprising an equivalent number of instances of both infected and uninfected conditions.	2	Uninfected & infected cells	Accuracy: 99.51
Dong *et al.*, 2017 [12]	Pre-trained LeNet, AlexNet, with GoogLeNet	Infected cells are 1,034, and non-infected cells are 1,531.	2	Normal & infected erythrocyte	Accuracy: 98.13 (GoogLeNet)
Vijayalakshmi *et al.*, 2020 [20]	Unifying VGG and SVM	Infected 1030 images of falciparum with 1520 non-infected images.	2	Falciparum infected & uninfected	Accuracy: 93.13
Fuhad *et al.*, 2020 [21]	CNN combined with SVM	27,558 cellular images, comprising an equivalent number of instances of both infected and uninfected.	2	Uninfected & parasitized cells	Accuracy: 99.23
Liang *et al.*, 2016 [29]	CNN model with Custom 16 layer	27,578 images with an infected and uninfected ratio of 1:1.	2	Normal & abnormal	Accuracy: 97.37

(*Continued*)

Table 8.1 Analyzing the differences in the approaches taken by various authors in comparison. (*Continued*)

Author with year	Method utilization	Image acquisition	Classification	Classification type	Performance statistics (%)
Rajaraman *et al.*, 2018 [30]	Sequential CNN	27,558 cellular images, comprising an equivalent number of instances of both infected and uninfected conditions.	2	Uninfected & infected cells	Accuracy: 98.60
Çinar and Yildirim, 2020 [31]	Alex Net, Dense Net, GoogLeNet, ResNet, and Inception-v3, VGG-19	A total of 6730 images in between 3,730 parasitized and 3,000 uninfected images.	2	Uninfected & parasitized cells	Accuracy: 97.83 (Dense Net)
Juliet *et al.*, 2019 [33]	ResNet-50 for transfer learning	27,558 cellular images, comprising an equivalent number of instances of both infected and uninfected.	2	Uninfected & parasitized cells	Training accuracy: 95.91 Validation accuracy: 95.4
Peñas *et al.*, 2017 [34]	Inception-v3	Among 363 photos, Vivax images are 142 and images of falciparum are 221.	3	Gametocyte of vivax & falciparum, ring of falciparum	Accuracy: 87.9
Suriya *et al.*, 2019 [36]	DCNN model with Convolutional Neural Network	26,188 cell images with 13,105 parasitized and 13,083 uninfected images.	2	Uninfected & parasitized cells	Accuracy 98.9

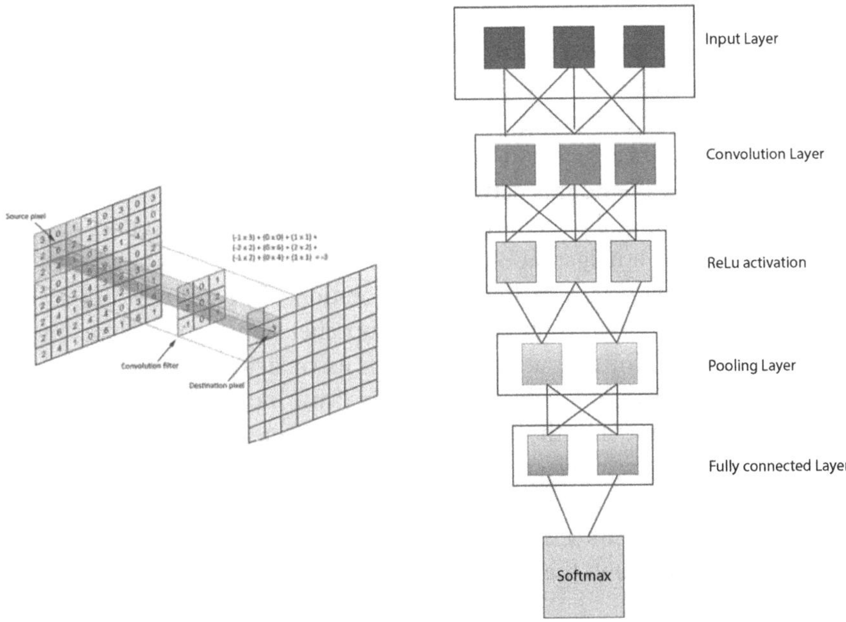

Figure 8.4 CNN architectural view.

aligns with the nuanced functioning of the neural network inherent in the human brain. Within the domain of neural networks, the aggregation and categorization of data adhere to a preconceived design guided by mathematical functions termed "neurons." The operational paradigm of the network closely emulates statistical methodologies such as curve fitting and regression analysis. Figure 8.5 elucidates the nuanced functioning of convolution within the intricate fabric of the neural network.

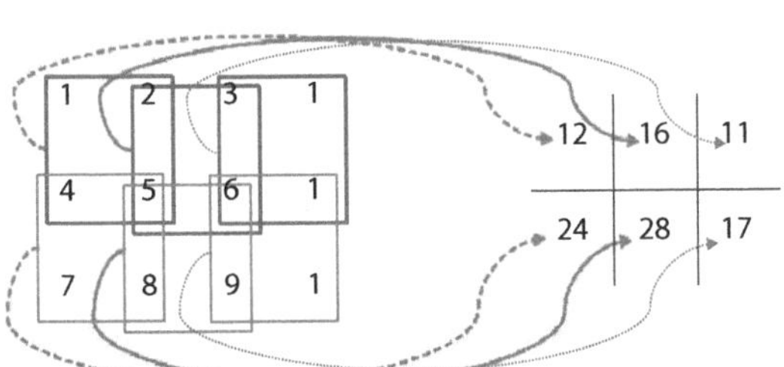

Figure 8.5 Illustration of the convolution operation.

A neural network comprises strata of interconnected nodes, with each node embodying a perceptron reminiscent of the principles underpinning multiple linear regression. The activation function of the perceptron processes the signals stemming from multiple linear regression, potentially introducing nonlinearities into the system. This intricate architectural composition endows the neural network with the capacity to learn and adapt, discerning meaningful patterns embedded within the input data.

In essence, the amalgamation of the Structured System Assessment and Design Technique with a meticulous exploration of neural network architecture contributes to a comprehensive comprehension of the system's functional intricacies. The neural network, with its capacity to replicate human cognitive processes and its adaptability to dynamic input variations, emerges as a potent instrument in the discernment of intricate patterns latent within datasets. The article underscores the pivotal role played by neural networks in attaining optimal outcomes and elucidates the underlying principles through elaborate architectural depictions and explications of network operations. Figure 8.6 shows the overall workflow of the proposed methdology.

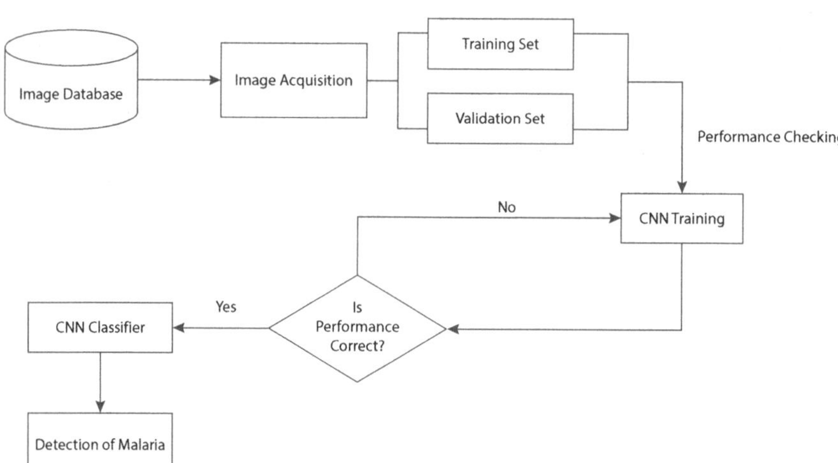

Figure 8.6 A framework of the proposed system.

8.4.1 Proposed Algorithm

Here asterisk (*) is the mathematical symbol for convolution in this article. The expression would be as follows if an input image were represented by 1 and a filter by F:

Z=I*F the training algorithm for an image datest is provided as follows;

Step 1: Load the incoming images into a variable, such as I.

Step 2: Create a filter matrix in step two by initializing it at random. With the filter Z1 = I * F, images are convolved.

Step 3: On the outcome, apply the Sigmoid activation function.

An equal sigmoid (Z1)

Step 4: Create a weight and bias matrix by initializing it at random. Transform the data using a linear formula.

Z2 = WT. A + b

Step 5: Use the Sigmoid function to analyze the data. The result will be this in the end.

O equals sigmoid (Z2)

These values are treated as parameters by the CNN model, which initializes them arbitrarily and teaches them as it rains.

8.5 Result Analysis

8.5.1 Dataset

The dataset under examination for this research comprises a total of 27,600 cell images, meticulously curated for analysis. Within this collection, 13,800 images depict parasitized cells, while the remaining 13,800 showcase non-parasitized counterparts. The visual representation of the blood smear images extracted from this dataset is presented in Figure 8.7, encompassing sub-figures 8.7(a) and 8.7(b).

8.5.2 Preprocessing of Data

The process of pre-processing plays a pivotal role in refining and improving the quality of images, simultaneously addressing challenges such as non-uniform illumination, blurring, and the unwanted inclusion of extraneous details. In the context of this discussion, the focus is on tailoring pre-processing techniques specifically for enhancing images of malarial bloodstains. This procedural refinement holds significant promise in ensuring semantically meaningful segmentation of images while preserving intricate details of the subject matter. A well-known strategy in this pre-processing journey involves the application of morphological tasks. These tasks contribute to further enhancing the overall quality of the images under consideration. The intricacies of the pre-processing steps are paramount in dealing with the nuances inherent in malarial bloodstain images.

In the quest for refining the dataset, several essential steps were undertaken. This includes the identification and handling of missing values within the dataset, the strategic division of the dataset into training and test datasets, and the crucial step of feature scaling. A meticulous approach was adopted to fine-tune the data, systematically removing outliers to ensure the generation of a clean dataset, instrumental in the experimental phase of this research. The tangible results of these efforts are showcased in Figure 8.7, where Figure 8.7(a) provides a visual representation

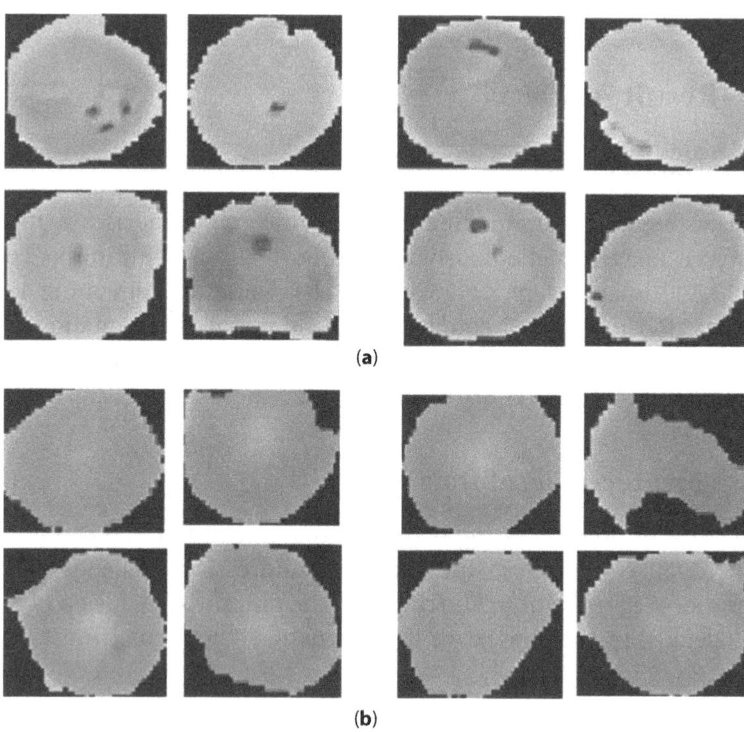

Figure 8.7 (a) Sample infected images; and (b) uninfected images.

of a parasitic image, and Figure 8.7(b) corresponds to an uninfected image. These illustrations serve as a testament to the effectiveness of the pre-processing techniques employed, offering a clear distinction between infected and uninfected images in the dataset.

8.5.3 Splitting of Dataset

The tabulated data in Table 8.2 delineates the number of occurrences within both the training and testing datasets.

8.5.4 Classification

Upon obtaining a meticulously refined dataset, the training data, accompanied by its corresponding labels, was fed into the classification model. The implementation was carried out with carefully chosen parameters: Learning rate set at 0.1, Activation function designated as ReLU, Batch size configured to 32, and the training epoch capped at 50. These parameters were meticulously fine-tuned to achieve a commendable accuracy rate of 96.67%. The success of this implementation underscores the efficacy of the selected parameters in facilitating precise classification within the model.

8.5.5 Model Prediction and Performance Metrics

After meticulous training, fine-tuning, and evaluation on the test dataset, the resulting metrics are presented in Table 8.2. Notably, the achieved accuracy surpasses that of other systems scrutinized in the course of this research, affirming the superiority of the proposed model in comparison to its counterparts. The presented metrics serve as a testament to the model's efficacy and its capacity to outperform existing systems, underscoring its potential for enhanced performance in the domain under investigation.

Table 8.2 Splitting of dataset.

Dataset type	Number of images	Percentage (%)
Train	19320	70
Test	8280	30
Total	27600	100

8.5.6 CNN Learning Curves

In this article, we discuss the outcome of the CNN learning process during training. Figure 8.8 shows the learning curve. This procedure was executed for every category or parameter throughout 50 epochs.

Table 8.3 encapsulates a confusion matrix delineating the outcomes of predictions rendered by a classification model applied to a malaria dataset. The tabulation meticulously enumerates the instances of accurate and erroneous predictions, providing count values and a detailed breakdown for each class, as illustrated in Figure 8.9.

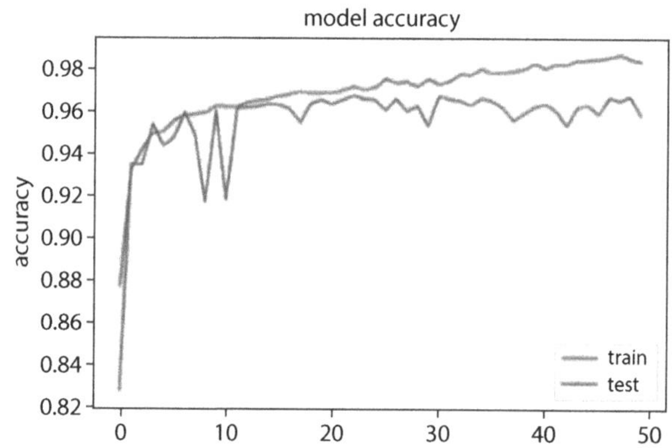

Figure 8.8 Model training accuracy.

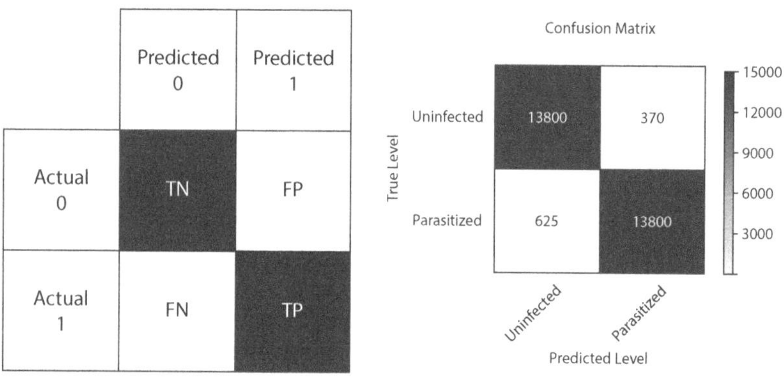

Figure 8.9 Confusion matrix.

8.6 Discussion

The data used for this research was fine-tuned to remove all the outliers from the dataset to get a clean dataset for the experimentation of this research work. After procuring a refined dataset, the training data and its associated labels were introduced into the classification model. For this model, we took a few parameters like accuracy, precision, recall, and F score which is shown in Table 8.3 below.

Table 8.3 Model's parameter value based on different matrices.

Parameter	Accuracy	Precision	Recall	F1- score
	96.67	96.25	94.23	97.10

8.7 Conclusion

This manuscript offers a comprehensive technical examination of recent advancements in malaria categorization utilizing CNNs. It is imperative to note that a CNN currently demonstrates its utility primarily in binary classification within the realm of malaria diagnosis. The domain of DL, a subset of artificial intelligence, has contributed a multitude of algorithms for the nuanced classification of diverse elements. The outcomes obtained during the testing phase of the developed system contribute significantly to enhancing the efficiency of malaria disease diagnosis from blood smears. Furthermore, the implementation of this system is poised to mitigate the financial burden associated with traditional microscopic diagnoses incurred by patients. This technological leap forward not only streamlines the diagnostic process but also holds promise for reducing the economic costs borne by individuals seeking medical evaluation for malaria.

8.8 Future Scope

In a forward-looking inquiry, it is judicious to recommend the utilization of publicly available benchmark datasets for the construction of a CNN model specifically designed for multi-class classification. The emphasis could be directed towards the categorization of various species and life stages of Plasmodium, the causative agent of malaria. Subsequent research undertakings should involve the assessment of the proposed CNN methodology using openly accessible benchmark datasets. Furthermore, there is an imperative necessity to present a CNN model explicitly tailored for the intricate task of multi-class classification. This exhortation is extended to fellow researchers, encouraging them to diversify data sources through the application of a spectrum of methodologies, encompassing optimizer techniques, bespoke models, ensemble models, evolutionary algorithms, and attention mechanisms. This collaborative endeavor aims to discern the optimal CNN technique and architecture for the exhaustive categorization of malaria. The trajectory of our approach may traverse compelling and advantageous directions by deploying a CNN for the identification of malaria parasites in peripheral blood smears. Hybrid ML methodologies, amalgamating both conventional techniques and DL, harbor the potential to yield outcomes of heightened precision compared to our ongoing efforts. This cooperative pursuit aspires to propel progress in the field and contribute to a more comprehensive understanding of methodologies for malaria categorization.

References

1. Maude, R.J., Beare, N.A., Sayeed, A.A., Chang, C.C., Charunwatthana, P., Faiz, M.A., Dondorp, A.M., The spectrum of retinopathy in adults with Plasmodium falciparum malaria. *Trans. R. Soc. Trop. Med. Hyg.*, 103, 7, 665–671, 2009.
2. Wassmer, S.C. and Grau, G.E.R., Severe malaria: what's new on the pathogenesis front? *Int. J. Parasitol.*, 47, 2-3, 145–152, 2017.
3. Björkman, A., Malaria associated anaemia, drug resistance and antimalarial combination therapy. *Int. J. Parasitol.*, 32, 13, 1637–1643, 2002.
4. World Malaria Report 2016, World Health Organization, pp. 1–280, 2016.
5. World Malaria Report 2020, World Health Organization, Geneva, pp. 1–299, 2020.
6. Tangpukdee, N., Duangdee, C., Wilairatana, P., Krudsood, S., Malaria diagnosis: A brief review. *Korean J. Parasitol.*, 47, 2, 93–102, 2009.
7. Yang, D., Subramanian, G., Duan, J., Gao, S., Bai, L., Chandramohanadas, R., Ai, Y., A portable image-based cytometer for rapid malaria detection and quantification. *PLoS One*, 12, 6, e0179161, 2017.
8. Mavandadi, S., Dimitrov, S., Feng, S., Yu, F., Sikora, U., Yaglidere, O., Padmanabhan, S., Nielsen, K., Ozcan, A., Distributed medical image analysis and diagnosis through crowd-sourced games: a malaria case study. *PLoS One*, 75, e37245, 2012.

9. Rajaraman, S., Jaeger, S., Antani, S.K., Performance evaluation of deep neural ensembles toward malaria parasite detection in thin-blood smear images. *PeerJ*, 7, e6977, 2019.
10. Suriya, M., Chandran, V., Sumithra, M.G., Enhanced deep convolutional neural network for malarial parasite classification. *Int. J. Comput. Appl.*, 44, 12, 1113–1122, 2022.
11. Rehman, A. *et al.*, Microscopic malaria parasitemia diagnosis and grading on benchmark datasets. *Microsc. Res. Tech.*, 81, 9, 1042–1058, 2018.
12. Pan, W.D., Dong, Y., Wu, D., Classification of malaria-infected cells using deep convolutional neural networks, in: *Machine learning: advanced techniques and emerging applications*, p. 159, 2018.
13. Litjens, G. *et al.*, A survey on deep learning in medical image analysis. *Med. Image Anal.*, 42, 60–88, 2017.
14. Fuhad, Faizullah, K.M. *et al.*, CNN Based Model for Malaria Diagnosis with Knowledge Distillation. *Proceedings of the 2020 4th International Conference on Digital Signal Processing*, 2020.
15. Szegedy, C. *et al.*, Rethinking the inception architecture for computer vision. *Proceedings of the IEEE conference on computer vision and pattern recognition*, 2016.
16. Hung, J. and Carpenter, A., Applying faster R-CNN for object detection on malaria images. *Proceedings of the IEEE conference on computer vision and pattern recognition workshops*, 2017.
17. Deng, J. *et al.*, Imagenet: A large-scale hierarchical image database. *2009 IEEE conference on computer vision and pattern recognition*, Ieee, 2009.
18. Bibin, D., Nair, M.S., Punitha, P., Malaria parasite detection from peripheral blood smear images using deep belief networks. *IEEE Access*, 5, 9099–9108, 2017.
19. Krizhevsky, A., Sutskever, I., Hinton, G.E., ImageNet classification with deep convolutional neural networks. *Commun. ACM*, 60, 6, 84–90, 2017.
20. Vijayalakshmi, A., Deep learning approach to detect malaria from microscopic images. *Multimedia Tools Appl.*, 79, 15297–15317, 2020.
21. Faizullah Fuhad, K.M. *et al.*, Deep learning based automatic malaria parasite detection from blood smear and its smartphone-based application. *Diagnostics*, 10, 5, 329, 2020.
22. Dang, N. *et al.*, Malaria Detection on Giemsa-Stained Blood Smears Using Deep Learning and Feature Extraction. *International Conference on Innovative Computing and Communications: Proceedings of ICICC 2019*, vol. 1, Springer Singapore, 2020.
23. Pattanaik, P.A. *et al.*, Malaria detection using deep residual networks with mobile microscopy. *J. King Saud Univ. Comput. Inf. Sci.*, 34, 5, 1700–1705, 2022.
24. Kundu, T.K. and Anguraj, D.K., Identification of Malaria Parasites in Thin Blood Smear Using SVM Classifier. *2023 2nd International Conference on Edge Computing and Applications (ICECAA)*, IEEE, 2023.

25. Brinker, T.J. *et al.*, Skin cancer classification using convolutional neural networks: systematic review. *J. Med. Internet Res.*, 20, 10, e11936, 2018.
26. Simonyan, K. and Zisserman, A., Very deep convolutional networks for large-scale image recognition. 2014, arXiv preprint arXiv:1409.1556.
27. Szegedy, C. *et al.*, Going deeper with convolutions. *Proceedings of the IEEE conference on computer vision and pattern recognition*, 2015.
28. He, K. *et al.*, Deep residual learning for image recognition. *Proceedings of the IEEE conference on computer vision and pattern recognition*, 2016.
29. Liang, Z. *et al.*, CNN-based image analysis for malaria diagnosis. *2016 IEEE international conference on bioinformatics and biomedicine (BIBM)*, IEEE, 2016.
30. Rajaraman, S. *et al.*, Understanding the learned behaviour of customized convolutional neural networks toward malaria parasite detection in thin blood smear images. *J. Med. Imaging*, 5, 3, 034501–034501, 2018.
31. Çınar, N., Kaya, B., Kaya, M., Comparison of deep learning models for brain tumor classification using MRI images. *2022 International Conference on Decision Aid Sciences and Applications (DASA)*, IEEE, 2022.
32. Kundu, T.K., Anguraj, D.K., Sudha, S.V., Modeling a Novel Hyper-Parameter Tuned Deep Learning Enabled Malaria Parasite Detection and Classification.
33. Reddy, A.S.B. and Sujitha Juliet, D., Transfer learning with ResNet-50 for malaria cell-image classification. *2019 International Conference on Communication and Signal Processing (ICCSP)*, IEEE, 2019.
34. Peñas, K.E.D., Rivera, P.T., Naval, P.C., Malaria parasite detection and species identification on thin blood smears using a convolutional neural network. *2017 IEEE/ACM International Conference on Connected Health: Applications, Systems and Engineering Technologies (CHASE)*, IEEE, 2017.
35. Kundu, T.K. and Anguraj, D.K., Optimal Machine Learning Based Automated Malaria Parasite Detection and Classification Model Using Blood Smear Images. *Trait. Signal*, 40, 1, 91–99, 2023.
36. Suriya, M., Chandran, V., Sumithra, M.G., Design of deep convolutional neural network for efficient classification of malaria parasite. *2nd EAI International Conference on Big Data Innovation for Sustainable Cognitive Computing: BDCC 2019*, Springer International Publishing, 2021.

9

Exploring the Efficacy of Generative AI in Constructing Dynamic Predictive Models for Cybersecurity Threats: A Research Perspective

T. Manasa* **and K. Padmanaban**

Department of Computer Science and Engineering, Koneru Lakshmaiah Education Foundation, Vaddeswaram, Guntur, Andhra Pradesh, India

Abstract

The rapid expansion of the Internet of Things (IoT) in smart buildings demands a continuous assessment of potential dangers and their consequences. Conventional techniques are becoming less and less effective in assessing risk and reducing related hazards, hence new strategies must be developed. The IoT cybersecurity systems are essential for many aspects of daily life, not only prediction applications. Specifically, botnet-initiated distributed denial of service (DDoS) attacks on key BMS software present significant dangers to security and resources. In this work, we provide a novel technique that combines the hybrid learning model (HLM), which incorporates random forest (RF) and C4.5-based decision trees, with the stochastic gradient boosting (SGB) predictor. Our improved algorithm achieves a remarkable 99.2% accuracy rate when evaluating DDoS attack risk indicators in the context of a cyber-system. In addition, it exhibits a remarkable 99% precision in anticipating DDoS assaults, proficiently preventing system disturbances, and successfully handling cyber hazards. We do a comparison study utilizing the 95% accuracy rate k-nearest neighbor classifier (KNN) to further confirm our findings.

Keywords: Internet of Things, machine learning, prediction, denial of service, attack

**Corresponding author*: thirumanasa@gmail.com

R. Nidhya, D. Pavithra, Manish Kumar, A. Dinesh Kumar and S. Balamurugan (eds.) Generative Artificial Intelligence: Concepts and Applications, (143–154) © 2025 Scrivener Publishing LLC

9.1 Introduction

The Internet of Things (IoT) is a revolutionary idea that is evolving in an attempt to safeguard consumers, promote internal IoT trust, and maintain privacy [1]. The IoT is envisioned to operate akin to a social network, incorporating aspects of community and collaboration. Utilizing technology such as sensors, CPUs, software, and others, data exchange and integration are made easier by the ability of common objects to link to computers and other devices over the Internet and other networks. These social connections make it easier for people and gadgets to communicate, strengthening social networks and streamlining information sharing [2]. These IoT concerns may be handled by adopting models inspired by human social networks since IoT employs human social networking principles to resolve IoT-related issues [3].

The IoT security solutions continue to struggle with scalability, centralization, and unclear architecture despite developments. Furthermore, these systems ignore the social knowledge gained from user-technology interactions in favor of an excessive emphasis on the physical characteristics of gadgets [4]. Building relationships in settings like friendships, corporations, and families is important for building trust. However, these ideas frequently fall short of improving interpersonal connections in the real world [5]. Devices connected to the IoT face particular vulnerabilities and the dangers of network assaults, including spoofing, fraud, and distributed denial of service (DDoS) attacks. Cyberattacks, threats, and attack vectors such as botnets and novel attack techniques are examined in this research [6].

The IoT paradigm harnesses subjective social interaction qualities to ensure accurate data processing, expert services, and improved security [7]. Research gaps that IoT can bridge consist of scalability similar to that of human social networking sites, item identification, efficient service administration, and social interaction management between socially intelligent things [7]. It is important to conduct additional study using the concept of the "smart world" phenomena, network navigability connections between items, and participant smart item trustworthiness management [8]. By merging tangible IoT devices with social interactions between people, IoT systems may provide people with pervasive connection. Computation offloading becomes important when IoT systems start prioritizing user happiness above information distribution becomes vital for expediting program execution. Over the past decade, the IoT has experienced significant growth, introducing several challenges in selecting reliable service components [9].

In these scenarios, establishing and maintaining relative trust among objects is crucial to selecting the most suitable tools for interaction and gathering precise data. However, rogue devices may exploit this trust to conduct various attacks on other IoT nodes. The "IoT nodes," the components of an IoT ecosystem, are what make links between the online and offline worlds possible. These gadgets are designed to aggregate data from diverse sources, often serving as data aggregators for multiple sensors. They may control an entire category of services by operating independently, forming networks of collaborative devices, or making up concepts or services. Ineffective management might lead to assaults and failures within. The IoT could outweigh its benefits. This study introduces a novel technique for detecting attacks on IoT networks. The structured approach of this work involves:

1. Initial preprocessing of the provided online dataset.
2. Employing a hybrid learning model (HLM), specifically embedded C4.5 with random forest (CRF), for prediction.
3. Assessing and quantifying the model's effectiveness using a range of parameters, including loss, recall, accuracy, and precision.

The paper is organized as follows: A comprehensive study of various methodologies is presented in Section 9.2, and the hybrid methodology is suggested in Section 9.3. The numerical findings are covered in Section 9.4, and the conclusion is provided in Section 9.5.

9.2 Related Works

The survey conducted by Alrehan and Alhaidari focused on various techniques based on machine learning (ML) for identifying DDoS assaults in vehicular ad hoc networks (VANET), a subsection of the IoT [10]. Although they briefly presented certain datasets, their research did not include a complete list of datasets or a detailed taxonomy of detection techniques until 2018. In their assessment of DDoS attack prevention, detection, and mitigation techniques, Loukas and Gülay provided historical context and techniques [11]. Nevertheless, their survey lacked a taxonomy of discussed techniques and did not provide a dataset list suitable for ML algorithms. Furthermore, they did not investigate assessed techniques in IoT or software-defined networking (SDN) contexts.

In [12], the author examined DDoS assaults in cloud computing settings and suggested a categorization scheme for them. Despite introducing a taxonomy for detection techniques, it lacked comprehensiveness focusing less on ML approaches and excluding strategies applicable to SDN and IoT environments. The author in [13] provided an overview of DDoS attack structure, functionality, and existing solutions but did not establish a taxonomy of various approaches or offer thorough explanations of the methodologies. This research seeks to rectify the deficiencies found in the previously stated surveys. In particular, it offers a more thorough and up-to-date literature review in addition to a thorough taxonomy of detection techniques, some of which are relevant to developing SDN and IoT networks [14]. This study also offers extensive explanations and introduces a broader range of surveyed methods for detecting DDoS assaults. Interestingly, it also includes datasets that were absent from some earlier surveys yet are appropriate for testing and training machine learning algorithms.

9.3 Methodology

This section provides a wider analysis of the proposed model for DDoS attacks. Figure 9.1 shows the block diagram of the projected model.

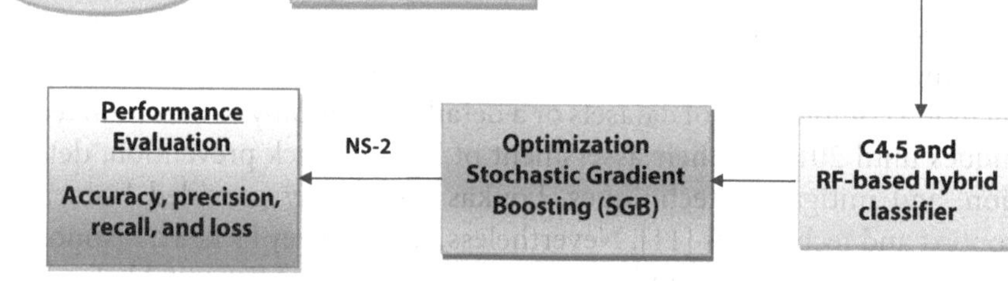

Figure 9.1 Block diagram.

9.3.1 Pre-Processing

Remove Duplicate Records: Identify and remove any identical records to ensure each entry in the dataset is unique.
Handle Missing Values: Identify instances with missing values in features related to the attack and network connection.
For Numerical Features: Use methods such as mean, median, or mode imputation to impute missing data.
For Categorical Variables (like attack type): Consider imputing missing values with the most frequent category or a separate category indicating missing data. Alternatively, if the missing data is extensive, you may remove instances with missing values after careful consideration of the impact on the dataset's integrity.
Eliminate Irrelevant or Redundant Features: Assess each feature's relevance to predicting attack flow. Remove features that do not contribute significantly to the predictive power of the model or those that are redundant. Features like sample ID, if present, might not be relevant for prediction and can be removed.
Encode Categorical Variables: Transform numerical values from categorical variables (like type) using methods like label encoding or one-hot encoding. For example, if gender is a categorical feature, use one-hot encoding to transform it into numerical values (0,1) where each category becomes a binary column.
Scale Numerical Features: To bring numerical properties to a common scale, scale them. Use techniques like Min-Max scaling or StandardScalar to normalize the features. As a result, during training, characteristics with wider ranges are kept from taking center stage. By following these steps, you can preprocess the attack-based records dataset effectively, ensuring data cleanliness, addressing missing values, scaling numerical characteristics, and encoding categorical variables for better model performance in predicting an attack.

9.3.2 Classifier

The HLM, specifically embedded CRF classifier, is the primary component of an ensemble learning model is a decision tree (C4.5). The bagging approach is used to create a framework consisting of many trained decision trees, as illustrated by the HLM block diagram. When a sample has to be categorized, the final classification decision is determined based on a majority vote from the output of each decision tree. The HLM model outperforms solo decision trees for processing high-dimensional data because it can effectively reduce overfitting, is robust against noise and outliers, and can process data in parallel. The power of HLMs is primarily found in the fact that they are parameter-free and represent a data-driven methodology. The model is excellent at training classification rules based on observed cases and does not require the user to have any prior understanding of classification. The flexibility of the model to different data circumstances is enhanced by this data-centric characteristic. The fundamental principle of the HLM model is the use of KC4.5, whereby each one provides a single "vote" to the category that it believes is most suitable. This helps choose which class the independent variable X is assigned to. This method successfully combines the aggregate expertise of several trees, enabling reliable and accurate classification results that take advantage of the various insights that each decision tree has to offer.

$$\{h(X,\theta_K), k = 1,2,\ldots,K\} \tag{9.1}$$

K stands for the number of C4.5 in the RF in this instance. A set of independent random vectors (θ_k) that are evenly distributed among themselves is used to build each tree. The K distinct decision trees make up the ensemble, and for the category that most closely matches the independent variable X, each person adds a prediction. These forecasts from the K decision trees are totaled via a voting process to establish the final category assignment for the independent variable X. Equation 9.1 highlights the ensemble component of the HLM model, wherein several decision trees collaborate to increase prediction accuracy and durability. The combination of predictions from diverse trees allows for a more comprehensive evaluation and ultimately leads to an improved and more reliable final category assignment for the independent variable X.

9.3.3 Optimization

The approach you are describing seems to outline the optimization steps for stochastic gradient boosting (SGB) when used in regression tasks. Here is a breakdown of the steps involved:

Initialization: Set the first prediction to the mean to begin initializing the model (or any other suitable value) of the target labels in the training data.

Gradient Calculation: Determine the loss function's negative gradient about the predictions of the present model. This gradient shows which way and how much the model's predictions must be adjusted to minimize the loss function.

Train C4.5: With the negative gradient serving as the target variable, construct a new weak learner decision tree. The purpose of this new tree is to learn and address the mistakes made by earlier iterations of the model.
Update Model Predictions: By including the new decision tree's predictions, scaled by a learning rate, the model's predictions are updated. The learning rate helps the model get closer to producing accurate predictions by regulating the update's amplitude to avoid overfitting.
Iteration: Perform each step again for a certain number of times (or until a specific stopping condition is satisfied). The goal of each iteration is to enhance the model's predictions by learning from the mistakes made in the previous rounds. The Stochastic Gradient Boosting technique iteratively builds an ensemble of weak learners (C4.5 in this case), with each new learner attempting to correct the errors of the ensemble up to that point. By combining the predictions of multiple weak learners systematically, the model gradually improves its ability to predict the target variable accurately. This methodology is effective in ensemble learning, allowing for powerful predictive models by leveraging the strengths of individual weak learners while minimizing the overall error in predictions.

9.4 Numerical Results and Discussion

After conducting an extensive literature review and developing our results are based on ML models that use the DDoS detection technique. To verify and evaluate the outcomes, our method compares the outputs with a specific SVM. To assess the effectiveness and usefulness of our proposed method, researchers conducted an analysis using the NS-2 network simulation and the CIC IoT Dataset 2022 attack data. In the following figures, we present the graphical representation depicting the distribution of data outcomes determined by byte counts, flows, and packet counts. The label '1' designates the assaulted data points in the visual representation shown in Figure 9.1 while the normal data traffic points are marked with '0'. This graphical representation showcases the data according to various parameters such as traffic flows, byte count, traffic density, and packet count, allowing for a visual understanding of the distinctions between attacked and normal data.

The simulation assessments conducted on the implemented algorithm demonstrated its superior performance compared to individual NN models in detecting complex DDoS techniques. These sophisticated attacks include combinations such as ping of death assaults, UDP floods, SYN floods, Zero-day, and fragmented packets. Prior research on single NN projects revealed

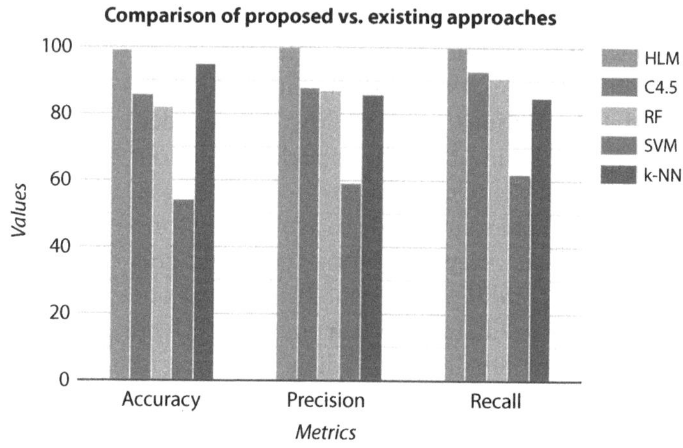

Figure 9.2 Comparison of proposed vs. existing approaches.

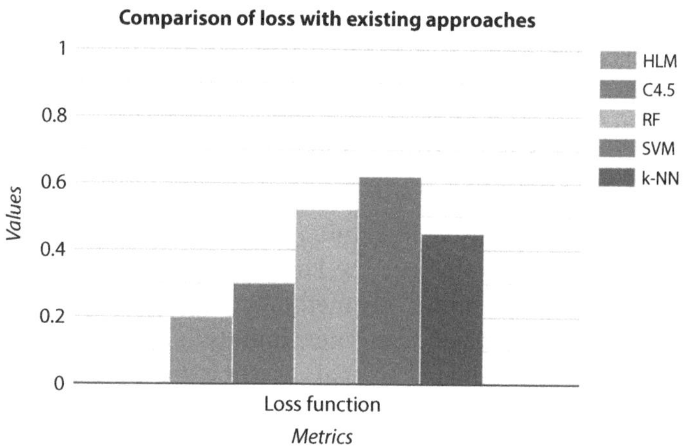

Figure 9.3 Comparison of loss with existing approaches.

accuracy levels between 75% and 80%; nevertheless, our system, integrating C4.5 and RF networks showcased remarkable accuracy, utilizing the CIC dataset to attain 99.19%, as shown in Table 9.1. The Figure 9.2 and Figure 9.3 presents a visual representation of the accuracy of training and validation throughout several epochs, illustrating the progression and consistency of our algorithm's performance during the learning process. The DDoS attacks have the potential to cause significant disruptions to technical infrastructure, causing significant harm or jeopardizing system functionality.

Table 9.1 Overall assessment of performance.

Iterations	Accuracy	Precision	Recall	Loss
Hybrid Learning Model (HLM)	**99.2%**	**99.89**	**99.89**	**0.2**
C4.5	86	88	93	0.3
RF	82	87	91	0.52
SVM	54	59	62	0.65
k-NN	95	86	85	0.45

When it comes to fending off sophisticated DDoS attacks, traditional IoT protocols like the message queuing telemetry transport (MQTT) protocol frequently fall short. The use of ML algorithms for DDoS attack detection in IoT systems has been the subject of several research. Still, most of these studies reveal only moderate success rates in identifying advanced DDoS attacks. Our suggested strategy is distinct from previous approaches that prioritize features based on top scores from several classifiers. Table 9.1 illustrates how our methods showed greater accuracy even with a smaller collection of characteristics. This comparison considers several characteristics, including the kind of categorization, the number of features, and the techniques used.

There are several significant variations in the dataset and methodology that we used when comparing our suggested procedure to the publications, approaches, and datasets that we examined in our literature study. The main difference between our method and others is that we use hybrid modeling methods. Our model's correctness is confirmed by the F1-Score, which is shown in Table 9.1. Moreover, it is well recognized that the recall metric measures the proportion of correctly identified positive transactions—indicates the minimum error tolerance level of our model. The researchers previously demonstrated, through the implementation of a learning network, shown in certain flying conditions, that a C4.5 with a dynamic structure may produce the same control settings ensuring consistent responses, as observed previously. Tools for mathematical modelling that are well-established include game theory techniques. The successful outcomes of these theories indicate that they have been effectively incorporated into traditional artificial intelligence decision-making systems.

9.5 Conclusion

The rise of intelligent building applications introduces potential cybersecurity vulnerabilities for individuals, organizations, and the technologies they depend on. Among the notable risks requiring attention are DDoS attacks orchestrated by botnets. These attacks try to undermine websites and the IoT infrastructure as a whole by overloading connections with data. Despite the availability of several machine-learning-assisted detection techniques, our study presents a new defensive strategy. Our study utilizes an ML model, primarily focused on a learning model for identifying DDoS threats. Additionally, we use HLM to improve the detection process' accuracy. We use SGB for feature selection, which greatly increases the sensitivity and efficacy of DDoS detection. By offering strong security mechanisms against DDoS attacks, this architecture deftly detects and neutralizes incursion attempts.

The results of our investigation confirm that the suggested technique is quite successful, especially when it comes to identifying intricate DDoS attacks. Nevertheless, certain noteworthy restrictions are present, including the discrepancy between our study's focus on DDoS attacks and the evaluation dataset's predominance of DoS attacks. Besides, our system model does not accurately represent the SDN-enabled smart building environment due to a disagreement with the dataset's testing circumstances. Notwithstanding these constraints, our study demonstrates substantial progress in identifying and mitigating DDoS attacks. When the hybrid model is used, our method of defending against DDoS attacks becomes much more effective. When evaluated using the CIC dataset paradigms, our proposed model achieved an accuracy rate of 99.19%. Our approach has the potential to be much more effective after resolving these identified restrictions, which bodes well for the future development of smart buildings. In the future, we will be carrying out critical actions to strengthen security by putting in place several protection layers against various cyberattack techniques.

References

1. LeCun, Y., Bengio, Y., Hinton, G., Deep learning. *Nature*, 521, 7553, 436–444, May 2015.
2. Reddy, Ramadevi, Y., Sunitha, K.V.N., Effective discriminant function for intrusion detection using SVM, in: *Proc. Int. Conf. Adv. Comput., Commun. Inform. (ICAC)*, Sep. 2016, pp. 1148–1153.

3. Ingre, and Yadav, A., Performance analysis of NSL-KDD dataset using ANN, in: *Proc. Int. Conf. Signal Process. Commun. Eng. Syst.*, pp. 92–96, Jan. 2015.
4. Farnaaz, and Jabbar, M.A., Random-forest modeling for network intrusion detection system. *Procedia Comput. Sci.*, 89, 213–217, Jan. 2016.
5. Khan, and Jain, N., A survey on intrusion detection systems and classification techniques. *Int. J. Sci. Res. Sci. Eng. Technol.*, 2, 5, 202–208, 2016.
6. Tang, Mhamdi, L., McLernon, D., Zaidi, S.A.R., Ghogho, M., Deep learning approach for network intrusion detection in software-defined networking. *Proc. Int. Conf. Wireless Netw. Mobile Commun. (WINCOM)*, Oct. 2016, pp. 258–263.
7. Ashfaq, Wang, X.-Z., Huang, J.Z., Abbas, H., He, Y.-L., Fuzziness based semi-supervised learning approach for an intrusion detection system. *Inf. Sci.*, 378, 484–497, Feb. 2017.
8. Chang, Li, W., Yang, Z., Network intrusion detection based on random forest and support vector machine. *Proc. IEEE Int. Conf. Comput. Sci. Eng./IEEE Int. Conf. Embedded Ubiquitous Comput.*, Jul. 2017, pp. 635–638.
9. Zhao, Yan, R., Chen, Z., Mao, K., Wang, P., Gao, R.X., Deep learning and its applications to machine health monitoring: A survey. *IEEE Trans. Neural Netw. Learn. Syst.*, 2016, [Online]. Available: http://arxiv.org/abs/1612.07640.
10. Vincent, P., Larochelle, H., Lajoie, I., Bengio, Y., Manzagol, P. A., Bottou, L., Stacked denoising autoencoders: Learning useful representations in a deep network with a local denoising criterion. *J. Mach. Learn. Res.*, 11, 12, 3371-3408, 2010.
11. You, Li, Y., Wang, Y., Zhang, J., Yang, Y., A deep learning-based RNNs model for automatic security audit of short messages, in: *Proc. 16th Int. Symp. Commun. Inf. Technol.*, Qingdao, China, pp. 225–229, Sep. 2016.
12. Alrawashdeh, and Purdy, C., Toward an online anomaly intrusion detection system based on deep learning, in: *Proc. 15th IEEE Int. Conf. Mach. Learn. Appl.*, Anaheim, CA, USA, pp. 195–200, Dec. 2016.
13. Potluri, and Diedrich, C., Accelerated deep neural networks for an enhanced intrusion detection system. *Proc. IEEE 21st Int. Conf. Emerg. Technol. Factory Autom.*, Berlin, Germany, pp. 1–8, Sep. 2016.
14. Sherubha, P., Sasirekha, S. P., Manikandan, V., Gowsic, K., Mohanasundaram, N., Graph based event measurement for analyzing distributed anomalies in sensor networks. *Sādhanā*, 45, 1–5, 2020.

10

Poultry Disease Detection: A Comparative Analysis of CNN, SVM, and YOLO v3 Algorithms for Accurate Diagnosis

Spoorthi Shetty and Mangala Shetty*

MCA, NMAM Institute of Technology, Nitte, Karkala, Karnataka, India

Abstract

Poultry farming plays a vital role in the global food industry, with chickens being one of the most commonly raised birds. However, the presence of diseases among chicken populations poses significant challenges to the industry's productivity and profitability. Early detection and accurate diagnosis of diseases are crucial for effective disease management and prevention. In this paper, we propose an integrated approach for chicken disease detection using support vector machines (SVMs), convolutional neural networks (CNNs), and the YOLO v3 object detection algorithm. The proposed integrated approach is evaluated using a large-scale dataset comprising diverse chicken diseases. Experimental results demonstrate the effectiveness and robustness of the combined SVM, CNN, and YOLO v3 framework, achieving high accuracy in disease detection across different samples.

The developed system holds great promise for the poultry industry, enabling early detection and prompt intervention, ultimately reducing economic losses and improving animal welfare. Furthermore, the integration of machine learning and computer vision techniques in chicken disease detection highlights the potential for similar applications in other livestock domains, contributing to overall agricultural advancements.

Keywords: YOLO v3, convolutional neural networks (CNNs), support vector machine

**Corresponding author*: mangalapshetty@nitte.edu.in

R. Nidhya, D. Pavithra, Manish Kumar, A. Dinesh Kumar and S. Balamurugan (eds.) Generative Artificial Intelligence: Concepts and Applications, (155–172) © 2025 Scrivener Publishing LLC

10.1 Introduction

Chicken diseases pose significant challenges to the poultry industry worldwide, leading to significant economic losses and impacting animal welfare. Early detection and accurate diagnosis of these diseases are crucial for effective disease management and prevention of widespread outbreaks. Traditionally, disease detection in chickens has relied on manual observation and veterinary expertise. However, these methods are time-consuming, labor-intensive, and subjective, often leading to delayed interventions and increased disease transmission.

In recent years, the advancement of computer vision and machine learning techniques has opened new possibilities for automating and improving the accuracy of disease detection in poultry. One promising approach is the utilization of chicken droppings and eye images as valuable sources of information for disease identification.

Chicken droppings can provide valuable insights into the overall health and well-being of chickens. Various diseases can manifest specific characteristics in the appearance and composition of droppings, such as changes in color, consistency, or the presence of pathogens. By analyzing these patterns, it is possible to develop automated systems that can accurately classify and identify diseases based on chicken droppings images.

Diseased chickens often exhibit specific ocular abnormalities, such as inflammation, discoloration, or lesions. Leveraging computer vision techniques, these eye abnormalities can be captured and analyzed to detect and diagnose diseases in a non-invasive and efficient manner.

This research aims to develop a comprehensive approach for chicken disease detection using chicken droppings and eyes. By leveraging the power of advanced image processing techniques, including convolutional neural networks (CNN), support vector machines (SVM), and the YOLO v3 algorithm, we aim to achieve accurate and real-time detection of common chicken diseases.

The proposed system will involve the collection of a diverse dataset of chicken droppings and eye images, which will be labeled by veterinary experts to train and evaluate the performance of the machine learning models. The CNN will be utilized to extract discriminative features from chicken droppings images, while the SVM algorithm will be employed for disease classification based on eye images. Additionally, the YOLO v3 algorithm will facilitate the precise localization and detection of disease-related indicators in chicken eyes.

The outcomes of this research have the potential to revolutionize chicken disease detection and management practices in the poultry industry. By enabling early and accurate disease detection, interventions can be implemented promptly, minimizing the spread of diseases and reducing economic losses. Moreover, the proposed approach offers a non-invasive and efficient method for disease monitoring, reducing stress on chickens and improving animal welfare.

There are several reasons why we chose to focus on chicken disease detection specifically, rather than other diseases. Firstly, poultry farming plays a significant role in the global food industry, with chickens being one of the most commonly raised livestock animals. By detecting and addressing diseases in chickens promptly, we can ensure the health and welfare of these animals, prevent potential outbreaks, and minimize economic losses for poultry farmers.

10.2 Literature Review

Authors in papers (Zelalem *et al.*) (Hossain *et al.*, 2023) (Elsayed *et al.*, 2021) [1, 5, 6] provide the smartphone-based system for poultry disease detection and classification using deep learning techniques. By combining YOLO v3 for region of interest segmentation and a pre-trained ResNet50 model, the system achieved high accuracy in identifying common poultry diseases from chicken fecal images.

Machuve *et al.* (2022) and Wang *et al.* (2019) [2, 7] explain the developed model utilized a deep CNN to distinguish between healthy and unhealthy poultry fecal images. The results highlight the effectiveness of deep learning in accurately detecting and classifying poultry diseases based on fecal images, offering potential benefits for efficient disease diagnosis and management in the poultry industry.

Min Zhou *et al.* (2023) [3] explains the detecting abnormal chicken droppings in practical farming environments. By incorporating deformable convolution, PA-FPN, K-means++ algorithm, and classification Focal loss function, the model achieved an impressive accuracy of 98.8% and a 27.8% improvement in mean average precision (mAP) compared to the original network. The study's findings contribute to efficient online monitoring of abnormal chicken droppings and accurate discrimination of various types of chicken diseases.

Hemalatha *et al.* (2014) [4] provides the extreme learning machine (ELM) and SVM with Gaussian radial function classifier is used to classify an avian pox disease. Texture features were extracted using the gray level co-occurrence matrix, and statistical features were extracted using mean, standard deviation, kurtosis and skewness. Based on the confusion matrix results, ELM gives higher accuracy against the SVM (GRBF). From the results, it is noted that ELM classifies the disease better than SVM (GRBF).

In paper, (Zhuang *et al.*, 2018), (Hepworth *et al.*, 2012) [8, 9], authors obtain the images of sick broilers and identify healthy and unhealthy chickens using SVM model, and in paper, (Srivastava *et al.*, 2023) [10], the author identifies the disease using CNN algorithm.

In all the above papers, most of the authors have considered chicken fecal image for identification of disease and few have considered chicken eye image. But in our research, we considered both for disease identification, which makes the work unique.

10.3 Objectives

10.3.1 Accurate Disease and Early Disease Identification

Early Disease Detection: The main objective is to identify diseases in chickens as early as possible. By monitoring the droppings and examining the eyes, veterinarians and poultry farmers can detect signs and symptoms of diseases before they become severe or widespread. Early detection allows for timely intervention and treatment, minimizing the impact on the affected chickens and preventing the spread of diseases within the flock.

10.3.2 Multi-Class Disease Identification

Multi-class disease identification in chicken disease detection using droppings and eyes refers to the classification of different diseases or health conditions in chickens based on the analysis of droppings and eye examination. The objective is to develop a system or method that can accurately identify and classify various diseases or health issues in the chicken. By achieving accurate multi-class disease identification in chicken disease detection using droppings and eyes, it becomes possible to implement targeted interventions, improve disease management, and minimize the impact of diseases on poultry health, welfare, and productivity.

10.3.3 Automation and Real-Time Disease Monitoring

Automation and real-time disease monitoring in chicken disease detection using droppings and eyes involve the use of technology and data analysis to enable continuous, efficient, and timely detection and monitoring of diseases in chickens. Here are the key aspects of this objective: monitor various parameters such as droppings consistency, temperature, humidity, or eye health indicators. These sensors can continuously collect data, providing a constant stream of information for disease monitoring.

10.3.4 Better Accuracy

Increase the overall accuracy of the model in correctly identifying and classifying chicken diseases. This can be measured by the proportion of correctly classified disease samples compared to the total number of samples.

10.4 Methodology

10.4.1 Dataset

Data is collected from the popular dataset platform, Kaggle. However, in order to ensure the quality and reliability of the collected data, we have implemented a criterion to discard certain images based on their clarity.

To determine the clarity of the images, various factors such as blurriness, pixelation, and overall visual quality are considered. Images that do not meet the desired level of clarity are excluded from the dataset. This selection process helps ensure that the collected images are of sufficient quality and provide clear visual representations for further analysis and modeling.

Out of the available dataset containing 8000 images, we have chosen 6812 images for further analysis and usage. The 6812 images are distributed to four class labels such as Health with 2057 images, Coccidiosis with 2103 images, Newcastle disease (NCD) with 376 images, and Salmonella with 2276 images. We managed to have a dataset that meets our exact specifications of different images were then split into 70% for training and 30% for testing. The types of sample fecal images are shown in Figure 10.1, and eye images are shown in Figure 10.2.

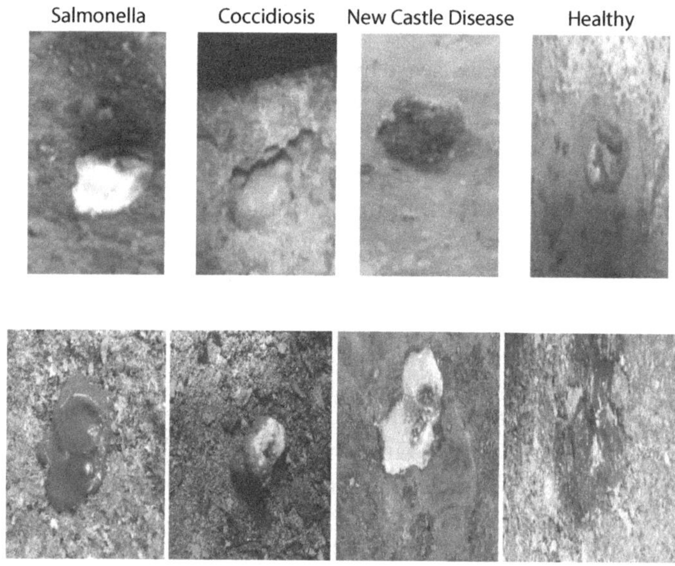

Figure 10.1 Sample images from the fecal image dataset.

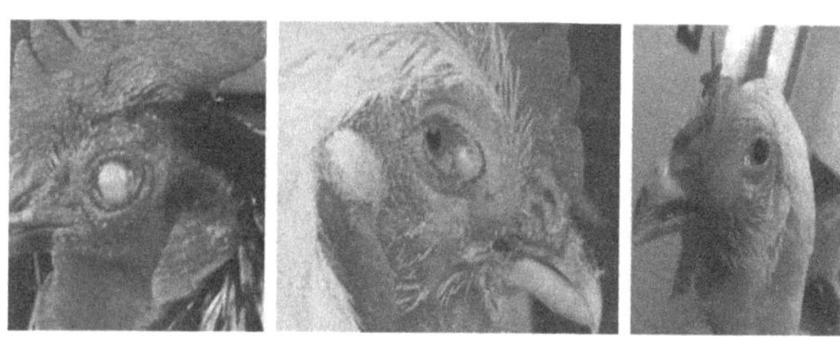

Figure 10.2 Sample images from the eyes image dataset.

10.4.2 Data Preprocessing

The dataset consists of four image classes: Salmonella, Coccidiosis, Healthy, and NCD. These classes have varying sizes, with Salmonella accounting for 32.5% of the dataset, Coccidiosis for 30.7%, Healthy for 30%, and NCD for 6.96%. This distribution results in a skewed dataset, where Salmonella is the most common class, and NCD is the least common. However, the performance of standard classifier learning methods, which assume balanced class distribution and equal costs of misclassification, can be significantly hindered when dealing with data that has an uneven class distribution.

10.4.3 Image Preprocessing

Before feeding the images to the deep learning classifier model, two pre-processing steps were performed: region of interest (ROI) segmentation and data augmentation. The ROI segmentation involved isolating and extracting the relevant regions from the images to focus on the important features. Data augmentation techniques were then applied to increase the size and diversity of the dataset by generating additional variations of the existing images. These pre-processing steps aimed to improve the performance and robustness of the deep learning classifier model.

10.4.4 Data Augmentation

Data augmentation is a technique used to enhance the size and quality of training datasets, leading to the development of improved deep learning models. It is particularly beneficial in computer vision tasks as it helps prevent overfitting during training. Overfitting happens when a network learns a function that overly fits the training data, resulting in poor generalization. In this step, geometric transformation augmentation techniques, such as rotation, zooming, flipping, and shifting, were randomly applied to the training images. This augmentation process introduces variations to the images, creating new training examples that can improve the model's ability to handle diverse data. Augmented images are depicted in Figure 10.3.

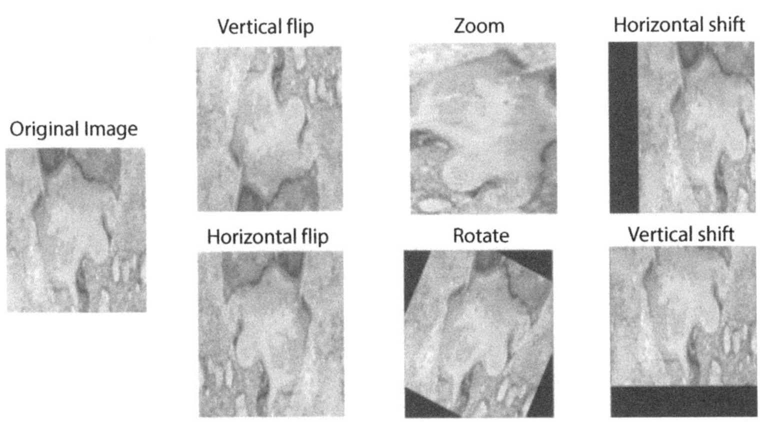

Figure 10.3 Data augmentation.

10.4.5 Extracting Region of Interest

To extract the region of interest (ROI) for chicken disease detection, the algorithm used in our work are combinations of CNN, and YOLO v3. Here is a general approach:

1. CNN for Feature Extraction: Train a CNN model on a large dataset of chicken disease images. This model will learn to extract relevant features from the input images, which can help identify disease-specific patterns.
2. SVM for Classification: Use the extracted features from the CNN as input to an SVM classifier. Train the SVM on labeled data, where each image is associated with a specific disease class. The SVM will learn to classify the images into different disease categories based on the extracted features.
3. YOLO v3 for Object Detection: YOLO v3 is an object detection algorithm that can identify and locate objects within an image. Adapt YOLO v3 to detect specific disease related objects or regions within chicken images. Train the YOLO v3 model on annotated data, where the disease-related regions in the images are labeled. The object detection model of YOLO v3 is shown in Figure 10.4.
4. ROI Extraction: Apply the trained YOLO v3 model to new chicken images. It will detect and localize the disease-related

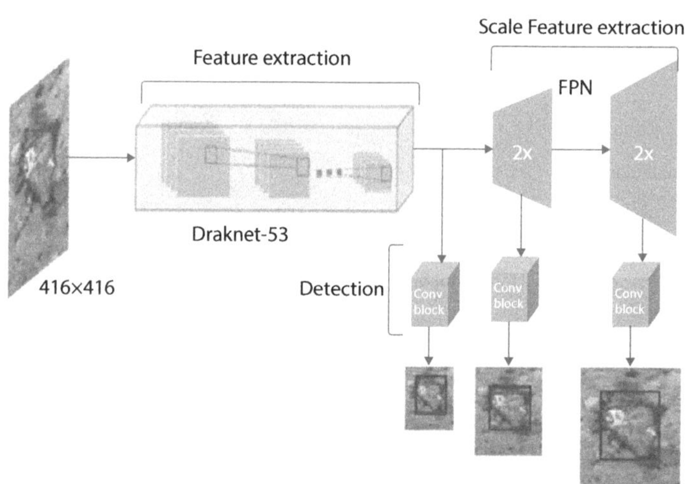

Figure 10.4 Architecture of YOLO v3 object detection model.

regions or objects within the images. These regions will be the ROIs indicating the presence of disease.

By combining these algorithms, you can leverage CNN for feature extraction, SVM for classification, and YOLO v3 for precise object detection to accurately extract ROIs related to chicken diseases in the images.

To evaluate the performance of chicken disease detection using CNN, SVM, and YOLO v3 algorithms, you can utilize various performance evaluation metrics. Here are some commonly used metrics:

1. Accuracy: Accuracy measures the overall correctness of the predictions made by the models. It calculates the ratio of correctly classified disease instances to the total number of instances.
2. Precision: Precision represents the ability of the models to correctly identify the disease instances among the predicted positive cases. It is the ratio of true positives to the sum of true positives and false positives.
3. Recall (Sensitivity or True Positive Rate): Recall measures the ability of the models to identify all the positive instances correctly.
4. F1 Score: The F1 score is the harmonic mean of precision and recall. It provides a balanced measure of the models' performance, considering both precision and recall.
5. Intersection over Union (IoU): IoU is commonly used in object detection tasks. It calculates the overlap between the predicted bounding box (ROI) and the ground truth bounding box. A higher IoU indicates better localization accuracy.
6. Mean Average Precision (mAP): mAP is a widely used evaluation metric for object detection tasks. It calculates the average precision across different levels of detection confidence thresholds. A higher mAP indicates better overall performance.
7. Receiver Operating Characteristic (ROC) Curve: The ROC curve plots the true positive rate (sensitivity) against the false positive rate. It helps assess the models' performance at different classification thresholds.
8. Precision-Recall Curve: The precision-recall curve plots precision against recall at various classification thresholds. It provides insight into the trade-off between precision and recall for different models.

It is important to choose evaluation metrics that are relevant to the specific task and align with the goals of the chicken disease detection system. Additionally, cross-validation or separate test datasets can be used to obtain reliable and unbiased performance evaluation results. The formulas to calculate Accuracy, Recall, precision and F-measure are:

$$Accuracy = \frac{TP + TN}{TP + TN + FP + FN}$$
$$Recall = \frac{TP}{TP + FN}$$
$$precision = \frac{TN}{TN + FP}$$
$$F - measure = \frac{2 * Recall * precision}{Recall + precision}$$

The process of classification from the input data is shown in Figure 10.5.

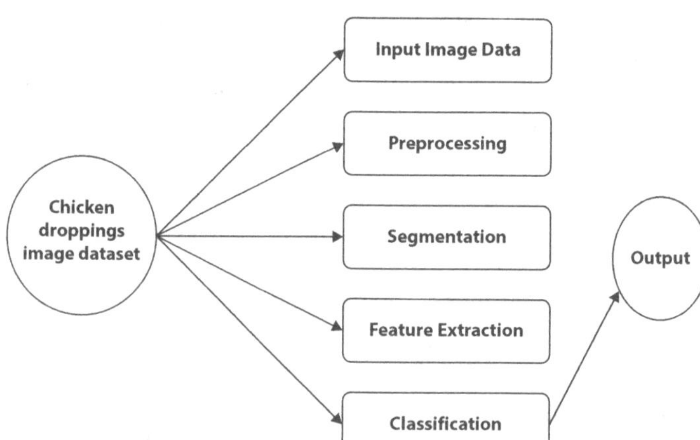

Figure 10.5 Flowchart.

10.5 Results and Discussion

Chicken disease detection using CNN, SVM, and YOLO v3 involves training machine learning models to analyze images of chicken droppings and classify them into different disease categories. The goal is to accurately identify the presence of diseases such as Coccidiosis, Salmonella, or NCD and provide appropriate treatment recommendations based on the characteristics of the droppings. When a user uploads an image of chicken droppings to the system, the trained models (CNN, SVM, or YOLO v3) analyze the image and make predictions. If the image is classified as healthy by all three models, then result is determined as "healthy." However, if any of the models classify the image as a specific disease (e.g., Coccidiosis, Salmonella, or NCD), the system provides a corresponding disease diagnosis.

Based on the color, pattern, and column size pattern observed in the chicken droppings, the system can provide treatment recommendations specific to the diagnosed disease. These recommendations can be predefined based on veterinary guidelines and expertise. For example, if Coccidiosis, Salmonella and NCD is diagnosed, then system can suggest appropriate anticoccidial medications, dosage, and treatment duration. The developed poultry disease detection model to upload the image is shown in Figure 10.6. After uploading the fecal image, the model identifies it as healthy.

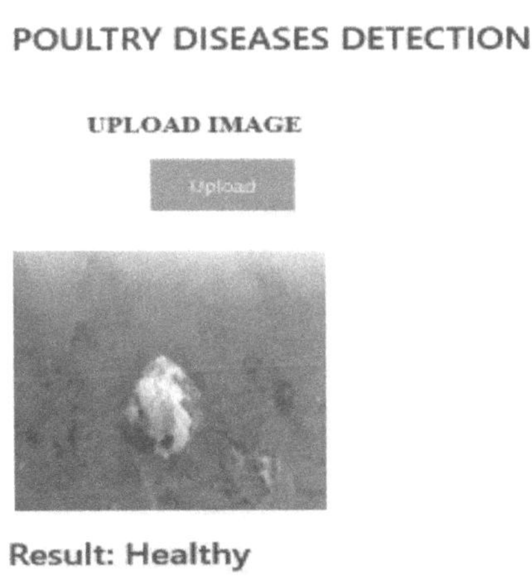

Figure 10.6 Healthy fecal samples of chicken.

However, if any issues are detected in the image, such as Coccidiosis, NCD or Salmonella, it will provide an alert or display the specific disease detected. In Figure 10.7, an unhealthy image is uploaded in the model, and the model identifies it as a chicken suffering from the Coccidiosis disease primarily based on color variations, and the model also suggests treatments, such as anticoccidial medications and antibiotics, and it also alerts the user that supportive care is necessary for the disease. This way, the chicken disease detection system helps identify the specific disease and offers guidance on addressing Coccidiosis in the flock. Figure 10.8 and Figure 10.9 depict the identification of NCD and Salmonella disease based on the color of fecal images, respectively.

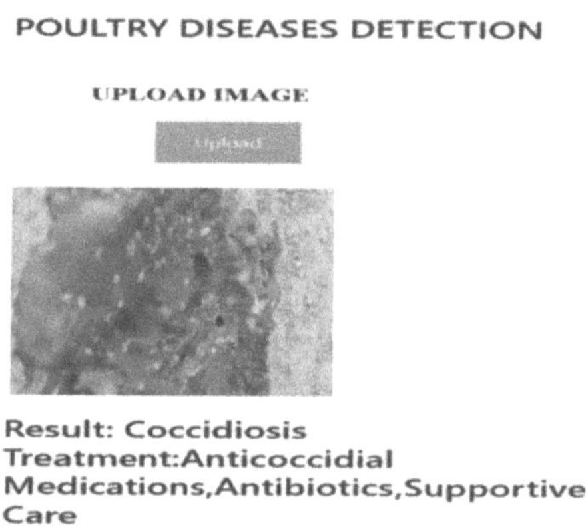

Figure 10.7 Coccidiosis fecal samples of chicken.

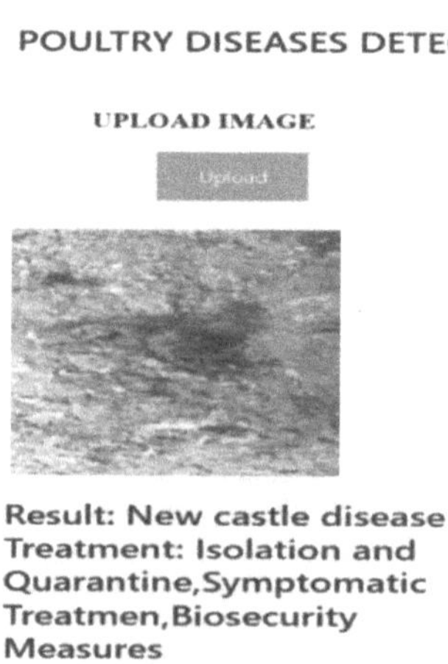

Figure 10.8 NCD fecal samples of chicken.

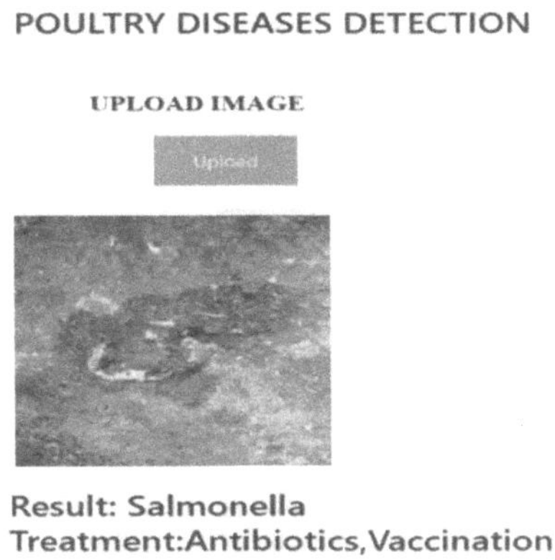

Figure 10.9 Salmonella fecal samples of chicken.

Based on the analysis of four cases of chicken droppings, a fecal image detection system can effectively identify and classify the condition of the droppings. It can detect and differentiate between healthy droppings and those indicating potential diseases. Specifically, the system can identify and display messages indicating specific treatments for various diseases such as Coccidiosis, NCD, and Salmonella.

This detection system proves to be valuable in assessing the health of chickens based on their droppings. By providing specific treatment recommendations, it enables prompt intervention and appropriate management of the detected diseases. Ultimately, this technology assists poultry farmers in maintaining the well-being of their flocks and implementing targeted treatments to mitigate the impact of potential illnesses.

By analyzing the eyes of chickens, a system can distinguish between healthy and unhealthy conditions as shown in Figure 10.10, offering valuable insights to poultry farmers. Healthy chicken eyes typically exhibit clear and bright appearance, with no visible signs of redness, swelling, discharge, or abnormal cloudiness. They appear alert and free from any apparent discomfort.

On the other hand, unhealthy chicken eyes may display various indicators of potential issues. These could include redness, inflammation, discharge, cloudiness, or excessive tearing. Such symptoms might be associated with infections, injuries, or underlying diseases affecting the eyes.

The performance of three algorithms SVM, CNN and YOLO v3 are compared and depicted in Figure 10.11.

The graph indicates that SVM performs at a relatively lower level compared to the other two models. The SVM is known for its effectiveness in

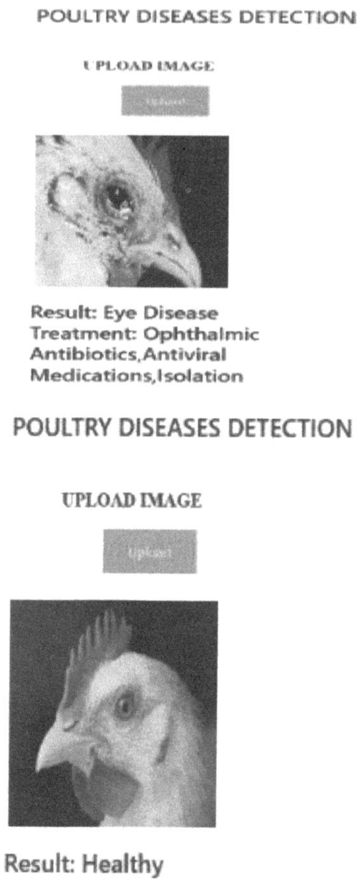

Figure 10.10 Healthy and unhealthy eye images.

handling binary classification tasks but may face limitations in more complex scenarios such as identifying multiple diseases or detecting intricate patterns in chicken images.

On the other hand, the CNN demonstrates a higher level of accuracy, surpassing SVM in disease detection. The CNNs excel in image recognition and classification tasks, making them suitable for identifying diseases based on visual cues present in chicken images. Their ability to learn hierarchical representations and capture intricate patterns within the images contributes to their improved performance.

At the top of the accuracy spectrum lies YOLO v3, showcasing the highest accuracy among the three models. YOLO v3 is a state-of-the-art object detection algorithm that can identify and localize objects within images,

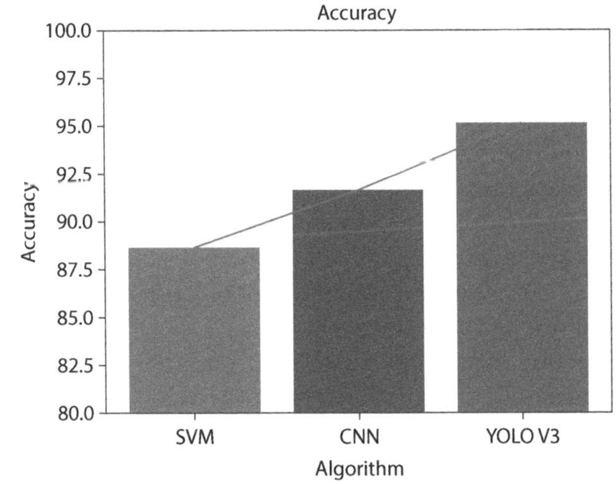

Figure 10.11 Accuracy of SVM, CNN, and YOLO v3.

including disease-related characteristics in chicken images. Its ability to detect multiple diseases simultaneously and provide precise bounding box information makes it a robust choice for comprehensive chicken disease detection.

$$\text{Accuracy} = (\text{Number of correctly classified samples}) / (\text{Total number of samples}).$$

In summary, while the SVM offers a lower accuracy level, CNN and YOLO v3 demonstrate higher accuracy in chicken disease detection tasks. The CNN excels in recognizing disease-related patterns, while YOLO v3 provides superior object detection capabilities. Choosing the appropriate model depends on the specific requirements of the detection system, considering factors such as the complexity of diseases to be identified and the need for precise localization.

10.6 Conclusion

In conclusion, chicken disease detection is a critical task for maintaining the health and productivity of poultry farms. Various methods and techniques can be employed for this purpose, and the choice depends on factors such as accuracy, efficiency, data availability, and computational resources.

Machine learning algorithms like SVM can be utilized to classify chicken images based on extracted features, such as color, texture, and shape descriptors. Support vector machines offer simplicity and interpretability, but they may not capture complex spatial patterns effectively.

Convolutional neural networks are powerful deep learning architectures that can learn hierarchical features directly from raw pixel data. They excel at capturing complex spatial patterns and have achieved remarkable success in image classification tasks, including disease detection in chickens. However, CNNs require a large amount of labeled data and significant computational resources for training.

Object detection algorithms like YOLO v3 can be employed to detect and localize various diseases or abnormalities in chicken images. YOLO v3 divides the image into a grid, predicts bounding boxes, and assigns class probabilities for each grid cell, providing both localization classification information.

References

1. Zelalem, M. and Simegn, G., Smartphone Based Detection and Classification of Poultry Diseases from Chicken Fecal Images Using Deep Learning Techniques. *Smart Agric. Technol.*, 4, 100221, 2023, 10.1016/j.atech.2023.100221.
2. Machuve, D., Nwankwo, E., Mduma, N., Mbelwa, J., Poultry diseases diagnostics models using deep learning. *Front. Artif. Intell.*, 5, 733345, 2022 Aug 1, doi: 10.3389/frai.2022.733345, Erratum in: Front Artif Intell. 2022 Sep 01;5:1016695. PMID: 35978651; PMCID: PMC9376463.
3. Zhou, M., Zhu, J., Cui, Z., Wang, H., Sun, X., Detection of abnormal chicken droppings based on improved Faster R-CNN. *Int. J. Agric. Biol. Eng.*, 16, 243–249, 2023, 10.25165/j.ijabe.20231601.7732.
4. Oakley, B.B., Lillehoj, H.S., Kogut, M.H., Kim, W.K., Maurer, J.J., Pedroso, A., Lee, M.D., Collett, S.R., Johnson, T.J., Cox, N.A., The chicken gastrointestinal microbiome. *FEMS Microbiol. Lett.*, 360, 2, 100–12, 2014 Nov. doi: 10.1111/1574-6968.12608. Epub 2014 Oct 13. PMID: 25263745.
5. Hossain, M.S., Salsabil, U.S., Syeed, M.M.M., Rahman, M.M., Fatema, K., Uddin, M.F., SmartPoultry: Early Detection of Poultry Disease from Smartphone Captured Fecal Image. *2023 20th International Joint Conference on Computer Science and Software Engineering (JCSSE)*, Phitsanulok, Thailand, pp. 345–350, 2023, doi: 10.1109/JCSSE58229.2023.10202054.
6. Elsayed, A. and Hazman, M., Framework for Mobile based Expert System for Poultry Diseases. *Int. J. Comput. Appl.*, 183, 1–5, 2021, 10.5120/ijca2021921319.

7. Wang, J., Shen, M., Liu, L., Xu, Y., Okinda, C., Recognition and Classification of Broiler Droppings Based on Deep Convolutional Neural Network. *J. Sens.*, 2019, 10, 2019, Article ID 3823515, https://doi.org/10.1155/2019/3823515.
8. Zhuang, X., Bi, M., Guo, J., Wu, S., Zhang, T., Development of an early warning algorithm to detect sick broilers. *Comput. Electron. Agric.*, 144, 102–113, 2018.
9. Hepworth, P., Nefedov, A., Muchnik, I., Morgan, K., Broiler chickens can benefit from machine learning: Support vector machine analysis of observational epidemiological data. *J. R. Soc. Interface*, 9, 1934–42, 02 2012.
10. Srivastava, K. and Pandey, P., Deep Learning Based Classification of Poultry Disease. *Int. J. Autom. Smart Technol.*, 13, 2439, 2023, https://doi.org/10.5875/ausmt.v13i1.2439.

11

Generative AI-Enhanced Deep Learning Model for Crop Type Analysis Based on Clustered Feature Vectors and Remote Sensing Imagery

B. Bazeer Ahamed[1*], D. Yuvaraj[2] and Saif Saad Alnuaimi[2]

[1]*University of Technology and Applied Sciences, College of Computing and Information Sciences-Al Musannah, Sultanate of Oman*
[2]*Department of Computer Science, Cihan - Duhok, Duhok, Kurdistan Region, Iraq*

Abstract
Unmanned aerial vehicles (UAVs) have become a popular tool for increasing productivity in agriculture in the past few years, decreasing labor costs, time spent on inspections, and drudgery. It also takes them only a few minutes to traverse vast distances. The tremendous advances in technology have led to an increasing variety of precision agriculture applications, such as crop/plant categorization, that obtain vital data with the implementation of UAV-based remote sensing technology. Solid tools and algorithms, including deep learning techniques, are required to process these data effectively. The most advanced method for vision applications is the deep belief network with clustered feature vectors (DBN-CFV). They have shown remarkable achievements in image processing tasks and have recently become a powerful tool. In the current study, we investigated the most recent learning-based approaches utilized in UAV-based remote sensing image analysis for crop/plant classification, with the purpose of assisting researchers and farmers in selecting the best algorithms for their evaluated crops and the hardware being used. Accurately classifying different crop varieties has been made possible by combining deep learning techniques with various UAV-based data sets. The review's readers will get knowledge of the most challenging problems that academics are trying to solve to understand better how different crop kinds can be

**Corresponding author*: Bazeer.bagrudeen@utas.edu.om

R. Nidhya, D. Pavithra, Manish Kumar, A. Dinesh Kumar and S. Balamurugan (eds.) Generative Artificial Intelligence: Concepts and Applications, (173–196) © 2025 Scrivener Publishing LLC

classified from UAV pictures and how to solve them so that deep learning-based algorithms work better.

***Keywords*:** Unmanned aerial, agriculture, deep learning, remote sensing, prediction

11.1 Introduction

The function and contributions of agriculture are very significant in the modern era of globalization. Due to the twofold rise in the world population over the last 50 years, agriculture has faced numerous obstacles in meeting the growing demands of society. Multiple estimations of this phenomenal growth imply that the world's population will reach 9 billion by 2050 [1]. Furthermore, the estimates indicate a notable decline in the retired or employed population proportion, coupled with a rise in the number of individuals residing in metropolitan areas [2]. This implies that there is a need for human labor and that agriculture production must be significantly raised worldwide. Tractors were among the technological advances brought to agriculture more than a century ago to help with this kind of issue. Many technologies exist today, with mechanical technology currently exhibiting an incredible rate of advancement. The widespread application of current technology in business, particularly in the agricultural sector, such as robotic platforms, remote sensing, and the Internet of Things (IoT), has led to smart and efficient farming [3]. According to Maggiori *et al.* [4], deep learning (DL) is an advanced approach that is being employed effectively as a component of various machine-learning algorithms. It is more accurate since it has better learning capabilities than artificial neural networks (ANNs), which are similar to them [5]. Recent years have seen a wide range of research disciplines, including farming and agriculture, use and study DL technologies, including recurrent neural networks (RNNs), convolutional neural networks (CNNs) and generative adversarial networks (GANs). Using various software systems, agriculturalists and researchers frequently disregard the concepts and workings of the GANs, RNNs, and CNNs—three standard techniques used in DL algorithms. Very deep convolutional networks (VGGNets), deep convolutional generative adversarial networks (DCGANs), and long short-term memory (LSTM) networks are just a few examples of the subcategories of DL algorithms that one must understand in order to understand standard DL algorithms [6] fully.

Regarding data analysis and image processing, DL is a relatively new and current method and technique with a lot of promise and potential, as stated by Goeau *et al.* [7]. Deep learning (DL) has recently successfully transitioned from other fields to agriculture. Because it uses complicated models that allow for huge parallelization, it also has the ability to address complex issues more rapidly and efficiently. These multidimensional DL models are expected to increase classification accuracy and decrease mistakes in regression issues, given that there are sufficiently large datasets to explain regression problems [8]. Because drone technology provides an effective means of monitoring, assessing, and scanning crops through the utilization of high-quality and high-resolution images, the authors of [9] claim that the application of drone technology for DL in agriculture and farming is significant. This kind of technology makes evaluating quality and identifying field advancements easier. Farmers and agriculturalists, for instance, can assess whether crops are appropriately prepared for harvesting with the use of drone technology's images. Farmers can make more informed judgments about farming by using machine learning (ML) and DL techniques to understand the soil's characteristics better [10]. Decisions regarding the best time to plant and harvest crops are also made using DL, along with an evaluation of how water and nutrients should be managed. Crop returns on investment (ROI) can be estimated by considering market margin and cost, and yields are more significant and efficient [11, 12]. The fact that DL has been shown to outperform traditional techniques like random forest (RF) algorithms, support vector machines (SVMs), and ANNs further supports its efficiency. Several technologies are being used in conjunction with DL to enhance performance in classification and prediction linked to agricultural concerns. Time and memory dimensions are present in the RNN and LSTM models.

These instruments can, therefore, be used to estimate crop yield using the mining time dimensions and memory function, evaluate the need for water, and predict the growth of plants and animals based on data analysis [13]. Additionally, by utilizing past data to evaluate fruit yields or water requirements, they can be utilized to compute the growth of both plants and animals. For example, Schwarz *et al.* [14] predicted many occurrences and climate changes using both models. For the timely detection of agricultural diseases, the use of infrared thermal imaging and hyperspectral images to offer data and information is the proper way. The topic of agriculture is growing exponentially, so it is essential to give a current overview of the literature that focuses on innovative techniques for research that use DL. Therefore, this study's goal was to summarize the most recent developments in the agriculture industry related to DL [15]. With regard to fruit counting, water management, soil management, crop management, seed classification, weed detection, disease detection, harvesting, and yield prediction, in particular, the study sought to characterize the application of DL in agriculture. The new wave of technological adoption in agriculture has drastically changed and aided in crop growing and farming. However, because DL has been shown to boost agricultural productivity, scientists are now looking into the potential applications of DL in harvesting, agriculture, and yield prediction.

This document falls into the following categories: Section 11.2 describes the methodology for the study. The literature review in Section 11.3 highlights a brief history of the topic. In Section 11.4, the function of DL in the agriculture sector is highlighted. Model development-related DL tools are included. Section 11.5 presents the findings and a commentary. The study's general conclusion is given in this section.

11.2 Related Works

Over the years, numerous academics have proposed novel strategies to boost agricultural production, such as implementing vertical agriculture, greenhouses, and even utilizing current technologies like satellites and aircraft [16]. The continual improvement of several fields, including chemistry, biology, agronomy, and technology, enables farmers to accurately determine a plant's nutrient and water requirements in addition to its diseases. The agricultural industry will be substantially altered from how we currently see it in 10 to 20 years due to changes in the future. Farmers are relying increasingly on modern technologies that offer quick and accurate information on crop conditions, guaranteeing higher yields. In addition, major corporations like Google and Amazon have made the most significant expenditures in agricultural technologies ever [17]. These corporations no longer see investments from the same traditional standpoint. To boost food production globally, in addition to agriculture, they are making significant investments in several other industries [18].

Using effective remote sensing technology, it is possible to obtain timely and accurate information about the crop's condition, which is essential for increasing crop productivity. Furthermore, robust algorithms are necessary to use remote sensing data effectively. In modern agriculture, one of the most important concepts is crop classification, which tries to divide plant and crop varieties into several groups while specifying their geographic distribution. To enhance their capacity for making decisions, it can benefit farmers and government officials to have practical knowledge of their crops. Using different ML and DL methods, a great deal of research has been done with excellent findings on the successful classification of crops using satellite-based remote sensing images [19]. Nevertheless, they have certain drawbacks, including low temporal and spatial resolutions that may compromise the quality of the data and erratic weather that should make data collection more challenging. Inadequate algorithmic performance and incorrect crop classification could arise from these limitations [20].

Traditional ML techniques like SVM and RF have also been used in methods for categorizing different crop/plant types from aerial data. These strategies rely on the manual extraction of features using a variety of ways, including the historical of oriented gradients (HOG), scale invariant feature transform (SIFT), and local binary pattern (LBP), among others [21]. With complex data, these characteristics render conventional approaches difficult and ineffective. However, DL algorithms have found a potent remedy for these problems [22]. The past few decades have seen the rise of new technologies like DL and UAV-based remote sensing that could be essential to the future of agricultural and global food production. These are creative, useful methods that help farmers automate a number of tasks, such as plant and crop identification [23]. UAVs have several advantages over other remote sensing systems that are currently in use including excellent flexibility, low cost, compact size, real-time data collecting, and the optimal balance of temporal, spatial resolution and spectral [24, 25]. Furthermore, unmanned aerial vehicles (UAVs) are a non-destructive technology employed to inspect a variety of crops, in contrast to unmanned ground vehicles (UGVs), which have the ability to harm specific plants and disturb the field by compacting the soil, which affects agricultural production.

It could not have instantly determined the condition of the crop, the type of soil, or the presence of disease or pests a millennium ago. However, this should be achievable when combined with UAVs and DL models. Many applications in smart farming, like precise pesticide and liquid fertilizer spraying, water stress monitoring, crop surveying/monitoring [26, 27], and crop yield estimation [28], depend on accurate and automatic crop classification using DL techniques and UAV-based remote sensing imagery. These tasks have the potential to boost crop yield, lower costs, and save a significant amount of time by giving farmers valuable information that should enable them to make decisions quickly [29]. A few survey studies that looked into the uses of unmanned aerial vehicles (UAVs) or other DL algorithms in a variety of industries, including agriculture, can be found in the literature. The ability to identify things from low altitudes was assessed by Sethy *et al.* [30] using a variety of DL-based object identification systems. This research may greatly aid in understanding the concept underlying the existing object detection algorithms [31–35].

11.3 Methodology

Remote sensing technology assesses agricultural qualities by viewing the targeted object from a variety of distances, spanning several hundred kilometers to a few meters, with the aim of categorizing crops. It has proven to be one of the most promising agricultural and farm monitoring technologies. Some of the most dependable remote sensing technologies outperform traditional methods for agricultural scouting, which typically require a significant number of humans. These methods include manned airplanes, satellites, UAVs and UGVs. The performance of crop classification for smallholders, cost, and spatial/temporal resolution are still constraints in remote sensing systems based on satellites and aircraft despite their on-going advancements. Similarly, UGVs offer high-resolution imagery, but covering vast agricultural areas takes a very long time. Temporal, spectral and very high spatial image resolutions are needed in small-scale, mixed-plant agricultural fields to identify different crops or plant species and monitor a broad region in a reasonable amount of time.

The foundation of our suggested approach is using a set of features acquired through an unsupervised feature extractor that was previously presented to represent and classify a tissue image. Rather than considering the characteristics of every point in the image, this extractor quantifies only the significant sub-regions to find the features. It first recommends establishing significant sub-regions surrounding the cytological tissue components with the objective of doing this. To characterize the sub-regions/components in an unsupervised way, it then learns their local features using a deep belief network composed of successive restricted Boltzmann machine (RBM). Lastly, it clusters the local attributes employing the k-means algorithm to quantize them. The image is finally represented and classified using the distribution of its quantized sub-regions/components. The recommended process is schematically shown in Figure 11.1, and each step is thoroughly explained in the subsections that follow.

This suggested approach is motivated by the following: Different crop types within a tissue fulfil distinct roles within the plant. Depending on the kind and function of the crop type, the external surroundings and visual appearance can change. Additionally, specific crop types may develop into

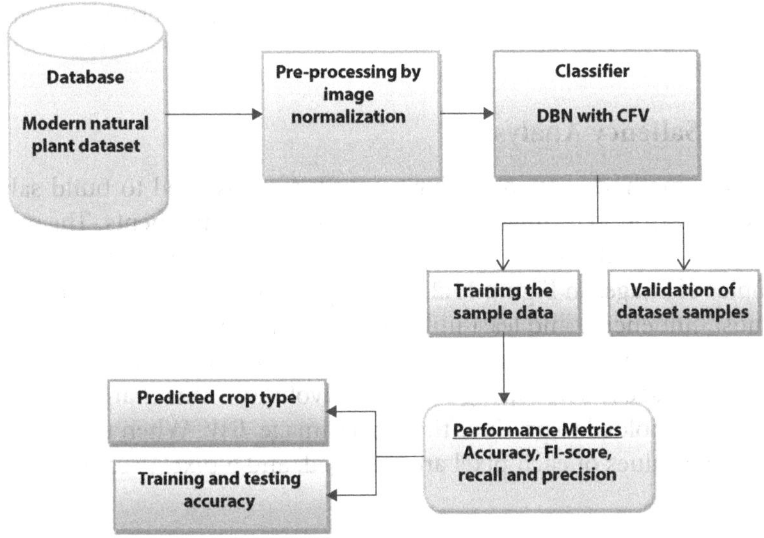

Figure 11.1 Flow of the proposed model.

specialized structures. These crop-based components' characteristics collectively define the plant's visual characteristics. Specific crop type and related components change in appearance and distribution depending on the type of crop. In the prediction process, for example, various kinds of connective crop types have been positioned in between the external factors to support the growth, and they arrange around a coverage region to form an environmental structure. The crop-based features form a single layer and are grouped to form the features, i.e. most influencing and least influencing. As this crop prediction continues to advance, the regular shape of a crop completely disappears, and the epithelial cells become scattered throughout the connective regions.

The researchers may easily define some of these visual observations, while others may be difficult to describe. Even for the human eye, segmentation becomes a highly challenging challenge when there is no clear description for an observation. Moreover, perfect component localization is often required for both the expression and quantification of such statements, making them very arduous to annotate when used in a supervised classifier. Our methodology approximates the crop components using a set of multi-typed circular objects. After that, it takes advantage of the local windows clipped around these objects to choose which salient sub-regions to describe automatically. This is only an approximation, and that one object may correlate to several components or vice versa. It is also crucial to remember that the features roughly depicted by the salient sub-regions clipped around the objects will also be applied to characterizing the entire image.

11.3.1 Saliency Analysis

An earlier method created by our research team is used to build salient sub-regions around estimated crop-based feature components. The salient sub-region identification and approximation are demonstrated using examples of images in Figure 11.2, with explanations provided below. Both the most influencing and least influencing features are used in the approximation technique for object representation. To do so, the remote sensing image I is first extracted using color deconvolution. This channel is subsequently thresholded to produce the binary image BW. When thresholding is used, the values of each pixel are averaged, and a pixel is categorized as

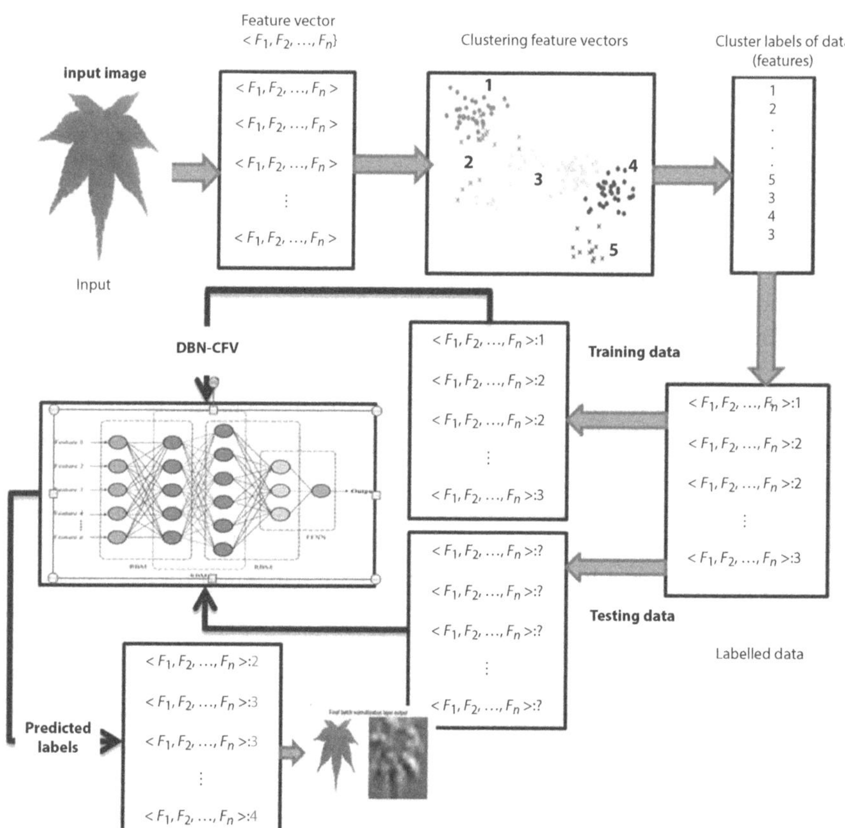

Figure 11.2 Proposed architecture.

crop type if its value is below the threshold and as non-influencing otherwise. The following step is to individually apply the circle-fit method on each group's BW pixels to determine a set of most and least influencing objects. Starting from the most significant pixel, the circle-fit algorithm iteratively finds non-overlapping circles on the given pixels when the circle radii are more critical than the threshold r_{min}. Upon defining a salient zone i around each object c_i, a window is ultimately sliced out of the binary image BW. The object centroid determines the window's center, and its size is defined by the parameter ω size. Although the approximation technique labels the located objects as either influencing or non-influencing, the object centroids are not used in any way; we use them to build the salient regions. Instead, these objects will be retyped or re-characterized using the local properties that a deep belief network will learn.

11.3.2 Saliency Region Analysis with Belief Networking

This step involves two learning mechanisms: dense belief network (DBN) first acts as an unsupervised feature extractor for objects that correspond to the salient sub-regions. The local deep characteristics of the salient sub-regions are determined by using the activation values of the hidden unit nodes in the final RBM which are learned by means of a deep belief network of RBMs. To obtain the clustering vectors, the second system, known as feature clustering vectors, makes use of the local deep features. Any salient sub-region will be quantized using this clustering, equivalent to retyping the object for which this salient sub-region is declared. Below are the specifics of various learning systems. An RBM-based deep belief network is pre-trained by the DBN method. A graphical model that is undirected and composed of symmetric weights between visible and hidden layers is called an RBM. It is possible to think of the units in an RBM's hidden layer as a higher representation of the units in its visible layer input. A set of RBMs is stacked sequentially to generate the representations at different levels of abstraction by linking the output of one RBM to the input of the following RBM. The procedure involves cropping a salient sub-region (i) from the binary image BW and feeding its pixels into the first RBM. Next, this salient subregion's local feature set $(\varnothing_i)$ is created using the output of the previous RBM. The jth RBM's weight matrix and bias vector are denoted by W_j and B_j, respectively in this approach. Weights and biases of the network are determined by the DBN function, which pre-trains the deep belief network layer by layer using the contrastive divergence approach. This is accomplished by randomly selecting salient sub-regions from training images creating a dataset known as D_{dbn} in the process. This is the pseudocode for Algorithm 11.1. The DBN must additionally input the network's architectural characteristics; this includes the overall number of RBMs (hidden layers), as well as the number of hidden units in each layer.

Algorithm 11.1: Evaluation of Salient Object Detection Task.

Input: Remote sensing images, pre-trained network, weight, bias
Output: Clustered features
1. $D_{DBN-CFV} = \varnothing$
2. **for** every randomly chosen images **do** $// D_{DBN-CFV}$
3. $BW =$ image labelling;
4. $C =$ image-based saliency decomposition
5. **for** every randomly chosen images **do** $// c_i \in C$
6. $\Omega_i \rightarrow image\ window\ cropping$; $// BW, c_i, \omega_{size}$
7. $D_{DBN-CFV} = D_{DBN-CFV} \cup \Omega_i$
8. **end for**
9. **end for**
10. **Return** crop type

11.3.3 Group Analysis

After determining the DBN weights and biases, the local feature function can be used to specify the local deep features of a specific salient sub-region. This work aims to quantify the labels or qualities of the full crop image and the salient sub-regions. This results in the quantization of these continuous attributes into discrete labels. As previously said, it is very hard, if possible, to annotate every salient sub-region; hence, learning these labels in a supervised way is highly challenging. As a result, this paper suggests learning this labeling process through an unsupervised method. $K-$ means clustering on the local deep features of the salient subregions is used to achieve this. The local deep elements of randomly chosen salient sub-regions of randomly chosen training images comprise the training set $D_{cluster}$. To find the clustering vectors V, the $k-$means algorithm makes use of this training set. After this process, you will get a set V of K clustering vectors. The id of the nearest clustering vector is used to identify any salient sub-region in the following stage.

11.3.4 Classification

A set of global characteristics is extracted in the last phase to represent an arbitrary image I. This is accomplished by identifying and retrieving the local deep features of each of the image's salient sub-regions. The cluster vector's auxiliary function assigns the id l_i of its closest clustering vector to each salient sub-region I based on its deep features φ_i. Global features, or the attributes of the elements that comprise the group to which these sub-regions belong, are then extracted from the labels of each salient sub-region to represent image I. For this, a histogram is employed. Finally, image I is classified using an SVM with a linear kernel according to its global properties. This study makes use of SVM implementation which uses the one-against-one method for multiclass classifications.

11.3.5 Parameter Setup

The model parameters of the proposed technique that require external settings are the cluster number K, the salient subregion size ω_{size}, and the minimal circle radius r_{min}. Pixels are used for the parameters ω_{size} and r_{min}. The parameter C is also present in the SVM classifier. Without utilizing any test samples from the original dataset, we employ cross-validation on the training images in our tests to determine the values of these parameters. Furthermore, no performance indicator derived from the second dataset is considered. After taking into consideration several combinations of the following values: size = {19, 29, 39}, r_{min} = {3, 4, 5}, K = {500, 1000, 1500}, C = {1, 5, 10, 25, 50, 100, 250, 500, 1000, 2500, 5000, 10000}. Eventually, the parameters are changed to size = 29, r_{min} = 4, C = 500 and K = 1500. We will go into more depth about how this parameter selection affects the performance of the technique. One should choose the deep belief network's architecture in addition to these parameters. Generally speaking, the network's representation of abstraction levels is based on the number of hidden layers. This number is fixed at four. Then, taking into account the following factors, we decide on 2000, 1000, 500, and 100 hidden units arranged from bottom to top levels. To accurately represent the pixels in a local sub-region, we must choose the hidden unit number of the first layer with a sufficient value. On the other hand, choosing a value in the final layer small enough to quantize the sub-regions efficiently is essential. It is crucial to select the middle-hidden unit numbers in a manner that is consistent with the hidden unit selections made for the first and last levels. Future studies will likely include investigating other network designs.

11.4 Numerical Results and Discussion

This part discusses the numerical results obtained with the predicted model. In comparison to several other existing techniques, such as RF, SVM, Regional Convolutional Neural Networks (RCNN), standard CNN, DNN and LSTM for better classification accuracy is shown in this simulation, which is carried out in the MATLAB 2020a environment. Numerous performance measures, including the kappa coefficient, Mathews correlation coefficient (MCC), mean absolute error (MAE), F-measure, accuracy, precision, and recall. All these metrics' evaluation formulas are given in the equations below. The DBN-CFV model is run using the MatConvNet package, which is used to validate the model. The 200*200 rows and columns of the original input image are used for image resizing in this experiment, and the data augmentation technique is employed to increase the number of samples in the real-time dataset. Two sets are randomly selected from the input dataset: 70% is used for training, and 30% is used for testing. The suggested DBN-CFV model is tested with a number of alternative methods in order to increase the experimentation's dependability. The image resizing procedure is carried out within the training set. The classifier's performance is assessed using the total prediction accuracy. Conv_1, conv_2, conv_3, and conv_4 were run in DBN-CFV with a padding size of 1. For the pooling layer, the stride is 2, and the kernel size is [2, 2]. In this case, dropout layers are added to prevent over-fitting problems when the ratio is 0.5. Finally, fully connected (FC) layers and the SoftMax layer for model training are located at the top. The learning rate is 10^{-5}, and the batch size is 100.

1) **Accuracy:** indicates the correct percentage of all records in the specified testing set. Equation 11.1 provides a mathematical expression for it.

$$Accuracy = \frac{TP + TN}{TP + TN + FP + FN} \tag{11.1}$$

2) **Precision:** illustrates the ratio of correctly predicted weed to predicted weed during the testing procedure. Equation 11.2 provides a mathematical expression for it.

$$Precision = \frac{TP}{TP + FP} \tag{11.2}$$

3) **Recall:** reveals the percentage of correctly predicted weed to all weed samples collected throughout the testing set. Equation 11.3 provides a mathematical expression for it.

$$Recall = \frac{TP}{TP + FN} \tag{11.3}$$

4) **F-measure:** According to Equation 11.4, it is the recall and precision measure.

$$F - measure = \frac{2 * Precision * Recall}{Precision + Recall} \tag{11.4}$$

Standard samples that were identified and correctly assessed as normal are referred to as true negative (TN), while true positive (TP) samples have been appropriately labelled as weeds. Whereas false negatives (FN) are sample paddy cases that are incorrectly labeled as weeds, false positives (FP) are normal samples that have been incorrectly classified as weeds. Take two classes, for example: '0' and '1', respectively.

5) **MCC:** A phi coefficient, also known as Matthews' correlation coefficient, is used to quantify the quality of binary classification. Equation 11.5 provides a mathematical expression for it.

$$MCC = \frac{TP * TN - FP * FN}{\sqrt{(TP + FP)(TP + FN)(TN + FP)(TN + FN)}} \tag{11.5}$$

6) **Kappa co-efficient:** It is employed to assess the inter-rate reliability for the qualitative terms. It is regarded as a strong measure. Equation 11.6 is how it is represented.

$$k = \frac{Pr(a) - Pr(e)}{1 - Pr(e)} \tag{11.6}$$

In this case, the measured probability is represented by $Pr(a)$ and the probability rate, yes or no, by random agreement, is represented by $Pr(e)$.

7) **Mean absolute error (MAE):** The phenomena are specified by measuring the errors between the paired observations. Equation 11.7 provides an expression for it.

$$MAE = \frac{\sum_{i=1}^{n} \mid y_i - x_i \mid}{n} \tag{11.7}$$

Here, y_i stands for prediction, x_i for true value, and 'n' for the total number of data points. The saliency maps are created and fed into the segmentation process during the segmentation process. In this case, the salient item is represented using the saliency model. It is known from the observation that objectness integration allows saliency segmentation to achieve higher segmentation accuracy and to be robust across all classes. The suggested segmentation model achieves the salient items with clearly defined borders and removes the unnecessary background areas from the background regions' images, including grass, water, and shadow, which contrast sharply with the primary image background. Additionally, the saliency model's segmentation quality is higher and better illustrates objectness and saliency to improve the salient object segmentation process. Segmentation may be done effectively with this method, and the quality of the segmentation is enhanced. The percentages of saliency object pixels that have been segregated according to all of the segmented object pixels are used to illustrate the metrics precision. The percentage of correctly separated salient object pixels to ground truth pixels is known as the recall. As a result, segmentation using saliency mapping works better than current methods and produces superior segmentation results.

11.4.1 Dataset

The dataset originates from https://flavia.sourceforge.net/, representing a contemporary collection of color images of natural plants encompassing diverse attributes such as various features, percentage details of specific plant regions, and relevant information. Only certain regions affected by particular conditions are included in the dataset, adhering to established standards for dataset preparation. However, the acquisition of these images does not follow uniform protocols. Image acquisition necessitates capturing leaves from similar species across different plants in varied environmental conditions and scenarios over different periods. The selection process solely revolves around this criterion without considering other factors. Consequently, the dataset exhibits inconsistencies in image sizes, varying across different images. Creating a comprehensive and practical natural dataset entails considering various elements of the natural environment. Integrating continuum aspects helps generate a more pragmatic and coherent collection of data, crucial for addressing the challenge of identifying plant species in outdoor settings. This dataset compensates for the absence of a standardized dataset. The insights derived from cautiously collecting and utilizing this information have the potential to enhance numerous applications, particularly those concerning plant identification, by providing a broader perspective. Additionally, this dataset contributes valuable information that sheds light on existing challenges related to plant identification.

11.4.2 Classification Results and Discussions

The comparison of several metrics, including recall, precision, accuracy, MCC, F-measure, kappa, and MAE, is shown in Table 11.1. The features retrieved from the higher-level layers do not clearly separate the weed category based on the results obtained via DBN-CFV. It is often built with image resolution in mind, allowing for attaining creative features at higher layers. It is seen from the literature that there are better choices than multi-resolution images for the traditional CNN-based method. Edges and corners, or lower-level features, are removed. A few discriminative characteristics are taken from the middle layer to handle the lower-resolution images. The results of the experiments provide proof of this. The concatenation and categorization of middle-level features improves the overall classification accuracy by 96.50%. In order to increase recognition accuracy for the given real-time dataset, it is emphasized that the added information is a feature representation. Thus, the importance of the model, the overall experiments, and the expected robustness of the model are examined. Table 11.1 compares the proposed model's performance with other techniques. The following Figures 11.3 to 11.7 shows the different layers and the normalized layers outcome.

Table 11.1 Overall performance comparison.

Methods	DBN-CFV	RCNN	CNN	DNN	LSTM	RF	SVM
Accuracy	92%	83%	72%	64%	60%	56%	54%
Precision	95%	83%	79%	79%	77%	76%	76%
Recall	81%	80%	72%	64%	60%	56%	54%
F-measure	86%	83%	71%	59%	53%	45%	41%
MCC	75%	66%	51%	41%	34%	25%	20%
MAE	0.0750	0.1667	0.2708	0.3542	0.3958	0.4375	0.4583
Kappa	72%	66%	45%	29%	20%	12%	8%

Figure 11.3 Input sample.

Figure 11.4 Second layer outcome.

Figure 11.5 Successive layer outcome.

Figure 11.6 Third layer outcome.

Figure 11.7 Batch normalization outcome.

The DBN-CFV model has a 92% prediction accuracy, which is higher than that of RCNN, CNN, DNN, LSTM, RF, and SVM by 9%, 19%, 27%, 32%, 36%, and 38%. In comparison to alternative methods, the suggested DBN-CFV has a precision of 95%, which is 12%, 12%, 12%, 28%, 79%, and 29% higher (see Figure 11.8). Compared to other methods, the suggested DBN-CFV has a recall of 81%, which is 2%, 8%, 9%, 29%, 24%, and 35% higher. Compared to alternative methods, the suggested DBN-CFV has an F-measure of 86%, which is 6%, 21%, 26%, 44%, 50%, and 57% higher (see Figure 11.9). The suggested DBN-CFV has an MCC of 75%, which is greater than other techniques by 15%, 22%, 41%, 36%, 54%, and 2% less than RCNN. The suggested DBN-CFV has an MAE of 0.0750, which is 0.05, 0.6917, 0.4875, 0.3839, 0.1832, 0.3625, and 0.6917 times smaller than previous methods. The suggested DBN-CFV's kappa coefficient is 72.72, which is greater than earlier methods by 18%, 30%, 51%, 26%, and 64%, and 3% less than DBN-CFV. Figures 11.10 to 11.13 shows the different comparison of results of DBN-CFV model.

For this reason, it is commonly known that some basic pre-processing operations like thresholding and saliency mapping are required to address the weed classification problem. To properly categorize the weeds, the whole feature representation must be provided. The outcomes obtained through the utilization of the suggested framework exhibit potential; nevertheless, additional investigation is necessary to improve the precision of categorization and reduce false positives. Though some advanced methods exist, which also provide higher prediction accuracy, this model is very simple for separating the different crop type.

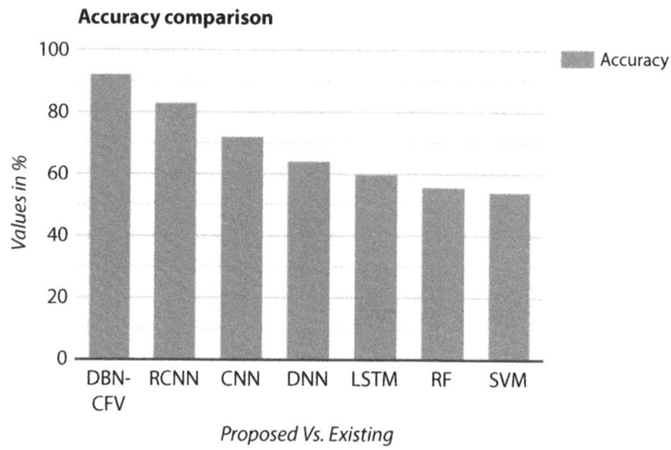

Figure 11.8 Accuracy comparison.

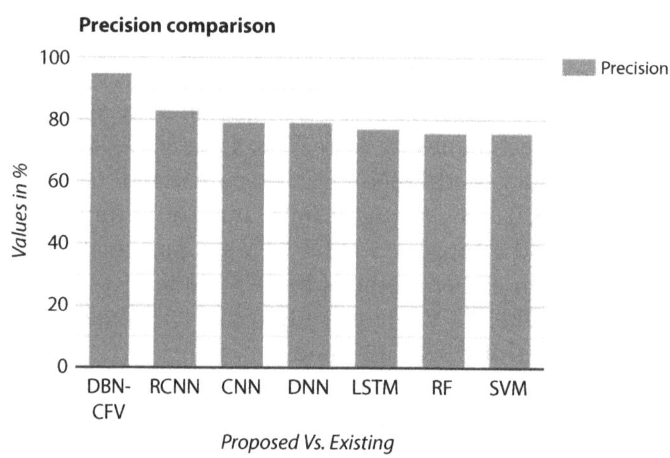

Figure 11.9 Precision comparison.

11.5 Conclusion

To achieve more effective prediction results, this research focuses on modelling DBN-CFV framework that incorporates multiple stages of preprocessing, such as image scaling, thresholding, binary segmentation, and saliency segmentation. The green color contrast during the segmentation process is emphasized. Through this procedure, the foreground items' contrast is superior to that of the background regions' contrast. The classifier

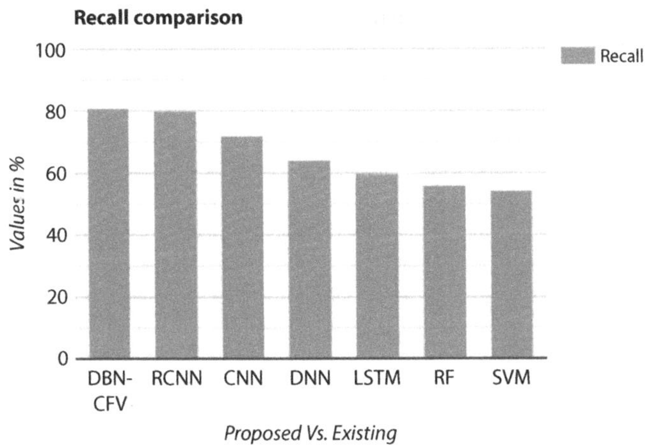

Figure 11.10 Recall comparison.

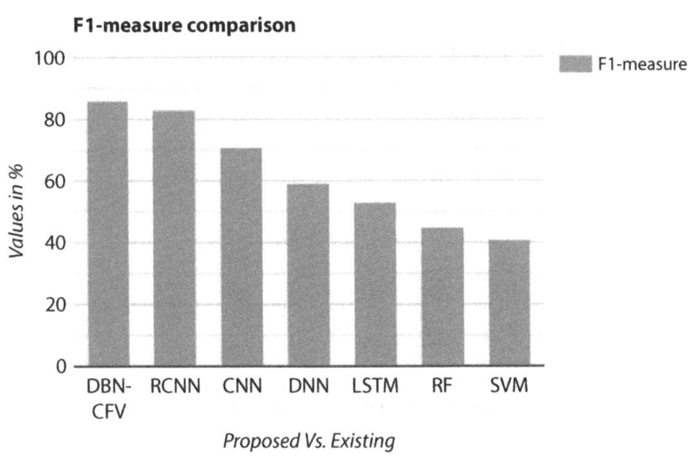

Figure 11.11 F1-measure comparison.

model receives the segmented images as input, and classification is carried out to distinguish between the types of crops. To improve classification accuracy, the multi-layered CNN model takes into account both lower-level and semantic information (features). Thanks to data augmentation, outfitting problems resulting from smaller sample sizes are effectively managed. This proposed framework considerably improves the overall system performance in managing multi-resolution data. The results of the experiment show that the suggested DBN-CFV model performs better in

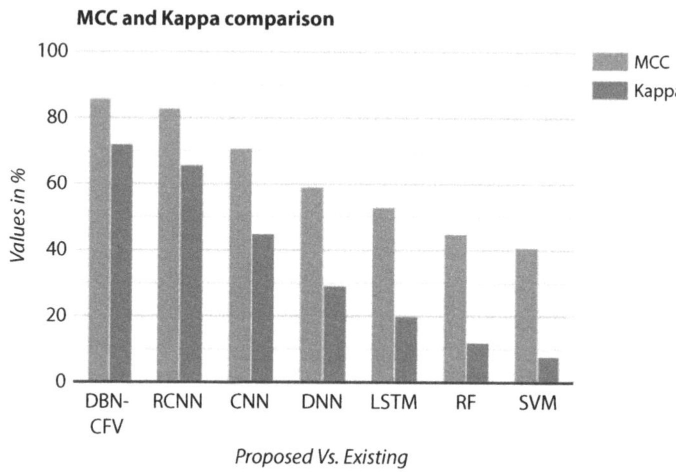

Figure 11.12 MCC and Kappa comparison.

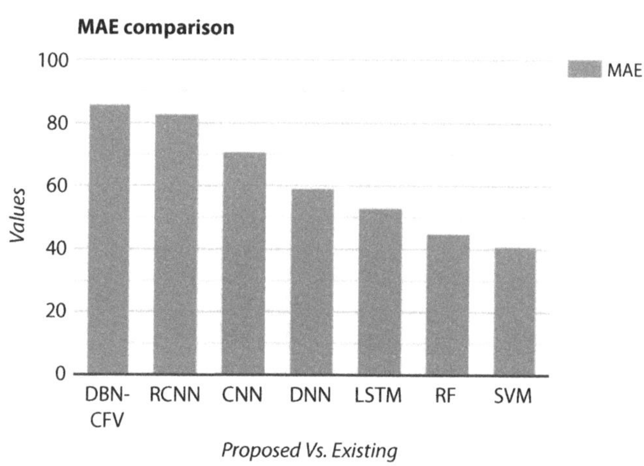

Figure 11.13 MAE comparison.

a number of performance metrics, including 81% F-measure, 91% recall, 95% accuracy, MCC of 0.7559, MAE of 0.0750, and 72% kappa coefficient. The suggested DBN-CFV model performs better than a number of current methods, including SVM classifier, DNN, LSTM, CNN, RCNN, and RF. It is more beneficial to perform these validations using the real-time dataset. However, the construction of the dataset and the gathering of dataset samples represent the main study limitations. Future versions of the model may incorporate appropriate methods for image processing and learning, leveraging the advantages to fine-tune the distinction between crops and weed kinds. The notable breakthroughs in crop identification should be enhanced to ensure that the system functions in challenging environmental circumstances.

References

1. White, J.C., Coops, N.C., Wulder, M.A., Vastaranta, M., Hilker, T., Tompalski, P., Remote sensing technologies for enhancing forest inventories: A review. *Can. J. Remote Sens.*, 42, 5, 619–641, 2016.
2. Toth, C. and Jóźków, G., Remote sensing platforms and sensors: A survey. *ISPRS J. Photogramm. Remote Sens.*, 115, 22–36, 2016.
3. Chollet, F., Xception: Deep Learning with Depthwise Separable Convolutions. *Proc. IEEE Conf. Comput. Vis. Pattern Recognit.*, 7, 3, 1251–1258, 2017, https://doi.org/10.4271/2014-01-0975.
4. Maggiori, E., Tarabalka, Y., Charpiat, G., Alliez, P., High-Resolution Semantic Labeling with Convolutional Neural Networks. *IEEE Trans. Geosci. Remote Sens.*, 55, 12, 7092–7103, 2017.
5. Huang, B. *et al.*, Large-scale semantic classification: Outcome of the first year of Inria aerial image labelling benchmark. *Int. Geosci. Remote Sens. Symp.*, 2018-July, pp. 6947–6950, 2018, https://doi.org/10.1109/IGARSS.2018.8518525.
6. Wagner, F.H., Sanchez, A., Tarabalka, Y., Lotte, R.G., Ferreira, M.P., Aidar, M.P., Aragao, L.E., Using the U-net convolutional network to map forest types and disturbance in the Atlantic rainforest with very high resolution images. *Remote Sens. Ecol. Conserv.*, 5, 4, 360–375, 2019.
7. Goëau, H., Bonnet, P., Joly, A., Plant identification based on noisy web data: Te amazing performance of deep learning. *CEUR Workshop Proc. 2017*, vol. 1866(LifeCLEF), LifeCLEF 2017.
8. Ronneberger, O., Fischer, P., Brox, T., U-net: Convolutional networks for biomedical image segmentation, in: *International Conference on Medical Image Computing and Computer-Assisted Intervention*, pp. 234–241, Springer, Cham, 2015, https://doi. org/10.1007/978-3-319-24574-4_28.
9. Rzanny, M., Mäder, P., Deggelmann, A., Chen, M., Wäldchen, J., Flowers, leaves or both? How to obtain suitable images for automated plant identification. *Plant Methods*, 15, 1, 77, 2019, https://doi.org/10.1186/s13007-019-0462-4.
10. Lopatin, J., Dolos, K., Kattenborn, T., Fassnacht, F.E., How canopy shadow affects invasive plant species classification in high spatial resolution remote sensing. *Remote Sens. Ecol. Conserv.*, 5, 4, 302–317, 2019.

11. Angermueller, C., Pärnamaa, T., Parts, L., Stegle, O., Deep learning for computational biology. *Mol. Syst. Biol.*, 12, 7, 878, 2016, https://doi. org/10.15252/msb.20156651.
12. Lopatin, J., Fassnacht, F.E., Kattenborn, T., Schmidtlein, S., Mapping plant species in mixed grassland communities using close range imaging spectroscopy. *Remote Sens. Environ.*, 201, 12–23, 2017.
13. He, K., Zhang, X., Ren, S., Sun, J., Deep residual learning for image recognition, in: *Proceedings of the IEEE Computer Society Conference on Computer Vision and Pattern Recognition*, 2016, https://doi.org/10.1109/CVPR.2016.90.
14. Schwarz, M., Schulz, H., Behnke, S., RGB-D object recognition and pose estimation based on pre-trained convolutional neural network features, in: *Proceedings - IEEE International Conference on Robotics and Automation*, 2015, https://doi.org/10.1109/ ICRA.2015.7139363.
15. Chen, L.C., Papandreou, G., Kokkinos, I., Murphy, K., Yuille, A.L., Deeplab: Semantic image segmentation with deep convolutional nets, atrous convolution, and fully connected crfs. *IEEE Trans. Pattern Anal. Mach. Intell.*, 40, 4, 834–848, 2017.
16. Sure, C.H., Li, W., Vercauteren, T., Ourselin, S., Jorge Cardoso, M., Generalised dice overlap as a deep learning loss function for highly unbalanced segmentations, in: *Lecture Notes in Computer Science*, 2017, https://doi.org/10.1007/978-3-319-67558-9_28.
17. Phadikar, S., Sil, J., Das, A.K., Rice diseases classification using feature selection and rule generation techniques. *Comput. Electron. Agric.*, 90, 76–85, 2013.
18. Lee, S.H., Chan, C.S., Mayo, S.J., Remagnino, P., How deep learning extracts and learns leaf features for plant classification. *Pattern Recognit.*, 71, 1–13, 2017.
19. Shah, M.P., Singha, S., Awate, S.P., Leaf classification using marginalized shape context and shape+ texture dual-path deep convolutional neural network, in: *Proceedings of the 2017 IEEE International Conference on Image Processing (ICIP)*, Beijing, China, 17–20, pp. 860–864, September 2017.
20. Lee, S.H., Goëau, H., Bonnet, P., Joly, A., New perspectives on plant disease characterization based on deep learning. *Comput. Electron. Agric.*, 170, 105220, 2020.
21. Mohanty, S.P., Hughes, D.P., Salathé, M., Using deep learning for image-based plant disease detection. *Front. Plant Sci.*, 7, 1419, 2016.
22. Sladojevic, S., Arsenovic, M., Andela, A., Culibrk, D., Stefanovic, D., Deep neural networks based on plant diseases by leaf image classification. *Comput. Intell. Neurosci.*, 2016, 1–10, 2016.
23. Too, E.C., Yujian, L., Njuki, S., Yingchun, L., A comparative study of fine-tuning deep learning models for plant disease identification. *Comput. Electron. Agric.*, 161, 272–279, 2019.

24. Tan, M. and Le, Q., Efficientnet: Rethinking model scaling for convolutional neural networks, in: *Proceedings of the 2019 International Conference on Machine Learning*, Long Beach, CA, USA, pp. 6105–6114, 9–15 June 2019.
25. Kaur, S., Pandey, S., Goel, S., Semi-automatic Leaf Disease Detection and Classification System for Soybean Culture. *IET Image Proc.*, 12, 1038–1048, 2018.
26. Arora, J. and Agrawal, U., Classification of Maize leaf diseases from healthy leaves using Deep Forest. *J. Artif. Intell. Syst.*, 2, 14–26, 2020.
27. Ghazi, M.M., Yanikoglu, B., Aptoula, E., Plant identification using deep neural networks via optimization of transfer learning parameters. *Neurocomputing*, 235, 228–235, 2017.
28. Adedoja, A., Owolawi, P.A., Mapayi, T., Deep learning based on NASNet for plant disease recognition using leave images, in: *Proceedings of the 2019 International Conference on Advances in Big Data, Computing and Data Communication Systems (icABCD)*, pp. 1–5, Winterton, South Africa, 5–6 August 2019.
29. Russakovsky, O., Deng, J., Su, H., Krause, J., Satheesh, S., Ma, S., Huang, Z., Karpathy, A., Khosla, A., Bernstein, M. *et al.*, ImageNet Large Scale Visual Recognition Challenge. *Int. J. Comput. Vision (IJCV)*, 115, 211–252, 2015.
30. Sethy, P.K., Barpanda, N.K., Rath, A.K., Behera, S.K., Deep feature-based rice leaf disease identification using support vector machine. *Comput. Electron. Agric.*, 175, 105527, 2020.
31. Sherubha, P., Sasirekha, S.P., Manikandan, V., Gowsic, K., Mohanasundaram, N., Graph based event measurement for analyzing distributed anomalies in sensor networks. *Sādhanā*, 45, 1–5, 2020.
32. Sherubha, P., and Mohanasundaram, N., An efficient network threat detection and classification method using ANP-MVPS algorithm in wireless sensor networks. *Int. J. Innov. Technol. Explor. Eng.*, 8, 11, 1597–1606, 2019.
33. Meganathan, R., Anand, R., Murugesh, V., Security establishment using deep convolutional network model in cyber-physical systems. *Multimed. Tools Appl.*, 1–21, 2024.
34. Zhang, S. and Duan, X., Prediction of protein subcellular localization with oversampling approach and chou's general pseaac. *J. Theor. Biol.*, 437, 239–250, 2018.
35. Sherubha, P., Amudhavalli, P., Sasirekha, S.P., Clone attack detection using random forest and multi objective cuckoo search classification. In: *2019 International Conference on Communication and Signal Processing (ICCSP)*, pp. 0450–0454, IEEE, 2019, April.

12

Cardiovascular Disease Prediction with Machine Learning: An Ensemble-Based Regressive Neighborhood Model

Yuvaraj Duraisamy*, Salar Faisal Noori and Shakir Mahoomed Abas

Department of Computer Science, Cihan University - Duhok, Duhok, Kurdistan Region, Iraq

Abstract

Cardiovascular disease (CVD) is determined as a life-threatening disease globally with a high mortality rate. Over a certain period, there are some commonly overwhelming health issues noted in various countries. The major issues that influence CVD are family history, gender, stress, age, high blood pressure, cholesterol, BMI, and unhealthy life activities. Based on all these issues, researchers intend to propose various approaches for earlier prediction. Moreover, the proposed model's prediction accuracy and its enhancements are owing to the life-threatening risks and inherent criticality of CVD. This work concentrates on modeling an efficient ensemble-based regressive neighborhood model (ERN) is proposed for the effectual CVD prediction model. Various performance metrics are evaluated and compared with various other approaches.

***Keywords*:** Cardiovascular disease, machine learning, prediction, classification, accuracy

12.1 Introduction

Cardiovascular disease (CVD) is one of the most common causes of death in the modern world. In clinical domain data processing, predicting cardiovascular events is a major difficulty. Machine learning (ML) has been found to be useful in aiding with the decision-making and forecast of

**Corresponding author*: d.yuvaraj@duhokcihan.edu.krd

R. Nidhya, D. Pavithra, Manish Kumar, A. Dinesh Kumar and S. Balamurugan (eds.) Generative Artificial Intelligence: Concepts and Applications, (197–208) © 2025 Scrivener Publishing LLC

enormous amounts of data generated by the healthcare sector [1]. These ML approaches have also been employed in recent breakthroughs in several sectors of the Internet of Things (IoT). Various research merely scratch the surface of using ML to predict cardiac disease [2]. In this study, we provide a unique strategy for identifying key characteristics using ML approach, which enhance the accuracy of cardiovascular events forecasting. Possible variations of characteristics and numerous well-known classification algorithms are used to develop the statistical method [3]. Through into the estimation method for heart attacks with the hybrid random forest with a linear model, we achieve an improved quality performance with only an average precision of 88.7% [4].

Many contributing health conditions, such as obesity, increased blood pressure, excessive cholesterol, irregular heartbeat, and others, make it very hard to detect cardiac disease. The prevalence of cardiac cancer in human has been determined using a diversity of data gather and classification techniques approaches. a choice of approaches, such as genetic algorithm (GA), and Naïve Bayes (NB), the k-nearest neighbor algorithm (KNN), decision trees (DT) are used to organize the ruthlessness of the condition [5]. Since the mechanism of cardiac sickness is intricate, it has got to be treated with concern. Malfunction to do so may harm the heart or result in early death. Medical data and research mining are utilized to uncover dissimilar types of metabolic disorder [6]. In the forecast of heart sickness and statistical inquiry, business intelligence with categorization plays an essential part [7].

Decision tree algorithms have also been used to forecast the precision of measures connected to heart illness [7]. For the diagnosis of cardiac disease, several strategies of learning abstractions have been applied, including established data mining approaches. Several measurements were conducted in order to create a prediction model employing not just different approaches, but also by combining two methods. Methodologies [8] are the name given to these novel techniques that have been combined. We use cardiac moving average to establish ML. This process uses a mixture of clinical accounts for forecast such as left bundle branch block (LBBB), atrial flutter (AFL), normal sinus rhythm (NSR), premature ventricular contraction (PVC), sinus bradycardia (SBR), right bundle branch block (RBBB), atrial fibrillation (AFIB), and second degree block (BII) to determine the person's actual state in respect to heart attacks For classifying, a datasets containing a back - propagation neural network (RBFN) is employed, with 70% of the information use it for train and test 30% for classification [9].

In the sphere of advance studies, we also present the computer aided decision support system (CADSS). Previous studies have indicated that using data mining algorithms in the health sector reduces the time it takes to forecast disease and produces more precise results [10]. We propose utilizing the GA to diagnose cardiac disease. For random selection, crossovers, and recombination, this strategy competes effectively classification models learned from the GA, resulting in the new suggested genetic algorithm. We employ the well-known Cleveland datasets, which was acquired from a University of California, Irvine (UCI) ML repository, for experimental results. We will evaluate later on how our findings stack up against some of the most well-known supervised instructional methods [11]. Particle swarm optimization (PSO), the most powerful evolutionary method, is described, and even some parameters for heart attacks are produced. The rules were implemented at randomized using advanced capabilities, resulting in a massive increase in accuracy [12]. Symptoms such as heart rates, sex, gender, and others are used to indicate cardiovascular diseases. The deep neural network ML algorithm is developed, which produces more correct and reliable results.

In generally, neural networks (NNs) are thought to be the finest tool for predicting illnesses such as heart problems and neurological disease. We employ a suggested technique that contains 13 variables for predicting heart disease. When compared to previous approaches help in finding a higher degree of performance. In past years, carotid artery stenting (CAS) has also been a popular therapeutic option in the healthcare profession. The CAS alerts older myocardial infarction individuals to the incidence of significant adverse cardiovascular events (MACE). Their assessment becomes extremely crucial. We use an artificial neural network (ANN) to accomplish the research objectives, which has shown to be effective in the diagnosis of cardiovascular problems [14]. The use of artificial neural approaches, which include not just likelihood function but also coefficient of determination from many preceding techniques, is introduced. When opposed to past research, this model reaches an accuracy level of up to 89.01 percent, which is a significant outcome. To maximize the speed of heart diseases, the Cleveland heart information is employed in all studies, together with a NN [15].

We offer an approach called ensemble-based regressive neighborhood (ERN) model. The major goal of this study is to increase the accuracy of heart disease prediction abilities. Much research has been undertaken that resulted in a subset of features limitations for programmatic usage [16]. The ERN technique, on the other hand, employs all characteristics without regard to feature selection. We employ a hybrid strategy to run trials to determine the characteristics of a model. The findings of this research reveal that our suggested hybrid model is more capable of predicting cardiovascular disease than previous techniques [17].

12.2 Related Works

Investigators have recommended different deep learning strategy-based screening method to analyze HD in the fiction. This review discusses various active deep learning approaches to clarify the consequence, this revision mainly includes multiple active deep learning method detection tools. Tun *et al.* [11] created the HD categorization scheme utilize data mining and deep learning approach, and then system's exactness was 77%. The C level and information were worn in concurrence with the universal incremental approach and the description selection techniques. Ley *et al.* [12] formed an analytical structure for HD categorization that used multi-layer recurrent neural network and SVM strategies and reached an effectiveness of 80.41%. Meng *et al.* [13] created an HD grading classification-based on an NN with Fuzzy reason integrated. The categorization system has an effectiveness of 87.5%. Bashir *et al.* [14] used a quantitative system of measurement execute venture miner (5.2) to construct an ANN-based analysis scheme for HD, which had a precision of 89.01%, a sensitization of 80.09%, and a definite of 95.91%. Nai *et al.* [15] execute a deep learning (DL)-based HD analytical process. The efficiency of the ANN-DBP procedure in a mixture with the FS process was exceptional [18]. The system was developed using ML prediction models such as DT, and ANN, NB. NB had a reliability of 86.12%, ANN had an accuracy of 88.12%, and the DT decoder had a reliability of 80.4%.

12.3 Methodology

This work proposes a novel learning approach for cardiovascular disease prediction. The objective is to provide an appropriate ML model, which predicts the disease reliably based on the clinical parameters (see Figure 12.1). The model follows some pre-processing steps to enhance the prediction outcome [19]. They are: 1) data pre-processing like missing value replacement, outlier removal and dealing with imbalanced class; 2) feature selection; and 3) classification with an ERN model. The objective is to attain enhanced prediction outcomes with diminished amount of features [20].

12.3.1 Pre-Processing

In the initial phase, the data is explored for probable outliers, and the samples with outliers are deviates with the normal dataset characteristics.

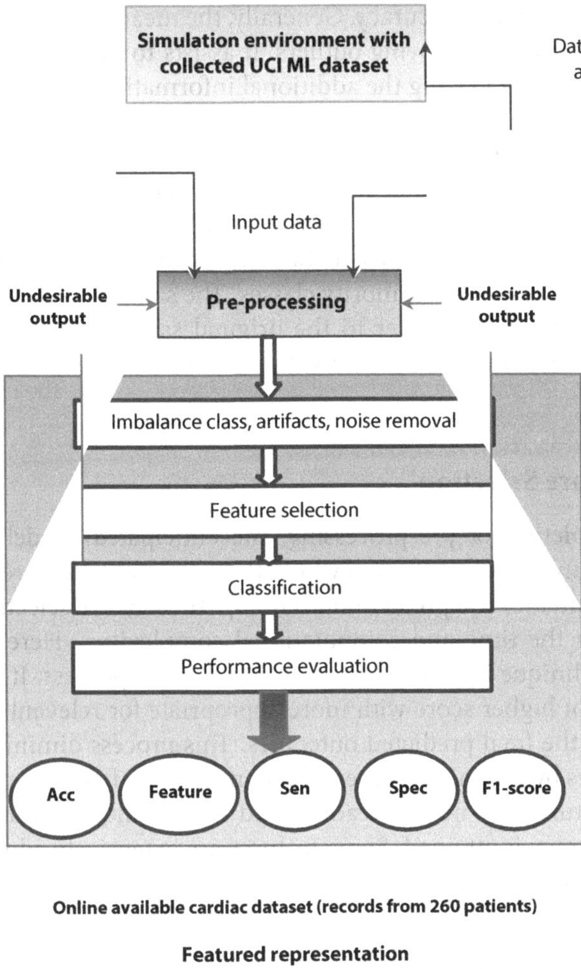

Figure 12.1 Flow diagram of anticipated model.

The outlier data is determined to be noisier with no significance data value and influences the model performance negatively [21]. The anticipated model adopts BoxPlot for outlier prediction and gives five number summaries, i.e. minimal first quartile (Q1), median (Q2), third quartile (Q3), and maximal. These points are plotted like box structure and determined as outliers. After the outlier removal process, the anticipated model verifies the missing values over the dataset. It is extremely common due to human error. When there are some missing values, then the model cannot be trained effectually owing to the reduced amount of training samples.

This influences the model accuracy. Generally, the mean substitution is the most common way for removing outliers. It assists to preserve the training data devoid of influencing the additional information and reduces the overfitting issues.

After the elimination of outliers and missing values, the imbalanced class needs to be resolved. This work adopts SMOTE where the model increases the minority class samples with the prediction of k-NN. The nearest neighbors are chosen randomly to enhance the minority class samples. It is used for the generation of various minority classes. The samples generated with this model are extremely nearer to the original samples with increased reliability and diminished randomness. It is effectually utilized by various researchers.

12.3.2 Feature Selection

After the completion of pre-processing, the anticipated model recommends the feature selection process where the appropriate feature subsets are chosen to enhance the prediction accuracy. This feature selection process diminishes the time and computational complexities. Here, feature significance technique is adopted for feature selection process. It helps in the evaluation of higher score with more appropriate for relevant features that turn to be the final predicted outcomes. This process diminishes the overfitting issues by diminishing the redundant features from the provided data. Some features are not misleading and redundant; thus, improved prediction accuracy is attained. Some features are extensively adopted for relevant feature selection.

12.3.3 Classification

At last, the anticipated model proposes an ensemble approach for classification. The model drives the prior experience, which assists in attaining superior results. Here, ensemble learning is attained with nearest neighbors and regression model. The former model works well with the huge amount of samples while the later model is categorically dependent on dataset variables even with the provided set of independent variables. It is extensively utilized by various prediction issues in the health care. It also provides superior outcomes for numerical attributes. At last, the proposed model examines the model accuracy with k-CV. It attains superior performance when testing the data. The parameter 'k' determines the fold that needs to split the data.

12.4 Numerical Results and Discussion

This work considers six performance metrics to compute the performance of the anticipated model. The potential model output includes true negative (TN), true positive (TP), false negative (FN), and false positive (FP). Here, TP and TN are depicted as the number of samples appropriately classified as 'positive' (occurrence of heart disease), and negative specifies the absences of heart disease, respectively. Then, FP and FN specify the number of samples inappropriately classified as 'positive' (heart disease occurrence) when it is usually 'negative' (absence of heart disease) and inappropriately classified as 'negative' (absence of heart disease) when it is actually 'positive' (heart disease occurrence) respectively. The execution of the proposed classifier model is done in MATLAB 2018a using various learning libraries. The experimentation is done in Intel-core i7 process, 16 GB RAM on Windows 10 OS. Additionally, the performance metrics are evaluated, and accuracy is expressed as in Equation 12.1:

$$Accuracy = \frac{TP + TN}{TP + FN + FP + TN} \tag{12.1}$$

Precision is expressed as in Equation 12.2:

$$Precision = \frac{TP}{TP + FP} \tag{12.2}$$

Sensitivity/recall/True Positive Rate (TPR) and f1- score is expressed as in Equation 12.3 and Equation 12.4:

$$Recall = \frac{TP}{TP + TN} \tag{12.3}$$

$$f = \frac{2pr}{p + r} \tag{12.4}$$

Table 12.1 depicts the comparison of overall performance metrics. The comparison is made among the existing LR, RF, L-GBM, SVM, BRT, DFN and the ERN (see Figure 12.2 to Figure 12.4). The metrics like accuracy,

Table 12.1 Overall comparison of the performance metrics.

Dataset	ML algorithm	Accuracy (%)		Sensitivity	Specificity	F1-score	No. of features		Time (min)	Area under region of curve (AUROC)
		Without feature	With feature				Without feature	With feature		
UCI machine learning repository	**LR**	88	94	0.69	0.67	0.36	13	11	1.60	88.55
	RF	79.	93	0.68	0.95	0.36	13	8	0.32	79.95
	L-GBM	95.	93	0.65	0.70	0.36	13	11	4.06	95.44
	SVM	95.	93	0.67	0.71	0.36	13	11	37.97	95.17
	BRT	85	92	0.68	0.69	0.36	13	9	2.57	85.64
	PDF	97	97	0.94	0.93	0.40	13	6	0.03	96.84
	Proposed	**98**	**98**	**0.98**	**0.98**	**0.45**	13	**5**	**0.02**	**97**

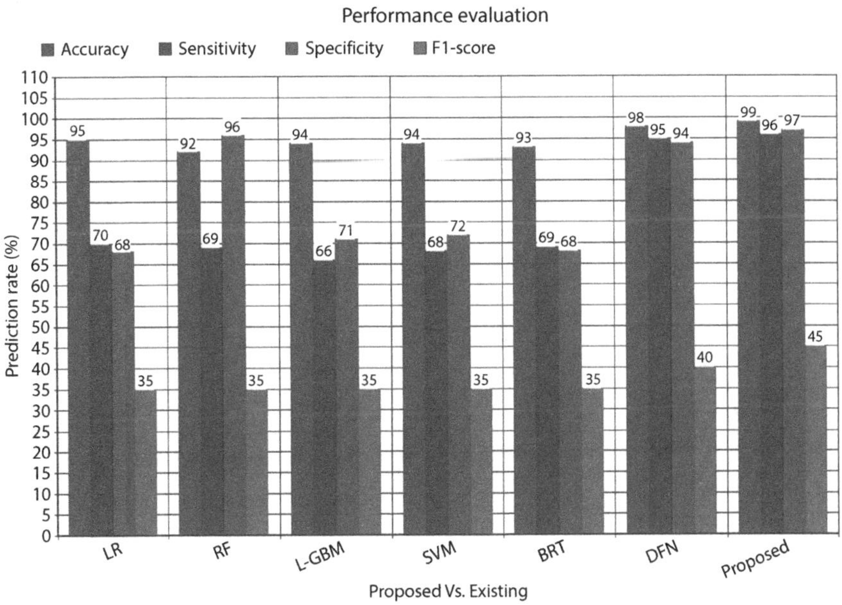

Figure 12.2 Performance metrics evaluation.

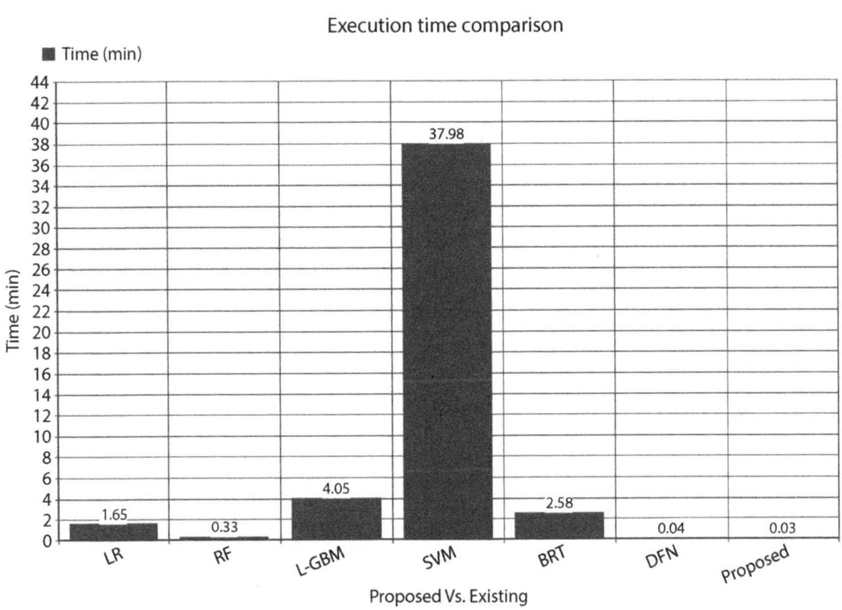

Figure 12.3 Execution time comparison.

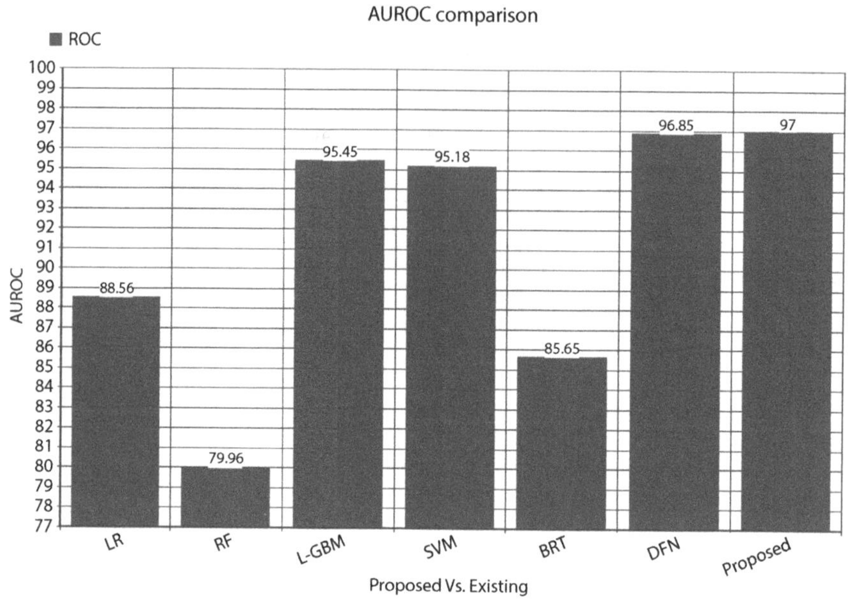

Figure 12.4 AUROC comparison.

sensitivity, specificity, F1-score, time, and AUROC are measured and compared with these methods [22]. The accuracy of the anticipated model is 99%, which is 9.44%, 18.41%, 2.55%, 2.82%, 12.35%, 0.35% higher than other approaches during data pattern analysis. The sensitivity of the anticipated model is 96%, which is 26%, 27%, 30%, 39%, and 1% higher than other approaches. The specificity of the anticipated model is 97%, which is 29%, 1%, 26%, 25%, 29%, and 3% higher than other approaches. The F1-score of the anticipated model is 45%, which is 10% higher than LR, RF, L-GBM, SVM, and BRT model and 5% higher than the DFN model. The execution time is 0.03 minutes, which is higher than other approaches. The AUROC is 97% higher than other approaches.

12.5 Conclusion

The prediction of unprocessed health information of CVD helps in long-term preservation of human lives and prior prediction of irregularities over cardiac issues. To examine the raw information and provide superior understanding regarding the CVD, ML algorithm is applied. Over the medical sector, the prediction of CVD is complex yet crucial. However, when the condition is identified earlier and prevention steps are required as quickly as feasible, the mortality rate is reduced dramatically. It is ideal the research is expanded to consider a real-time dataset of theoretical simulations and techniques. In cardiac disease prediction, the anticipated model proves the significance. The research is done with the integration of ML algorithms to enhance the prediction rate. The novelty relies on the gain of wider perspective of essential features and enhances computer-based prediction efficiency.

References

1. Jensen, Jensen, L.J., Brunak, S., Mining electronic health records: Towards better research applications and clinical care. *Nat. Rev. Genet.*, 13, 6, 395–405, Jun. 2012.
2. Li, Bai, C., Reddy, C.K., A distributed ensemble approach for mining health-care data under privacy constraints. *Inf. Sci.*, 330, 245–259, Feb. 2016.
3. Khedr, Aghbari, Z.A.L., Kamel, I., Privacy-preserving decomposable mining association rules on distributed data. *Int. J. Eng. Technol.*, 7, 3-13, 157–162, 2018.
4. Khedr, and Bhatnagar, R., New algorithm for clustering distributed data using K-means. *Comput. Inform.*, 33, 1001–1022, Oct. 2014.
5. Subhashini, and Jeyakumar, M.K., OF-KNN technique: An approach for chronic kidney disease prediction. *Int. J. Pure Appl. Math.*, 116, 24, 331–348, 2017.
6. Nathan, Kumar, P.M., Panchatcharam, P., Manogaran, G., Varadharajan, R., A novel Gini index decision tree data mining method with neural network classifiers for heart disease prediction. *Des. Autom. Embedded Syst.*, 22, 3, 225, 2018.
7. Hsu, Manogaran, G., Panchatcharam, P., Vivekanandan, S., A new approach for prediction of lung carcinoma using backpropagation neural network with decision tree classifiers, in: *Proc. IEEE 8th Int. Symp. Cloud Service Comput. (SC)*, pp. 111–115, Nov. 2018.
8. Ramasamy, and Nirmala, K., Disease prediction in data mining using association rule mining and keyword-based clustering algorithms. *Int. J. Comput. Appl.*, 42, 1, 1–8, Jan. 2020.
9. Bakar, Kefli, Z., Abdullah, S., Sahani, M., Predictive models for dengue outbreak using multiple rule-based classifiers, in: *Proc. Int. Conf. Electr. Eng. Information*, pp. 1–6, Jul. 2011.
10. Hariharan, Umadevi, R., Stephen, T., Pradeep, S., Burden of diabetes and hypertension among people attending health camps in an urban area of Kancheepuram district. *Int. J. Community Med. Public Health*, 5, 1, 140, Dec. 2017.

11. Tun, Arunagirinathan, G., Munshi, S.K., Pappachan, J.M., Diabetes mellitus and stroke: A clinical update. *World J. Diabetes*, 8, 6, 235–248, Jun. 2017.
12. Ley, Hamdy, O., Mohan, V., Hu, F.B., Prevention and management of type 2 diabetes: Dietary components and nutritional strategies. *Lancet*, 383, 9933, 1999–2007, Jun. 2014.
13. Meng, Huang, Y.-X., Rao, D.-P., Zhang, Q., Liu, Q., Comparison of three data mining models for predicting diabetes or prediabetes by risk factors. *Kaohsiung J. Med. Sci.*, 29, 2, 93–99, Feb. 2013.
14. Bashir, Qamar, U., Khan, F.H., IntelliHealth: A medical decision support application using a novel weighted multi-layer classifier ensemble framework. *J. Biomed. Inf.*, 59, 185–200, Feb. 2016.
15. Nai-Arun, and Moungmai, R., Comparison of classifiers for the risk of diabetes prediction. *Procedia Comput. Sci.*, 69, 132–142, Nov. 2015.
16. Nithya, S., Sundara Vadivel, P., Yuvaraj, D., Sivaram, M., Intelligent based IoT smart city on a traffic control system using raspberry Pi and robust waste anagement. *J. Adv. Res. Dyn. Control Syst.*, 2, 765–770, 2018.
17. Ahamed, B.B. and Yuvaraj, D., Framework for a faction of data in social network using link-based mining process, in: *International Conference on Intelligent Computing & Optimization*, Springer, Cham, pp. 300–309, 2018.
18. Krishnan, S.N., Vadivel, P.S., Yuvaraj, D., An Effective Document Category Prediction System Using Support Vector Machines, Mann-Whitney Techniques. *Int. J. Pure Appl. Math.*, 120, 6, 2267–2282, 2018.
19. Yuvaraj, D., Sivaram, M., Ahamed, A.M.U., Nageswari, S., An Efficient Lion Optimization Based Cluster Formation and Energy Management in WSN Based IoT, in: *International Conference on Intelligent Computing & Optimization*, Springer, Cham, pp. 591–607, 2019.
20. Priya, S.S., Sivaram, M., Yuvaraj, D., Jayanthiladevi, A., Machine Learning-based DDOS Detection. *2020 International Conference on Emerging Smart Computing and Informatics (ESCI)*, Pune, India, pp. 234–237, 2020, DOI: 10.1109/ESCI48226.2020.9167642.
21. Karthick, R. and Yuvaraj, D., Speech Emotion Identification Using Deep Neural Networks for Tamil Language. *J. Adv. Res. Dyn. Control Syst.*, 12, 10, 1171–1175, 2019.
22. Ahamed, B.B. and Yuvaraj, D., A Framework for Online Customer Reviews System Using Sentiment Scoring Method, in: *2021 22nd International Arab Conference on Information Technology (ACIT)*, pp. 1–8, IEEE, 2021, December.

13

Detection of IoT Attacks Using Hybrid RNN-DBN Model

Pavithra D.*, **Bharathraj R.**, **Poovizhi P.**, **Libitharan K.** and **Nivetha V.**

Information Technoloy, Dr. N.G.P. Institute of Technology, Coimbatore, India

Abstract

Cyberattacks are constantly evolving, becoming more complex and harder to detect. Hackers develop new exploits, malware, and phishing techniques faster than traditional security measures can adapt. Securing devices, against cyber threats is of importance in the context of the Internet of Things where all things are interconnected. The suggested framework presents a method, for detecting intrusions in networks by utilizing a model that combines recurrent neural networks (RNNs) and deep belief networks (DBNs). The RNNs excel at understanding patterns in sequential data, like network traffic flow in an Internet of Things environment. The DBNs are adept at extracting key features from data. By utilizing these methods, the goal is to create a system that can effectively identify and classify attacks. To assess its effectiveness this combined approach was applied to the UNSW NB15 dataset, which consists of both network traffic and malicious activity from a network. The outcomes show encouraging performance as the model accurately identified nine types of attacks such, as Backdoors, Denial of Service (DoS) Analysis, Exploits, Generic Threats, Reconnaissance activities, Fuzzers, for Abnormal Activity Shellcode Exploits, and Worms.

***Keywords*:** Intrusion detection system, Internet of Things, hybrid model, recurrent neural networks, deep belief networks

**Corresponding author*: pavimba07@gmail.com

R. Nidhya, D. Pavithra, Manish Kumar, A. Dinesh Kumar and S. Balamurugan (eds.) Generative Artificial Intelligence: Concepts and Applications, (209–226) © 2025 Scrivener Publishing LLC

13.1 Introduction

Intrusion detection systems (IDS) are incredibly important, in protecting computer networks and systems. They actively analyze network traffic to identify any signs of activities or security breaches; they act as a defense, against cyber threats enabling organizations to detect and respond to access, data theft and other harmful actions. One of the roles of an IDS is to actively observe network traffic for any abnormal patterns or behaviors. In its passive mode, the IDS monitors network packets and collects information without actively interfering with the flow of data. This enables it to observe and analyze communication patterns with the goal of establishing a standard, for network behavior. As a result the system becomes skilled at identifying any deviations, from this standard, which could potentially signal security risks or unusual occurrences. Conversely, in active monitoring, an IDS may take preventive measures when suspicious activities are detected. A proactive strategy entails the potential blocking or isolation of specific traffic identified as malicious, thus averting potential threats before they can compromise the system. In active mode, the IDS gains the capability not only to identify anomalies but also to respond swiftly to mitigate potential risks, thereby enhancing the overall security posture. The detection of abnormal patterns or behaviors encompasses diverse activities, including but not limited to unauthorized access attempts, atypical data transfer volumes, and unusual system activities.

Signature-based detection relies on predefined patterns or signatures associated with recognized threats. Essentially, these signatures serve as digital fingerprints encapsulating the attributes of known malware, viruses, or other malicious activities. The IDS consistently compares patterns observed in network traffic with a repository of these signatures. Upon detecting a correlation between the observed network traffic patterns and the signatures within its database, the system initiates an alert or executes pre-defined actions to counteract the threat. This method proves particularly effective against established and documented threats. It offers a fast and accurate way to detect known attack patterns, making it suitable for scenarios where the characteristics of potential threats are well understood. However, a limitation of signature-based detection is its inability to identify new or previously unseen threats, as it relies on predefined patterns.

Anomaly-based detection [1] represents a dynamic and behavior-centric strategy in contrast to traditional methods that hinge on predefined patterns. This approach involves continuous monitoring and learning from the regular activities within a system to establish a baseline of normal network behavior. In this method, the IDS identifies potential anomalies or security threats by flagging deviations from the established baseline. The distinct strength of anomaly-based detection lies in its capacity to recognize novel and previously unknown threats, enhancing its effectiveness in identifying emerging security risks. The strength of anomaly-based detection lies in its ability to identify novel and previously unknown threats. It can adapt to new attack vectors and tactics that may not have a predefined signature. Anomaly-based systems [10] are effective in detecting insider threats, zero-day exploits [15], and other advanced persistent threats that may not have recognizable patterns. However, the challenge with anomaly-based detection is the potential for false positives. Normal variations in network behavior or changes in system configurations may trigger alerts, leading to an increased risk of overlooking real security threats. Effective tuning and calibration are essential in minimizing the number of false positives while ensuring that anomaly-based detection remains accurate. The fine-tuning and proper adjustment are key aspects to reduce the errors of this detection method.

In the field of cybersecurity, artificial intelligence (AI) [14], machine learning (ML), and deep learning (DL) [7] are instrumental in enhancing the capabilities of IDS. Artificial intelligence, with its overarching umbrella, encompasses ML and DL, offering innovative solutions to mitigate evolving cyber threats. The ML algorithms in IDS analyze historical and real-time data, detecting patterns indicative of normal network behavior versus potential security threats. By continuously learning and adapting to new attack vectors, ML equips IDS to detect anomalies and previously unseen threats more effectively. A subset of ML, DL is specialized in processing complex and unstructured data. In the cybersecurity industry, it can be used to train deep networks to look for intricate patterns in large data sets and expose complex correlations. In intrusion detection, DL models can autonomously identify anomalies from normal network behavior, enabling the early detection of critical attacks. The DL approach is particularly beneficial in handling complex threats, providing advanced capabilities to counter increasingly complex threats.

The following proposed framework combines recurrent neural networks (RNN) and long short-term memory (LSTM) [2], and deep belief networks (DBN) [16] for intrusion detection within the context of cybersecurity and Internet of Things (IoT) environments. The RNNs are an architectural variety of neural network systems that have been specially developed for sequence data. In standard neural networks, each input and output is treated as independent of one another. However, when dealing with tasks like predicting the next word in a sentence becomes crucial.

The signature feature of an RNN is its hidden state, which retains information about the sequence of inputs it has processed. The iterative nature of RNNs, where the output from one step becomes the input for the next, enables the network to maintain a memory of previous steps, enhancing its ability to understand and generate sequential patterns.

The DBNs are a type of generative probabilistic model [14] that combines the advantages of restricted Boltzmann machines (RBMs) in a layered structure, which was explained in this section [6]. The first layer, known as the visible layer, receives input data. Each subsequent layer, referred to as a hidden layer, captures increasingly abstract and complex features through a stack of interconnected RBMs. The connections between layers are undirected, allowing for bidirectional information flow during both the learning and generative phases. The DBNs employ a pre-training approach where each layer is trained as an RBM, learning hierarchical representations of the input data. The network's output layer is the part which produces the desired results for classification, etc. On the other hand, DBNs manipulate data to extract hierarchical and distributed data representations, this property makes them useful in various domains such as feature learning, dimensionality reduction, and classification.

This framework provides an improved approach to attack detection using the UNSW-NB15 dataset. It involves nine categories of attack: Backdoors, Denial of Service (DoS) Analysis, Exploits, Generic Threats, Reconnaissance activities, Fuzzers, for Abnormal Activity Shellcode Exploits, and Worms.

13.2 Related Work

The recent publications of an intrusion detection framework designed for the IoT environment [5] make a significant advancement in the field of cybersecurity. In this proposed framework, the incorporation of AI techniques, specifically MLPs, RNNs, and DNNs, highlights a diverse and sophisticated approach to intrusion detection. Multi-layer perceptrons are known for their versatility in capturing intricate patterns in data, while RNNs excel in handling sequential information, making them adept at recognizing temporal dependencies in cyber threats. An intrusion detection framework designed for IoT ecosystems releases [5] and latest warnings for cybersecurity have made significant forward strides in the field.

Large-scale neural networks have, due to their hierarchical structure, the capacity to internalize complex representations, but the owner is usually able to detect subtle operating patterns whereas the malicious actor cannot be seen, and it evolves over time. The seven frameworks use different approaches and are classified into DL techniques like RNN, convolutional neural network (CNN), and deep neural network (DNN) and generative models such as RBN, deep belief networks (DBN), deep Boltzmann machines (DBM), and denoising autoencoders (DA) [17]. Including such datasets as NSL-KDD, KDDCup99, and UNSW-NB15 has been a widespread practice in the development and assessment of intrusion detection systems. These datasets are an invaluable asset to cybersecurity researchers and professionals, who need samples of typical network traffic or activities with which they can probe the performance of intrusion detection system. NSL-KDD is a modified and augmented form of the original KDD Cup, which surpassed some of the limitations and defects in the first version. It has attacked scenarios of a wider range, so it's more balanced in detecting many kinds of invasions. The KDDCup99 was a dataset that gained popularity for use as a standard in evaluating intrusion detection systems because of its association with competitive contestation. Although it is often used in research, some of the constraints of KDDCup99-namely lack refreshing network traffic and having many peculiar ones like such as NSL-KDD. The UNSW-NB15 [18] dataset represents a more recent addition to the available datasets for intrusion detection research. It is designed to reflect contemporary network traffic and includes a diverse set of attacks. The inclusion of this dataset in frameworks allows researchers to assess the performance of intrusion detection systems in a modern context, considering evolving cyber threats. The presented framework demonstrates the performance across multiple datasets commonly used in intrusion detection research.

Table 13.1 showcases the framework's robustness and accuracy in identifying both normal and malicious activities within this dataset. Similarly, using the UNSW-NB15 dataset, the framework delivered good results.

Table 13.1 Accuracy for identifying malicious activities in NSL-KDD dataset.

Dataset	Accuracy	Precision	Recall	F1s
NSL-KDD	96.90%	95.21%	94.50%	95.03%

Table 13.2 Accuracy for identifying malicious activities in UNSW-NB15 dataset.

Dataset	Accuracy	Precision	Recall	F1s
UNSW-NB15	95.90%	94.20%	91.41%	90.18%

Table 13.2 showcases the framework's effectiveness in handling diverse cyber threats present in contemporary network traffic. Additionally, the framework's performance on the KDDCup99 [18] dataset is notable.

Another framework uses CNN-LSTM layers to construct an intrusion detection system [2]. A CNN-LSTM design, which mixes CNN and LSTM architectures is one of the most powerful DL models found in the areas of time-series forecasting or video cognition, as well as natural language processing. The CNNs were effective in extracting spatial data, while LSTM could capture information about time. In combination, these two models worked well with mutually beneficial results. It is the responsibility of the CNN component in this architecture to learn hierarchical features from input data. Using convolutional filters, it picks out relevant patterns and features. In this way, the model is able to discern spatial representations in its input sequence. The output of the CNN layer learns spatial features on these maps. On the other hand, the LSTM component is intended through sequential data in order to compute correlation coefficients over longer distances. The LSTMs are particularly effective in addressing the long-term dependency problem associated with traditional recurrent neural networks. They maintain a memory cell to selectively store and retrieve information over extended sequences, allowing the model to capture temporal patterns and dependencies. In a CNN-LSTM layer, the output of the CNN component and uses it as a sequence. By condensing spatial features extracted by the CNN into a more manageable form, the model can optimize for both spatial and temporal data. This combined architecture is well suited to applications in which both spatial and temporal information is important in order for accurate predictions or classifications. Table 13.3 shows the accuracy of handling diverse cyber threats in KDDCup99 dataset.

Table 13.3 Accuracy in handling diverse cyber threats in KDDCup99.

Dataset	Accuracy	Precision	Recall	F1s
KDDCup99	90.01%	85.11%	89.23%	87.22%

The CNN-LSTM layers work well in the detection of internal network abnormal intrusion. Within DL models, this architecture is perfect for breaking down network traffic data. It is in this area that the spatial and temporal aspects deeply affect the ability to identify dangers to security. The CNN component of the layer excels at extracting spatial features from the input data, which could represent patterns and relationships in network traffic. Convolutional filters applied to the input sequences allow the model to discern relevant spatial information, such as unusual communication patterns or distinctive behaviors associated with malicious activities. The LSTM component complements this by capturing temporal dependencies in the sequence of network events. It enables the model to understand the sequential nature of activities and identify patterns that may unfold over time, a vital aspect in detecting sophisticated and persistent cyber threats. Since uniting CNN and LSTM into the same layer allows the model to learn spatial and temporal representations concurrently from the input data. This research utilizes the CIC-IDS2017 [13], UNSW-NB15, and WSN-DS datasets.

Table 13.4 shows the performance of CIC-IDS2017, UNSWNB15, and WSN-DS datasets.

Using a combined CNN [3] with machine techniques [4] results in lower accuracy understood solely from the CIC-IDS2017a dataset as a case in point at around 93%. In contrast, supervised learning algorithms like artificial neural networks, decision trees, k-nearest neighbors, Naïve Bayes, random forests, support vector machines, and CNN decide what to do with the training dataset in mind. These are typically labeled data collections, i.e., models trained on inputs and outputs. They go deep inside a mass of data to see the underlying patterns and relationships, so that they can predict or classify unknown instances by learning them with patterns. However, unsupervised learning algorithms such as k-means clustering, expectation-maximization (EM) clustering, and self-organizing maps are similar situations. They work together and try to identify patterns from unlabeled data that were previously unknown to us including natural

Table 13.4 Performance of CIC-IDS2017, UNSWNB15, and WSN-DS datasets.

Dataset	Accuracy	Precision	Recall	F1s
UNSW-NB15	94.10%	95.23%	94.5%	95%
WSN-DS	97.6%	80.5%	97%	97.6%
CIC-IDS2017	97.3%	95.8%	99%	95.8%

structures or groupings. There are many useful applications of unsupervised algorithms related to areas such as data exploration, pattern recognition and clustering. This is especially the case when extracting some unknown structures or hidden relationships within data with an unknown target variable.

13.3 Methodology

The proposed hybrid model for intrusion detection combines the strengths of RNNs and DBNs to detect attacks.

13.3.1 Dataset Used

The UNSW NB15 dataset is widely used in the field of network security and intrusion detection. It was created by the University of New South Wales (UNSW) in Australia to support research and development in network-based intrusion detection systems (NIDS) [9]. This dataset aims to capture a range of cyber threats and network activities. It includes 49 features that provide information about network traffic, such as source and destination IP addresses, port numbers, protocol types, payload data, packet sizes and other network characteristics. The dataset contains instances of types of attacks like Backdoors, DoS Analysis, Exploits, Generic Threats, Reconnaissance, Fuzzers, Shellcode Exploits, and Worms. Figure 13.1 presents a visual representation of the proposed framework.

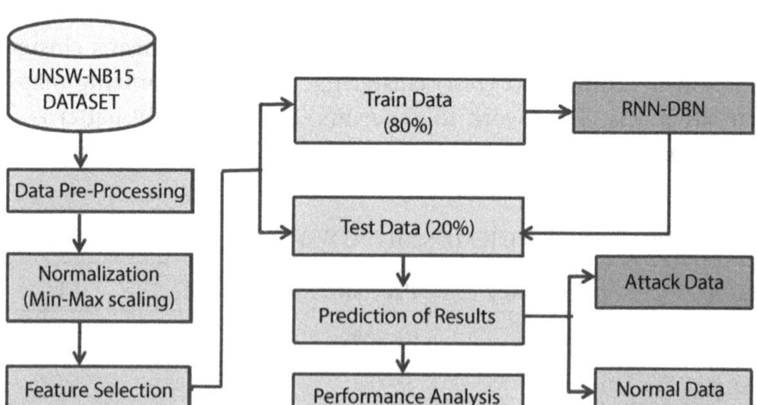

Figure 13.1 Proposed framework.

13.3.2 Data Preprocessing

Data pre-processing refers to a set of procedures applied to data to transform it into a suitable format for analysis or modeling purposes. It involves cleaning up the data transforming its structure as needed while addressing missing values and outliers. These steps ensure data quality and compatibility, within the dataset. In the context of the given dataset, the initial dataset contained 45 attributes and 175,341 rows. To address missing values, null values were dropped, resulting in a refined dataset with the same 45 attributes but reduced to 81,173 rows.

The next preprocessing step involved converting the data types of attributes based on the provided data type information from a features dataset. This ensures consistency and compatibility in the dataset. Additionally categorical variables were handled using one encoding [19]. Categorical variables can be converted into a matrix, known as one encoding (Table 13.5). This technique helps the model better understand and extract insights, from the data it is trained on. These preprocessing steps collectively contribute to creating a clean, standardized, and ready-to-use dataset for DL tasks, enabling more effective model training and analysis.

13.3.3 Data Normalization

Data normalization is a technique used in ML to make sure that numerical features, in a dataset have the scale. The aim is to bring features or variables to a scale, usually between 0 and 1 or centered around zero by rescaling them. The usage of MinMax Scaler [8] is a step in preparing the model. This technique. Transforms the input data so that it falls within a range typically between 0 and 1 ensuring consistency and minimizing the impact of varying scales across features. In the context of RNN-DBN models, which

Table 13.5 One encoding values.

Protocol_type	TCP	UDP	SNMP	FTP
TCP	1	0	0	0
UDP	0	1	0	0
SNMP	0	0	1	0
FTP	0	0	0	1

combine the temporal learning capabilities of recurrent neural networks with the hierarchical feature learning of deep belief networks, normalizing the input data becomes particularly important for enhancing model convergence and performance.

The MinMax Scaler [8] accomplishes this by mapping the minimum and maximum values of each feature to the desired range, effectively eliminating the influence of anomalies and providing a standardized foundation for the hybrid model to learn and generalize patterns across the dataset. This normalization step contributes to the overall stability and efficiency of the RNN-DBN model, facilitating better training and more robust predictions in diverse applications such as time series analysis and sequential data processing. The formula for Min-Max scaling is as follows in Equation 13.1.

$$Nscaled=(N-Nmin)/(Nmax-Nmin) \tag{13.1}$$

N is the original value of a feature. Nscaled is the scaled/normalized value of the feature. Nmin is the minimum value of the feature in the dataset. Nmax is the maximum value of the feature in the dataset.

13.3.4 Multi-Class Classification

For multi-class classification [12], a new data frame is generated, and the 'attack_cat' attribute is the focal point, encompassing nine distinct categories: Analysis, Backdoor, DoS, Exploits, Fuzzers, Generic, Normal, Reconnaissance, and Worms. To facilitate the model understanding of these categories, the 'LabelEncoder()' is employed to encode the 'attack_cat' labels, resulting in a transformation of categorical values into numerical representations. The encoded labels are stored in a variable named 'label.' To further enhance the model's performance, 'attack_cat' undergoes one-hot encoding, a process that converts categorical variables into binary vectors. Each category is represented by a binary column, and the presence or absence of a particular category is denoted by 1 or 0, respectively. This one-hot encoding not only ensures that the model accurately interprets and learns from the categorical information but also helps prevent any implicit ordinal relationships between the categories. Ultimately, this preprocessing strategy establishes a structured and numerical foundation for the multi-class classification model, enabling it to effectively discern and predict the various attack categories.

13.3.5 Splitting Dataset

Splitting datasets randomly into training and testing sets is a practice in learning to evaluate how well a model performs on unseen data. In an 80–20 split scenario this means allocating 80% of the dataset for training purposes while keeping aside the remaining 20% for testing. The main objective here is to ensure that the model learns patterns from most of the data during training while having a subset, for evaluation to measure its generalization capability. The random nature of the split helps mitigate biases that might arise from specific ordering or patterns in the original dataset.

13.3.6 RNN-DBN

The proposed framework introduces a model [11] that combines two types of networks: long short-term memory (LSTM) network and deep belief network (DBN) like network. This combination aims at detecting attacks. During the phase one important step involves reshaping both scaled training and test data so that they meet the input requirements of the LSTM network. Subsequently, the LSTM model is constructed with an input layer, an LSTM layer featuring 600 units to capture sequential patterns, and a dense layer employing a sigmoid activation function for binary classification. Following the training of the LSTM model, embedding generated by the LSTM layer is extracted and concatenated with the original scaled features. In the next step, a DBN-like neural network is established and trained on the combined data, aiming to leverage the learned sequential patterns from the LSTM.

Let us denote the output of the LSTM at time step t as y (t), and the corresponding input to the DBN as v. The hidden layer size for both LSTM and DBN is 600.

Output of LSTM with SoftMax Activation:

$$Y(t) = \text{Softmax}\,(W(hy) \cdot h(t) + b(hy)) \tag{13.2}$$

where W(hy) is the weight matrix for the output layer and b(hy) is the bias vector for the output layer.

The energy of the DBN Configuration (using RBM-like formulation):

$$E(v,h) = -\Sigma_{i=1}^{Nv} \Sigma_{j=1}^{Nh} w(ij)\ v(i)\ h(j) - \quad \Sigma_{i=1}^{Nv} b(i)\ v(i) - \Sigma_{j=1}^{Nh} c(j)\ h(j) \tag{13.3}$$

SoftMax Activation for Output of DBN:

$$P(y\ (t)\,|\,h) = \text{SoftMax}(W(oh) \cdot h + b(oh)) \tag{13.4}$$

where W(oh) is the weight matrix for the output layer of the DBN and b(oh) is the bias vector for the output layer of the DBN.

Equation 13.2 computes the LSTM output with SoftMax activation. Equation 13.3 defines the energy of the DBN configuration using RBM-like formulation, and Equation 13.4 applies SoftMax activation to the output of the DBN for final prediction probability.

The final step involves similarly transforming the test data and making predictions using the DBN-like model. The accuracy of the DBN-like model is then evaluated to assess its effectiveness in detecting attacks, offering insights into the overall performance of the hybrid model in enhancing intrusion detection capabilities.

Algorithm: Hybrid RNN-DBN Pseudo code

```
R_train, S_train = X_train, y_train_one_hot
R_test, S_test = X_test, y_test_one_hot
num_classes = 9
num_features_lstm = 600
Train LSTM model on R_train with S_train
Predictions_lstm = argmax(LSTM model predictions on R_test)
LSTM_embeddings_train = LSTM model layer 1 output on R_train
LSTM_embeddings_test = LSTM model layer 1 output on R_test
DBN_input_train=concatenate([Scaled
R_train, LSTM_embeddings _train], axis=1)
DBN_input_test= concatenate([Scaled R_test,Reshaped LSTM_embed-
dings _test], axis=1)
num_features_DBN = 600
Train DBN-like model on DBN_input_train with S_train
Predictions_dbn = argmax(DBN-like model predictions on DBN_input_
test)
```

Evaluate the LSTM model using S_test and Predictions_lstm
Evaluate the DBN-like model using S_test and Predictions_dbn
Print combined accuracy, recall, precision, and F1-score metrics

13.4 Experiments and Results

The proposed framework uses the following hyperparameter shown in Table 13.6.

This table outlines the chosen hyperparameters for the model: 25 epochs for training, a combination of Sigmoid and SoftMax activation functions (Sigmoid for hidden layers, SoftMax for the output) [16], Adam optimizer [20] for efficient weight adjustments, 600 hidden units to capture complex data patterns, a batch size of 500 for faster training and dropout value are used for avoiding overfitting.

Table 13.6 Hyperparameter values.

Hyperparameters	**Values**
Epochs	25
Activation	Sigmoid, Softmax
Optimization	Adam
Hidden Units	600
Batch Size	500
Dropout value	0.2

Table 13.7 Performance of proposed model.

Model	**Hybrid RNN-DBN**
Accuracy	97.87%
Recall	97.87%
Precision	98.20%
F1-Score	97.96%

This experiment is performed on Google Collab, and the system's performance is greater than 96% in terms of accuracy with mentioned hyper-parameters in Table 13.6.

In Table 13.7, the proposed Hybrid RNN-DBN model shows strength with high performance across key metrics. Its exceptional accuracy of 97.87% demonstrates a remarkable ability to correctly classify instances. Furthermore, the model performs well at both capturing true positives (recall of 97.87%) and minimizing false positives (precision of 98.20%). The balanced F1-Score of 97.96% further underscores its overall performance and strength.

Figure 13.2 represents the evolution of both training and validation accuracy. This model improves its ability to correctly classify instances on the training data while simultaneously maintaining good performance on the validation set.

Table 13.8 demonstrates system performance for the following attacks: Backdoors, DoS, Analysis, Exploits, Generic, Reconnaissance, Fuzzers for Abnormal Activity, Shellcode, and Worms.

Figure 13.3 represents the decrease in loss, a measure of error, as the model optimizes its parameters through the epochs. A steady downward trend in loss suggests successful learning and convergence to a minimum error state.

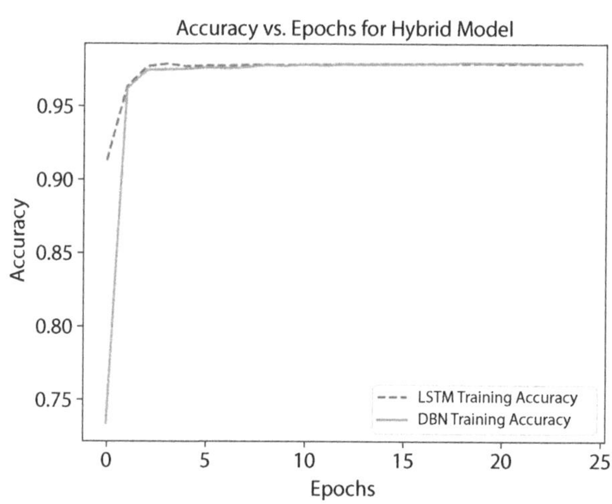

Figure 13.2 Accuracy and epochs on 25 epochs.

Table 13.8 Model Performance for different attacks.

Class	Precision	Recall	F1-Score	Support
Backdoor	0	0	0	2
DoS	1	1	1	143
Exploits	1	1	1	1059
Fuzzers	0.5	0.53	0.52	107
Generic	1	0.98	0.99	3692
Normal	1	1	1	1925
Reconnaissance	0.42	0.64	0.51	101
Worms	0	0	0	7
Accuracy			0.98	7036

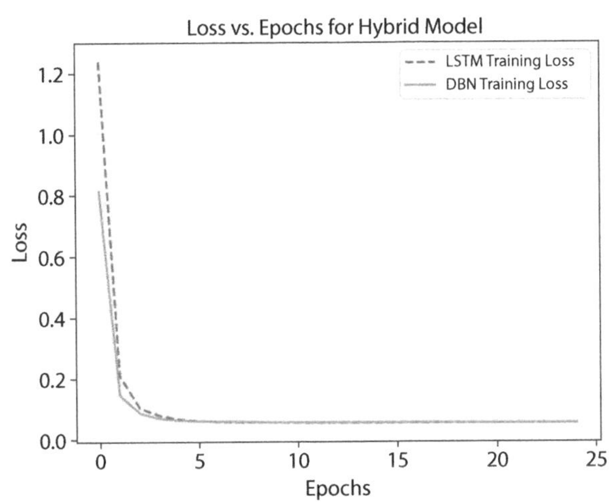

Figure 13.3 Loss and epochs on 25 epochs.

13.5 Conclusion and Future Scope

This paper discusses how the hybrid RNN-DBN model was developed and evaluated on the UNSW-NB15 dataset, with 80% of the data used for training and 20% for testing. The dataset was preprocessed using MinMax scaling for normalization. The model achieved an impressive accuracy exceeding 96%, effectively detecting various attacks such as Backdoors, DoS,Analysis, Exploits, Generic, Reconnaissance, Fuzzers for Abnormal Activity, Shellcode, and Worms. However, it faced challenges in accurately detecting Backdoors and Worms. Further investigation revealed that these specific attack types exhibited complex patterns that were difficult to capture accurately, leading to a lower detection rate compared to other attack categories.

For future work, enhancing the model's sensitivity to intricate patterns associated with Backdoors and Worms could be explored, possibly by fine-tuning the model architecture, experimenting with different feature representations, or employing advance techniques.

References

1. Kandhro, I.A., Alanazi, S.M., Ali, F., Kehar, A., Fatima, K., Uddin, M., Karuppayah, S., Detection of Real-Time Malicious Intrusions and Attacks in IoT Empowered Cybersecurity Infrastructures. *IEEE Access*, 11, 9136–9148, 2023.
2. Halbouni, A., Gunawan, T.S., Habaebi, M.H., Halbouni, M., Kartiwi, M., Ahmad, R., CNN-LSTM: hybrid deep neural network for network intrusion detection system. *IEEE Access*, 10, 99837–99849, 2022.
3. Kim, T. and Pak, W., Robust network intrusion detection system based on machine-learning with early classification. *IEEE Access*, 10, 10754–10767, 2022.
4. Azam, Z., Islam M.M., Huda, M.N., Comparative Analysis of Intrusion Detection Systems and Machine Learning-Based Model Analysis Through Decision Tree, in: *IEEE Access*, 11, pp. 80348–80391, 2023
5. Lansky, J., Ali, S., Mohammadi, M., Majeed, M.K., Karim, S.H.T., Rashidi, S., Rahmani, A.M., Deep learning-based intrusion detection systems: a systematic review. *IEEE Access*, 9, 101574–101599, 2021.
6. Deore, B. and Bhosale, S., Hybrid optimization enabled robust CNN-LSTM technique for network intrusion detection. *IEEE Access*, 10, 65611–65622, 2022.

7. Halbouni, A., Gunawan, T.S., Habaebi, M.H., Halbouni, M., Kartiwi, M., Ahmad, R., Machine learning and deep learning approaches for cybersecurity: A review. *IEEE Access*, 10, 19572–19585, 2022.
8. Wu, Z., Zhang, H., Wang, P., Sun, Z., RTIDS: A robust transformer-based approach for intrusion detection system. *IEEE Access*, 10, 64375–64387, 2022.
9. Dina, A.S., Siddique, A.B., Manivannan, D., Effect of balancing data using synthetic data on the performance of machine learning classifiers for intrusion detection in computer networks. *IEEE Access*, 10, 96731–96747, 2022.
10. Ullah, I. and Mahmoud, Q.H., Design and development of RNN anomaly detection model for IoT networks. *IEEE Access*, 10, 62722–62750, 2022.
11. Donkol, A.A.E.B., Hafez, A.G., Hussein, A.I., Mabrook, M.M., Optimization of Intrusion Detection Using Likely Point PSO and Enhanced LSTM-RNN Hybrid Technique in Communication Networks. *IEEE Access*, 11, 9469–9482, 2023.
12. Larriva-Novo, X., Sánchez-Zas, C., Villagrá, V.A., Vega-Barbas, M., Rivera, D., An approach for the application of a dynamic multi-class classifier for network intrusion detection systems. *Electronics*, 9, 11, 1759, 2020.
13. Maseer, Z.K., Yusof, R., Bahaman, N., Mostafa, S.A., Foozy, C.F.M., Benchmarking of Machine Learning for Anomaly Based Intrusion Detection Systems in the CICIDS2017 Dataset, in: *IEEE Access*, 9, pp. 22351–22370, 2021
14. Park, C., Lee, J., Kim, Y., Park, J.G., Kim, H., Hong, D., An enhanced ai-based network intrusion detection system using generative adversarial networks. *IEEE Internet Things J.*, 10, 3, 2330–2345, 2022.
15. Soltani, M., Ousat, B., Siavoshani, M.J., Jahangir, A.H., An adaptable deep learning-based Intrusion Detection System to zero-day attacks. *J. Inf. Secur. Appl.*, 76, 103516, 2023.
16. Süzen, A.A., Developing a multi-level intrusion detection system using hybrid-DBN. *J. Ambient Intell. Hum. Comput.*, 12, 2, 1913–1923, 2021.
17. Zavrak, S. and İskefiyeli, M., Anomaly-based intrusion detection from network flow features using variational autoencoder. *IEEE Access*, 8, 108346–108358, 2020.
18. Al-Daweri, M.S., Zainol Ariffin, K.A., Abdullah, S., Md. Senan, M.F.E., An analysis of the KDD99 and UNSW-NB15 datasets for the intrusion detection system. *Symmetry*, 12, 10, 1666, 2020.
19. Umar, M.A., Zhanfang, C., Liu, Y., Network intrusion detection using wrapper-based decision tree for feature selection, in: *Proceedings of the 2020 International Conference on Internet Computing for Science and Engineering*, pp. 5–13, 2020, January.
20. Awad, A.A., Ali, A.F., Gaber, T., An improved long short term memory network for intrusion detection. *PLoS One*, 18, 8, e0284795, 2023. Clerk Maxwell, J., *A Treatise on Electricity and Magnetism*, 3rd ed., vol. 2, pp. 68–73, Clarendon, Oxford, 1892.

14

Identification of Foliar Pathologies in Apple Foliage Utilizing Advanced Deep Learning Techniques

Tamal Kumar Kundu[1]*, Smritilekha Das[1] and R. Nidhya[2]

[1]*Department of Computer Science and Engineering, Koneru Lakshmaiah Education Foundation, Guntur, India*

[2]*Department of Computer Science and Engineering, Madanapalle Institute of Technology & Science, Madanapalle, Andhra Pradesh, India*

Abstract

The integration of generative artificial intelligence (AI) in plant pathology represents a revolutionary approach to addressing the challenges associated with foliar diseases in apple trees. The complex nature of diagnosing these diseases, coupled with the potential for significant agricultural losses, underscores the need for innovative and efficient solutions. Generative AI can play a pivotal role in automating the process of disease detection and diagnosis, mitigating the limitations of traditional methodologies. By leveraging generative models, we aim to enhance the accuracy and speed of identification, ultimately contributing to the overall health and productivity of apple crops.

Our approach involves harnessing the power of Generative Adversarial Networks (GANs) to generate synthetic images that simulate various manifestations of foliar diseases on apple leaves. This synthetic dataset, combined with existing real-world data, forms a comprehensive training set for our deep learning models. The generative models allow us to create diverse and realistic representations of foliar diseases, even in the absence of clear visual patterns. This addresses the challenge of diagnosing diseases without evident fungal fruiting bodies, reducing the risk of spread to neighbouring crops. Moreover, the inclusion of both biotic and abiotic factors in the generative dataset ensures a holistic approach to disease simulation. The core of our system involves the implementation of advanced generative algorithms to augment traditional machine-learning

**Corresponding author*: kundutamal007@gmail.com

R. Nidhya, D. Pavithra, Manish Kumar, A. Dinesh Kumar and S. Balamurugan (eds.) Generative Artificial Intelligence: Concepts and Applications, (227–248) © 2025 Scrivener Publishing LLC

techniques. By combining generative models with Convolutional Neural Networks (CNNs), VGG-16, ResNet50, and Support Vector Machines (SVM), we aim to achieve unparalleled accuracy in disease classification. Through the use of generative AI, our methodology not only minimizes human error but also significantly accelerates the process of disease identification. The ability to simulate a wide range of disease scenarios empowers our models to adapt to evolving threats and ensures robust performance in diverse agricultural environments. In conclusion, the integration of generative AI in disease detection for apple trees represents a cutting-edge solution to enhance accuracy, efficiency, and overall agricultural productivity. By revolutionizing the way we approach foliar disease identification, we contribute to the sustainable management of apple orchards and, consequently, the broader national economy.

Keywords: Apple leaf disease, machine learning, deep learning, detection of leaf disease

14.1 Introduction

In our quest to revolutionize the identification of foliar diseases in apple trees, we turn to the power of generative artificial intelligence (AI) to overcome existing challenges and empower farmers with advanced tools for crop management. Our approach integrates cutting-edge technologies to address the complexity of diagnosing crop ailments and provides a proactive solution to enhance food quality and reduce production costs. Generative adversarial networks (GANs) form the cornerstone of our initiative, enabling us to train apple leaves to distinguish between various states of health, rust infestations, scab infections, and instances of multiple diseases. By leveraging generative AI, we create a diverse and comprehensive dataset that simulates realistic scenarios, encompassing the complexities of crop health in different lighting conditions. China, with its rich agricultural history spanning over 2,000 years, serves as a focal point for our study, given its dominance in global apple production. Orchards in China have witnessed significant modernization, aligning with national economic policies. However, disease prevention and control continue to challenge farmers, prompting our initiative to bridge the gap between traditional knowledge and advanced technologies. Our plant pathology study employs a meticulously labeled dataset comprising 1821 training images of apple tree leaves, systematically classified into four categories: "healthy," "scab," "rust," and "multiple diseases." This dataset, enhanced by generative AI, becomes a powerful tool for training machine learning models to discern and understand various diseases affecting apple trees. The automated detection system we propose serves a dual purpose: it allows for real-time scrutiny of apple health during production and empowers orchard farmers with accurate disease discernment. Leaves, being easily accessible for observation and management, play a crucial role as a reference for disease identification. Despite the intricacies posed by blade vein complexity, our generative AI-driven automated disease detection remains indispensable for ensuring orchard health and maximizing economic benefits. By fusing generative AI with advanced machine learning techniques, our initiative not only addresses the challenges of misdiagnosis and visual expert costs but also provides a scalable and efficient solution for orchard farmers. As we navigate the complexities of plant pathology, we envision a future where generative AI transforms the landscape of crop disease identification, contributing to sustainable agriculture and economic prosperity.

14.2 Literature Survey

14.2.1 Disease Detection Using Machine and Deep Learning Techniques (2015–2021)

In times of yore, adept specialists utilized ocular scrutiny for the identification of botanical maladies. Nevertheless, owing to the inherent subjectivity of perception, the effectiveness and precision of disease recognition may exhibit considerable variance. In truth, executing the procedure in its entirety proves to be arduous. This is predominantly attributable to the considerable labor required for scrutinizing the foliage of a lone apple tree, a task only feasible by experts with specialized training. Furthermore, the scrutiny process is marked by capriciousness, given the propensity of professionals to experience fatigue. Consequently, there exists a need for the substitution of the conventional method of inspecting apple leaf diseases with stable, economical, and highly efficient precision methodologies. Given the recent noteworthy advancements in deep learning, it presents itself as a viable candidate for fulfilling this purpose.

Presently, the task of scrutinizing apple leaf diseases predominantly falls within the purview of adept professionals. The meticulous examination of individual apple leaves is incumbent upon this process. However, this undertaking is, in essence, insurmountable. The sheer abundance of leaves on a singular apple tree surpasses the human capacity for enumeration. Consequently, experts can only extend their scrutiny to a minute fraction of the apple trees within a given harvest. Predicating the identification of apple leaf diseases solely upon the scant number of sampled assessments necessitates reliance on the experiential acumen of these specialists. The resultant prognostication, rooted in this diminutive sampling, yields an inherently mercurial outcome. Moreover, the onus of detecting apple leaf diseases is born by a minute cohort of professionals, imposing an onerous burden upon them. In their state of fatigue, the evaluation of apple leaf maladies becomes susceptible to inaccuracies. The identification of diseases afflicting apple leaves poses a formidable challenge, prompting the dedicated efforts of numerous researchers endeavoring to devise diverse solutions. Their scholarly pursuits stand as a wellspring of inspiration for those seeking to tackle a similar quandary employing unique methodologies. This segment delves into the extensive body of research dedicated to the classification of leaf diseases, shedding light on recent and consequential findings. In conclusion, it has been ascertained that each method exhibited a commendable level of precision in discerning the presence of disease in apple leaves.

Padol *et al.* (2016) [1] employ a fusion classifier comprising SVM and ANN, achieving 100% accuracy in detecting downy and powdery mildew grape leaf diseases. However, the limited training and test data (137 images) raise concerns about overfitting. Departing from Johannes *et al.*'s (2017) [2] utilization of conventional machine learning algorithms, Picon *et al.* opted for a DCNN approach, employing ResNet50 for the early-stage detection of wheat leaf diseases. This strategic choice enables users to promptly respond and plan preventive measures. However, Ramesh *et al.* [3] (2018) utilizes a random forest algorithm for plant leaf disease detection, achieving 70% accuracy with a histogram of oriented gradient features. The introduction of additional local and global features like SIFT and SURF could potentially enhance accuracy. Wahab *et al.* [4] (2019) utilize SVM for classification and k-means clustering for image segmentation in identifying diseases of chili plant leaves. While accurate in determining healthy sections, accuracy drops to 57.1% when categorizing images of cucumber mosaic disease. Training with more affected plant images is recommended for improvement. rendering it redundant and time-consuming. In the realm of deep convolutional neural networks, Pandian *et al.* [5] (2019) discuss a nine-layer model covering six image enhancement techniques. For banana leaf diseases, Aruraj *et al.* [6] (2019) utilize local binary patterns with cubic SVM and refined KNN classifiers, achieving 89–90% accuracy. They suggest further improvement by extracting various texture and color features from images. Sethy *et al.* [7] (2019) employ multiclass SVM with particle swarm optimization for detecting and identifying rice leaf diseases. Gray level co-occurrence matrix (GLCM) is used for feature extraction, outperforming KNN and feed forward neural networks. In the context of tomato plant disease detection, Govardhan *et al.* [8] (2019) develop and evaluate multiple machine learning algorithms via k-fold cross-validation. Notably, SVM performs poorly (22.3%), while random forest outperforms other algorithms, contradicting the findings of other studies that favor SVM for leaf disease identification. In 2019, Picon *et al.* and their research team devised a crop protection application aimed at overcoming the limitations inherent in Johannes *et al.*'s work. Johannes' study utilized a restricted dataset comprising a mere 179 images depicting wheat diseases, a scope deemed insufficient by Picon *et al.* [9] Subsequently, Picon *et al.* rectified this limitation by expanding the dataset to encompass 3637 images. This augmentation proved instrumental in enhancing the efficacy of training the deep learning model compared to the antecedent methodology. They employ dropout to combat overfitting and apply batch gradient descent optimization, which could be refined by transitioning to Adam or Stochastic gradient descent (SGD) optimizers. Notably, despite the successful classification of grape leaf disease by Kamal *et al.* in [10] 2020 using CNN on a 1000-image dataset, challenges persist. For instance, when detecting tomato target spot disease, the system occasionally falters in achieving high confidence levels due to background noise in images. The integration of a dropout function aimed at mitigating overfitting issues is acknowledged, yet it is suggested that CNN might perform more effectively on extensive datasets. The authors' lack of comprehensive details regarding the CNN model, such as activation function and optimizer usage, implies that the model architecture may not have been rigorously adhered to in a controlled manner. Guo *et al.* [11] (2020) present a novel mathematical model for plant disease detection and recognition via deep learning, incorporating transfer learning (VGG-16) and the Chan–Vese segmentation algorithm. Despite achieving results, the Chan–Vese algorithm's time-intensive iterative calculations hinder rapid identification. To expedite training, the authors may have employed a neural network for generating a zero initial set corresponding to different leaves.

In 2021, the scholars Ahmed *et al.* [12] successfully addressed a multi-class classification issue by devising a three-tiered mobile-based architecture. This architecture incorporated a dataset comprising 96,206 images illustrating 38 prevalent plant disease categories across 14 crop species, encompassing both healthy and infected plants. The employed CNN model featured three layers: the intermediate representation model in Layer 1, the application layer in Layer 2, and the user layer in Layer 3. It is noteworthy that the authors could have enhanced the performance of Layer 1 by opting for superior activation functions like Tanh or ReLu instead of the log sigmoid function. The latter, due to its potential to cause neural network entrapment during model training, poses a significant drawback. Another issue highlighted is the Sigmoid function's saturation, leading to gradient elimination. Furthermore, Karnik *et al.* [13] (2021) adopt a two-step classification approach for pepper, potato, and tomato leaves, involving YOLO v3 and ResNet50 classifiers. Lakshmanarao *et al.* [14] (2021) claim an absence of overfitting without providing a compelling explanation or evidence. Jiang *et al.* [15] (2021) introduced an intricate network structure denoted as MobInc-Net, strategically devised for crop disease recognition and detection. The innovation lies in the refinement of the Inception module, where the conventional convolutions are substituted with depth-wise and point-wise convolutions. This alteration, referred to as the modified inception (M-Inception) M-module, is synergistically coupled with a pre-trained mobile net to effectively extract high-caliber from images. To facilitate precise classification and detection of various crop disease types, a fully interconnected SoftMax layer is incorporated, aligning with the specific number of categories. Subsequently, an SSD block is introduced to further refine the classification and detection process. Noteworthy is the tailored nature of this architecture, evidently crafted with a focus on the exigencies of crop disease recognition and detection. A notable characteristic of MobInc-Net is its adaptability for deployment on devices with limited computational resources. This adaptability is attributed to the incorporation of lightweight modules within the architecture, suggesting a potential suitability for implementation on resource-constrained devices.

14.2.2 Disease Detection Using Transfer Learning (2015–2021)

Ramcharan *et al.*'s [16] (2017) research challenges the notion that transfer learning alone is the most accurate algorithm for identifying cassava diseases. For cassava mosaic disease and red mite damage, SVM outperforms Inception v3 using both the original dataset and a leaflet dataset. Conversely, for cassava brown streak disease and green mite damage, Inception v3 surpasses support vector machines when utilizing the leaflet dataset. Discrepancies in disease classification arise when leaflets are employed instead of whole leaves. In the realm of citrus leaf disease detection in 2020, Luaibi *et al.* [17] employed and compared the CNN transfer learning architectures of AlexNet and ResNet. AlexNet demonstrated superior performance in terms of accuracy, with or without data augmentation, even without the application of optimization techniques. Andrushia *et al.* [18] (2020) introduced a method for discerning and categorizing maladies afflicting grape leaves, employing feature selection derived from the artificial bee colony (ABC) algorithm. In contrast, ResNet employed the SGD optimization technique but failed to outperform AlexNet. Interestingly, a

DCT image compression technique used as input for the ResNet50 algorithm yielded identical results to using the original image dataset. The advantage of working with small-sized images lies in the reduction of storage and computation costs, as highlighted by Sharma *et al.* [19] in 2021. Tunio *et al.*'s [20] (2021) approach to rice leaf disease detection involves a hybrid DCNN methodology. A distinctive addition to the existing literature is their utilization of the geometric transformation technique in data pre-processing. Despite innovative approaches, the authors encountered challenges related to overfitting and underfitting due to limited data, impacting the overall accuracy of the model. Hossain *et al.* [21] (2021) posited a scheme for the identification of plant leaf diseases through the utilization of models grounded in depth-wise separable convolution. Paymode *et al.* [22] (2022) postulated a methodology involving CNN techniques to discern instances of multi-crops leaf disease. Employing a deep learning-based model for feature extraction from images facilitated the classification of diseased and healthy leaves. The utilization of the CNN-based visual geometry group (VGG) model was implemented to enhance performance metrics. Here Table 14.1 below highlights the progress in detecting plant leaf diseases using sophisticated deep learning methodologies.

The number of parameters in deep learning models is a critical factor, as it contributes to the model's complexity, training time, and computational requirements. Larger models with more parameters often require more computing resources but may achieve better performance, especially on complex tasks and large datasets. It is important to choose a framework and model architecture based on the specific requirements. Table 14.2 enumerates various prominent deep learning frameworks alongside their respective parameter counts, which is shown below.

14.3 Different Diseases of Leaves

It is crucial to acknowledge that the severity of the symptoms mentioned may differ based on the disease stage and the general health of the apple tree. Detecting issues early on and implementing effective management practices, including pruning, utilizing disease-resistant varieties, and applying fungicides when needed, can significantly alleviate the impact of these diseases on apple trees.

Generative AI has proven instrumental in providing detailed descriptions. A vibrant green hue, indicative of robust chlorophyll levels and overall plant well-being, characterizes optimal apple leaf health. The surface of a healthy leaf is consistently smooth, with a uniform texture, devoid of any unusual spots,

Table 14.1 Advancements in plant leaf disease detection through complex deep learning approaches.

Techniques name	Author	Year	Method	Accuracy
Automatic Wheat Plant Disease Diagnosis using Mobile Capture Devices	Johannes *et al.* [2]	2017	Image processing with Naïve-Bayesian segmentation	80.00%
Deep Learning for Image-Based Cassava Disease Detection	Ramcharan *et al.* [16]	2017	Inception v3 with SVM and KNN	73%-91%
Reduced and modified Mobile Net	Kamal *et al.* [10]	2019	Depth-wise separable CNN	98.34%
Nine-Layer DCNN for Plant Leaf Disease Identification	Geetharamani *et al.* [5]	2019	Layered DCNN including various augmentation	96.46%
Grape Leaf Disease Identification	Andrushia *et al.* [18]	2020	Artificial bee colony optimization	93.01%
Smart Farming: Deep Learning Algorithm for Plant Disease Identification	Guo *et al.* [11]	2020	Segmentation (Chan -Vese) with VGG 16	83.57%
Citrus Leaf Disease Detection via Deep Learning Techniques	Luaibi *et al.* [17]	2021	AlexNet including ResNet	95.83% & 97.92%
Agricultural Plant Leaf Disease Detection Using Two-Stage Classifier	Karnik *et al.* [13]	2021	YOLO v3 & ResNet	94.00%

(Continued)

Table 14.1 Advancements in plant leaf disease detection through complex deep learning approaches. (*Continued*)

Techniques name	Author	Year	Method	Accuracy
Direct JPEG Compressed Domain Detection of Plant Leaf Disease Using Transfer Learning	Sharma *et al.* [19]	2021	Image compression with ResNet 50	98.94%
Mobile-Based Plant Leaf Disease Detection System	Ahmed *et al.* [12]	2021	CNN	94.00%
Custom CNN architecture	Hossian *et al.* [21]	2021	Depth-wise separable CNN	97.82%

Table 14.2 Several renowned deep learning frameworks and their corresponding parameter quantities.

Deep learning architecture	Parameter number
VGG 16	133–144M
Inception	132M
Efficient Net- B7	66M
AlexNet	60M
Xception	22.8M
EfficientNet-B0	5.3M
Mobile Net V1	4.2M
Mobile Net V2	3.4M

discolorations, or irregularities. These leaves maintain their distinctive shapes, which can vary among apple varieties but generally exhibit an elliptical or ovate form with serrated edges. Symmetry is a common trait in healthy leaves, and any deviation from this may signal a developmental concern. Furthermore, healthy leaves retain their normal size, with no significant reduction observed.

14.4 Dataset

The inaugural dataset, identified as the plant pathology dataset, encapsulates 3,651 images taken within a United States apple orchard. Proficient assessors have stratified these images into four discrete categories: rust, scab, healthy, and multiple diseases. In this instance, Figure 14.1 illustrates the leaves in an unblemished state, while Figure 14.2 presents exemplar images of apple leaves afflicted by various pathological conditions The images contained in this dataset manifest disparities in angles, illumination, and background, alongside heterogeneous shapes and sizes, thus endowing the dataset with intricacy and a close semblance to real-world conditions. Table 14.3 illustrates the disease nomenclature and their defining characteristics, accompanied by corresponding images which is shown below.

Figure 14.1 Healthy leaves.

Figure 14.2 Sample images of apple leaves.

Table 14.3 Disease names with their characteristics including images.

Disease name	Symptom	Color	Texture	Image
Scab	Dark, scaly lesions on the upper surface of the leaves. The lesions may coalesce, leading to defoliation in severe cases.	Dark brown to black spots	Lesions may have a rough texture	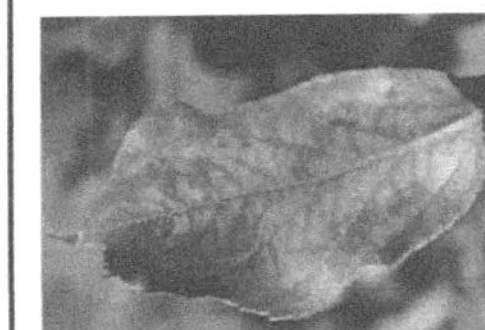
Powdery Mildew	White powdery substance on the upper surface of leaves, which can inhibit photosynthesis and stunt plant growth.	White or light grey patches	Powdery or dusty appearance	
Fire Blight	Wilting, blackening, and a "burned" appearance of leaves and branches. Can progress rapidly through the tree.	Blackened, scorched appearance on leaves and branches	Affected areas may have a slimy texture	

(*Continued*)

Table 14.3 Disease names with their characteristics including images. (*Continued*)

Disease name	Symptom	Color	Texture	Image
Cedar Rust	Rust-colored spots on the upper surface of leaves. May also affect fruit and other parts of the tree.	Rust-colored lesions with a yellow halo	Raised pustules on the underside of leaves	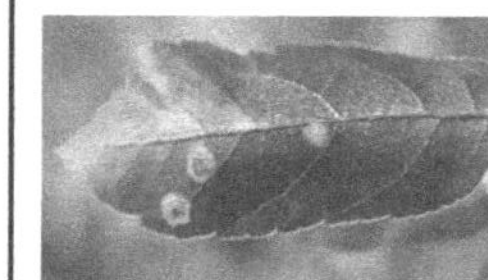
Leaf Spot	Circular or angular dark spots on the leaves, leading to premature leaf drop.	Dark brown to black spots	Lesions may have a defined border	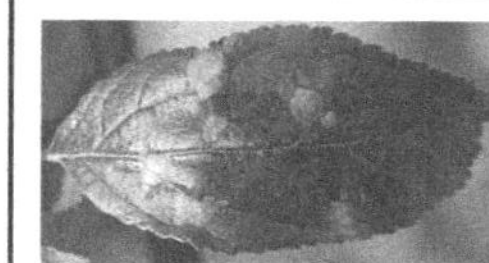
Tree Anthracnose	Irregular, dark lesions on leaves that can coalesce and cause leaf distortion.	Dark brown to black irregular lesions	Lesions may have a sunken appearance	

14.5 Proposed Methodology

In the domain of image classification, the ascendancy of CNN-based deep learning models is evident, eclipsing the conventional multilayer perceptron (MLP). The CNN, an ingenious creation within CNNs, establishes itself as the predominant methodology for extracting pivotal features from expansive datasets. Given the frequently substantial size of image datasets, the astute application of convolutional layers strategically reduces image dimensions, thereby alleviating computational burdens. The inherent elegance of weight sharing, synonymous with parameter sharing, in CNNs manifests through the utilization of filters (or kernels).

The incorporation of pooling introduces an additional layer of sophistication, achieving a noteworthy level of location invariance. Deviating from the customary approach embodied by MLPs, CNNs eschew the flattening of input images, opting instead for filters that skillfully unravel patterns within the intricate tapestry of image data. This nuanced approach enables CNNs to adeptly harness spatial information, reflecting the ingenuity embedded in the design of our bespoke CNN model. The model's pathway retains the vibrant spectrum of red-green-blue (RGB), rejecting the grayscale monotony found in conventional input images. The architectural composition unfurls with a symphony of diverse layers, commencing its melody with the sequential layer. It embarks on a rhythmic journey through convolutional strata, cascading through additional aggregative harmonies and activation orchestrations. The crescendo arrives at a dense layer, its filters tuned to a quartet, delicately extracting the melodic nuances within the dataset—be they scab, rust, the vitality of

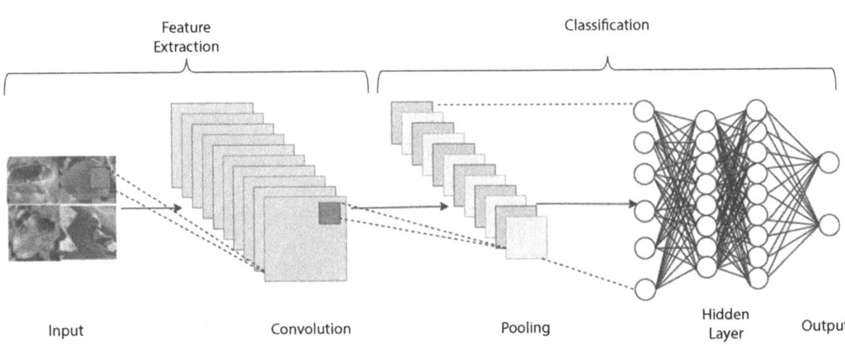

Figure 14.3 Proposed methodology.

health, or the intricate harmonies of multiple afflictions. Within the convolutional realm, a virtuoso performance of the convolution operation takes center stage, teasing out distinctive features that resonate through the layers. This musical progression finds its harmony in an encore layer, where the ReLu activation function steps into the spotlight. The choice of ReLu is not merely a note in passing; it is a deliberate composition, a crescendo of performance, harmonizing with superior finesse when compared to its alternative counterparts. Figure 14.3 shows the stage by stage steps involved in proposed methodology.

14.6 Data Analysis

From the antecedent graphical representation, discernment arises as follows:

- A noteworthy 70.7% of the images within the TRAIN subset manifest pathogenic conditions, while a mere 5.75% of the same subset exhibits the presence of multiple afflictions.
- A minority, constituting merely 29.3% of the entire dataset, is characterized by an absence of infection or the complete absence of maladies.
- Notably, within the dataset, there exists a near-equivalence in the quantities of both infected and uninfected instances of rust and scab.

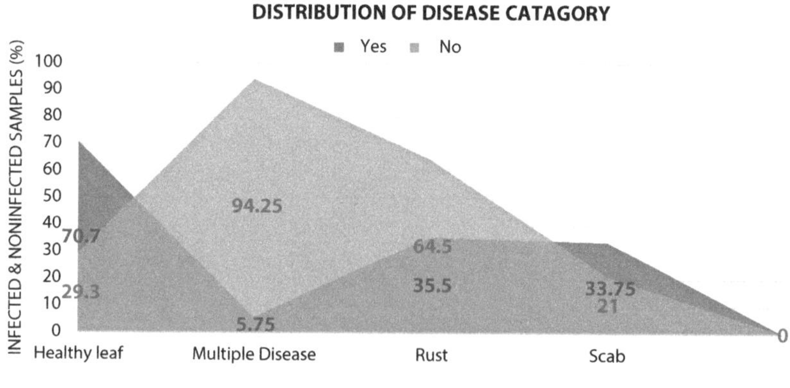

14.7 Pre-Processing Technique

Data preprocessing stands as a crucial prerequisite, focusing on eliminating undesirable disturbances and deviations from the dataset that may divert the model from its intended training trajectory. This phase thoroughly addresses obstacles that could impede the model's effectiveness. Once a relevant dataset is assembled, careful cleansing and preparation of the data become essential for subsequent model development. Within the dataset consisting of 3642 images, the identification of duplicate images has been observed, revealing a semblance of similarity. Here in Figure 14.4 shows the original image with the preprocessed image in cases where the dataset contains images of varying dimensions, resizing them to a standardized format becomes mandatory. This is particularly important as larger images require an increased number of trainable parameters, leading to heightened computational demands. Therefore, in situations with limited computing capabilities, reducing image dimensions becomes a significant strategy. The choice of resizing dimensions requires careful consideration to preserve information while avoiding an undue imposition of parameters that could result in prolonged training periods and resource exhaust errors. In the specific case under examination, the images were resized to dimensions (224, 224), yielding commendable outcomes. Label encoding, an integral part of data preparation, transforms string literals within the dataset into intelligible integer values, aligning with the computer's preference for numerical input. Given the computer's inclination towards numerical data, the conversion of strings to integers becomes imperative. The dataset in question comprises five columns with a string data type. Through the label encoding process, all textual representations are translated into numerical equivalents, effecting a comprehensive transformation of the dataset into a numerical ensemble. Notably, the dataset designated for stroke prediction exhibits a marked imbalance, indicating a significant incongruity in the distribution of target classes.

Figure 14.4 Data preprocessing.

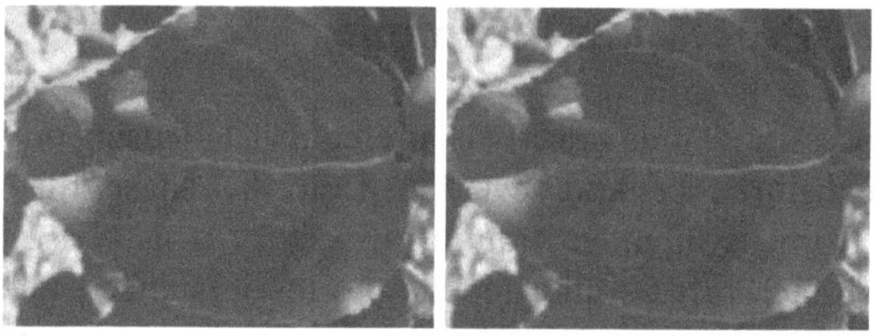

Figure 14.5 Converted RGB image to grayscale.

14.8 Data Visualization

Data visualizations play a pivotal role as indispensable tools in the quest to unveil concealed truths and discern emerging trends. These visual representations take on diverse formats, such as line charts adept at depicting temporal fluctuations. Bar and column charts, on the other hand, prove invaluable in scrutinizing interrelations and facilitating comparisons. When it comes to encapsulating the essence of constituent parts forming a whole, the pie chart emerges as a superlative choice. Geographical data, in turn, finds its most articulate expression through maps, elucidating spatial relationships in a visually cogent manner.

A meticulous examination of RGB channel values across all images unravels intriguing patterns. A cursory inspection hints at the RED channel values closely adhering to a normal distribution, exhibiting a bell-shaped curve. In contrast, scrutiny of the BLUE channel unveils a pronounced rightward skew, indicative of a heavy tail on the higher-value spectrum. The GREEN channel, in its distribution, features an elongated leftward tail, with overall values surpassing those observed in the other two channels. This nuanced analysis further attests that the BLUE channel's peak is not only broad but also flattened. Moreover, a discernible scarcity of images with extreme values is apparent, with most images in the RED and GREEN channels clustering around the mean. Here in Figure 14.5 shows the converted RGB image to gray scale image.

14.9 Evolutionary Progression and Genesis of Model

Generative AI has seen CNN-based deep learning models rise to prominence as the preferred choice for image classification tasks, outpacing MLP

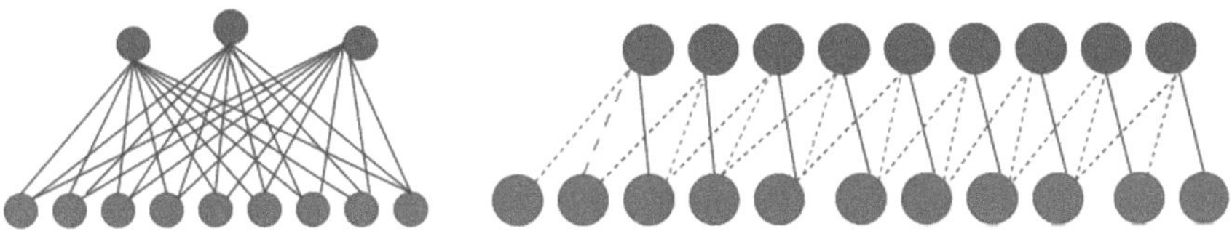

Figure 14.6 Differentiate fully connected and convolution layer.

approaches. A hallmark of CNNs lies in their utilization of weight sharing, or parameter sharing, facilitated by filters (kernels).

Moreover, CNNs incorporate pooling techniques to attain location invariance. In stark contrast to MLPs, CNNs refrain from flattening input images, relying instead on filters to discern patterns in image data. This distinctive approach empowers CNNs to adeptly exploit spatial information, contributing significantly to their effectiveness in tasks related to images. The adoption of CNN models proves advantageous, given their development through extensive research and training using high-end processors. Consequently, these models consistently yield impressive results across various scenarios. In Figure 14.6 presented above, a thorough distinction between fully connected layers and convolution layers is illustrated.

14.9.1 Evolution Model

The component responsible for model evolution is an integral part of a CNN system, assigned the task of utilizing the trained model to generate predictions for new data instances.

In the context of identifying foliar diseases in apple leaves through deep learning, images are categorized into distinct diseases such as healthy, multiple diseases, rust, and scab. The intricately designed model evolution module aims to produce a probability indicating the presence or absence of disease in apple leaves. It is crucial to acknowledge that the precise output from the model evolution module relies on the specific architecture of the CNN system and aligns with the project's defined objectives. Noteworthy is the fact that the accuracy of the prediction module is contingent on both the quality and quantity of data used for model training, as well as the model's proficiency in generalizing to new instances. The execution of the model evolution module within the realm of deep learning focused on detecting foliar diseases in apple leaves entails a series of intricate steps, employing advanced deep learning techniques. Figure 14.7 delineates the architectural framework of the proposed model as illustrated below.

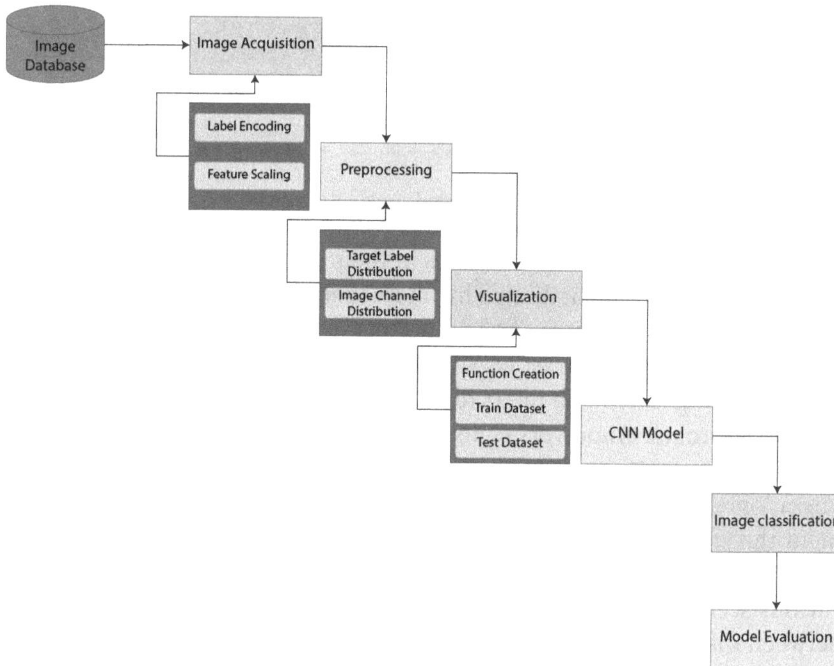

Figure 14.7 Proposed model architecture.

14.9.2 Model Performance

The evolution module within the comprehensive deep learning pipeline represents the culminating stage, encompassing phases such as data acquisition, preprocessing, training, and validation. This module harnesses the model trained through the preceding steps to make predictions when confronted with novel data. The availability of data for model construction is contingent upon prior processing. Constructing the model requires both a preprocessed dataset and the utilization of CNNs. Here it shows the dispersion of the RGB channel in Figure 14.8.

The following elucidation presents the block diagram of the envisioned system. A significant challenge in this scenario arises from the scarcity or minimal proportion of instances involving leaves affected by multiple diseases, in stark contrast to other categories. Here in Figure 14.9 delineates the predicted result of multiple disease of apple leaves. This results in a pronounced issue of substantial class imbalance. Consequently, using 'accuracy' as a metric would be ill-suited for assessing the effectiveness of deep learning models. As an imperative initial step, it becomes crucial to construct a visual representation of the confusion matrix. Subsequently, a

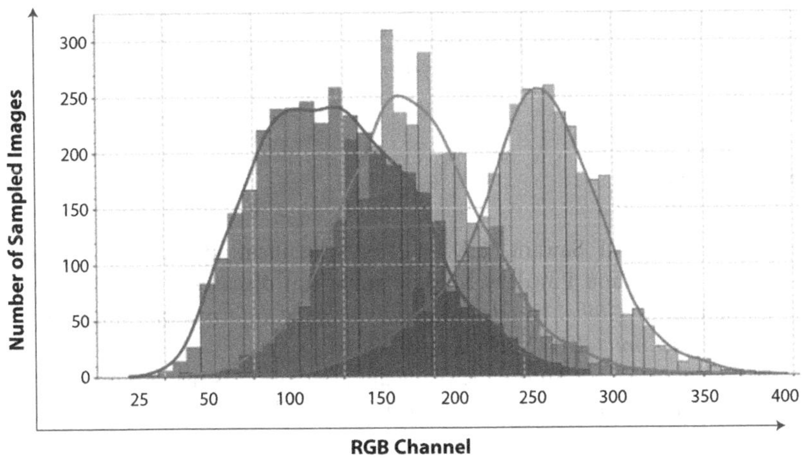

Figure 14.8 Dispersion of RGB channels.

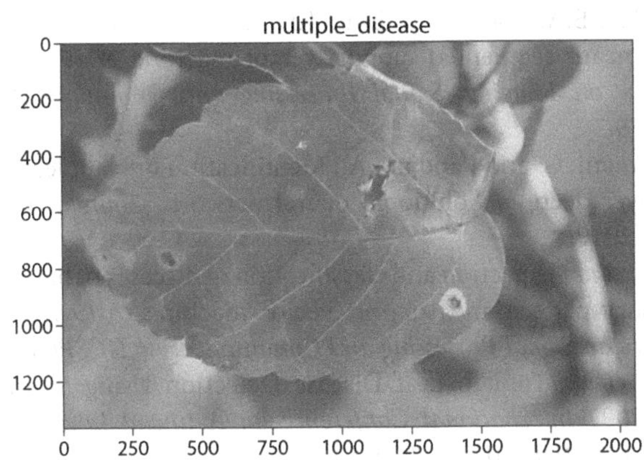

Figure 14.9 Predicted result of multiple disease.

meticulous examination of misclassifications, indicated by false positives (FP) and false negatives (FN), is imperative. In this context, FN signifies instances where the model erroneously predicts healthy leaves, which are, in reality, afflicted with ailments. Conversely, FP designates instances where the model incorrectly identifies leaves as diseased when, in fact, they are healthy.

$$Recall = \frac{TP}{TP + FN} \qquad Precision = \frac{TP}{TP + FP}$$

$$F1\ Score = 2 * \frac{Precision * Recall}{Precision + Recall}$$

References

1. Padol, P.B. and Sawant, S.D., Fusion classification technique used to detect downy and Powdery Mildew grape leaf diseases. *2016 International Conference on Global Trends in Signal Processing, Information Computing and Communication (ICGTSPICC)*, IEEE, 2016.
2. Johannes, A. *et al.*, Automatic plant disease diagnosis using mobile capture devices, applied on a wheat use case. *Comput. Electron. Agric.*, 138, 200–209, 2017.
3. Ramesh, S. *et al.*, Plant disease detection using machine learning. *2018 International conference on design innovations for 3Cs compute communicate control (ICDI3C)*, IEEE, 2018.
4. Wahab, A.H.B.A., Zahari, R., Lim, T.H., Detecting diseases in chilli plants using K-means segmented support vector machine. *2019 3rd International Conference on Imaging, Signal Processing and Communication (ICISPC)*, IEEE, 2019.
5. Geetharamani, G. and Pandian, A., Identification of plant leaf diseases using a nine-layer deep convolutional neural network. *Comput. Electr. Eng.*, 76, 323–338, 2019.
6. Aruraj, A. *et al.*, Detection and classification of diseases of banana plant using local binary pattern and support vector machine. *2019 2nd International Conference on Signal Processing and Communication (ICSPC)*, IEEE, 2019.
7. Shetty, P. *et al.*, Tomato Leaf Disease Detection Using Multiple Classifier System. *2022 International Conference on Artificial Intelligence and Data Engineering (AIDE)*, IEEE, 2022.
8. Govardhan, M. and Veena, M.B., Diagnosis of tomato plant diseases using random forest. *2019 Global Conference for Advancement in Technology (GCAT)*, IEEE, 2019.
9. Picon, A. *et al.*, Deep convolutional neural networks for mobile capture device-based crop disease classification in the wild. *Comput. Electron. Agric.*, 161, 280–290, 2019.
10. Kamal, K.C. *et al.*, Depthwise separable convolution architectures for plant disease classification. *Comput. Electron. Agric.*, 165, 104948, 2019.
11. Guo, Y. *et al.*, Plant disease identification based on deep learning algorithm in smart farming. *Discrete Dyn. Nat. Soc.*, 2020, 1–11, 2020.
12. Ahmed, A.A. and Reddy, G.H., A mobile-based system for detecting plant leaf diseases using deep learning. *AgriEngineering*, 3, 3, 478–493, 2021.

13. Karnik, J. and Suthar, A., Agricultural Plant Leaf Disease Detection Using Deep Learning Techniques. *Proceedings of the 3rd International Conference on Communication & Information Processing (ICCIP)*, 2021.
14. Lakshmanarao, A., Raja Babu, M., Srinivasa Ravi Kiran, T., Plant disease prediction and classification using deep learning ConvNets. *2021 International Conference on Artificial Intelligence and Machine Vision (AIMV)*, IEEE, 2021.
15. Jiang, P. *et al.*, Real-time detection of apple leaf diseases using deep learning approach based on improved convolutional neural networks. *IEEE Access*, 7, 59069–59080, 2019.
16. Ramcharan, A. *et al.*, Deep learning for image-based cassava disease detection. *Front. Plant Sci.*, 8, 1852, 2017.
17. Luaibi, A.R., Salman, T.M., Miry, A.H., Detection of citrus leaf diseases using a deep learning technique. *Int. J. Electr. Comput. Eng.*, 11, 2, 1719, 2021.
18. Andrushia, A.D. and Trephena Patricia, A., Artificial bee colony optimization (ABC) for grape leaves disease detection. *Evol. Syst.*, 11, 105–117, 2020.
19. Sharma, A., Rajesh, B., Javed, M., Detection of Plant Leaf Disease Directly in the JPEG Compressed Domain using Transfer Learning Technique, in: *Advanced Machine Intelligence and Signal Processing*, pp. 407–418, Springer Nature Singapore, Singapore, 2022.
20. Tunio, M.H. *et al.*, Identification and classification of rice plant disease using hybrid transfer learning. *2021 18th International computer conference on wavelet active media technology and information processing (ICCWAMTIP)*, IEEE, 2021.
21. Hossain, S.M.M. *et al.*, Plant leaf disease recognition using depth-wise separable convolution-based models. *Symmetry*, 13, 3, 511, 2021.
22. Paymode, A.S. and Malode, V.B., Transfer learning for multi-crop leaf disease image classification using convolutional neural network VGG. *Artif. Intell. Agric.*, 6, 23–33, 2022.

15

Enhancing Cloud Security Through AI-Driven Intrusion Detection Utilizing Deep Learning Methods and Autoencoder Technology

P.V. Sivarambabu[1*], Richa Agrawal[2], Arepalli Tirumala[3], Shaik Mahaboob Subani[4], Veeraswamy Parisae[5] and S. V. L. Sowjanya Nukala[3]

[1]*Department of Computer Science and Engineering, Koneru Lakshmaiah Educational Foundation, Guntur, Andhra Pradesh, India*
[2]*Department of Electronics and Communication Engineering, National Institute of Technology Patna, Bihar, India*
[3]*Department of Electronics and Communication Engineering, SRM University AP, Mangalagiri, Andhra Pradesh India*
[4]*Department of Electronics and Communication Engineering, Potti Sriramulu Chalavadi Mallikarjunarao College of Engineering & Technology, Vijayawada, Andhra Pradesh, India*
[5]*Department of Electronics and Communication Engineering, NRIIT, Agiripalli, Vijayawada, India*

Abstract
As cloud environments become increasingly prevalent, securing sensitive information from security attacks has become a critical challenge. Intrusion detection systems (IDS) play a crucial role in safeguarding cloud networks and preserving data integrity. Traditional signature-based detection approaches have limitations in handling emerging attack variants, necessitating the adoption of deep learning techniques (DLT) for more robust cloud security. In this article, we propose an AI-based IDS using DLT, specifically an autoencoder (AE) as a feature extractor, an autoencoder is a type of artificial intelligence (AI) system. Cloud traffic attributes are transformed into essential features by the AE, capturing relevant patterns

**Corresponding author*: sivarambabu424@gmail.com

R. Nidhya, D. Pavithra, Manish Kumar, A. Dinesh Kumar and S. Balamurugan (eds.) Generative Artificial Intelligence: Concepts and Applications, (249–264) © 2025 Scrivener Publishing LLC

and behaviors. The features are subsequently categorized using three binary classifiers: convolutional neural network (CNN), recurrent neural network (RNN), and long short-term memory (LSTM). The evaluation is conducted on the CICIDS 2018 dataset, an actual real-time cloud attack dataset, to assess the performance of the suggested approach in comparison to established methods. The outcomes reveal the effectiveness of the proposed methodology, attaining accuracy rates of 98.55%, 94.33%, and 95.08% for AE coupled with CNN, RNN, and LSTM, respectively. These results outperform existing intrusion detection methods, highlighting the efficacy of DLT in securing cloud environments. This article underscores the significance of adopting DLT-based intrusion detection for cloud security. The proposed behavior-based approach provides enhanced protection against security threats, offering a valuable solution for organizations relying on cloud infrastructures. The findings emphasize the potential of DLT in advancing cloud security, adapting to evolving attack challenges, and maintaining data confidentiality in cloud environments.

***Keywords*:** Cloud security, intrusion detection system, auto-encoder, deep learning techniques, cloud traffic

15.1 Introduction

The swift expansion of cloud computing has transformed the manner in which both organizations and individuals handle and process data. The inherent benefits of scalability, cost-efficiency, and ubiquitous access have made cloud environments an integral part of modern computing infrastructure. However, this paradigm shift towards cloud-based services has also introduced a host of security challenges, accentuating the critical need for robust mechanisms to safeguard sensitive information from a spectrum of potential threats. Cloud environments are inherently dynamic and virtualized, enabling the efficient allocation of resources and flexible deployment of services [1]. This virtualization, while advantageous, introduces vulnerabilities that can be exploited by malicious actors. Intrusions into cloud systems can result in devastating consequences, ranging from data breaches and service disruptions to compromised user privacy. Therefore, ensuring the security and integrity of cloud environments has become a paramount concern for cloud service providers and users alike. Traditional security approaches, such as signature-based detection, have been the cornerstone of intrusion detection systems (IDS) for years. Nevertheless, these approaches inherently face constraints in effectively identifying novel and sophisticated attacks. As cyber threats evolve and become increasingly complex, the inadequacies of signature-based detection become more apparent.

Attackers can easily modify their techniques, rendering predefined signatures ineffective. To address this challenge, a paradigm shift in intrusion detection strategies is imperative [2].

In recent times, deep learning (DL) has emerged as a transformative influence across diverse domains, encompassing computer vision, natural language processing, and now, the realm of cyber security. Deep learning techniques, powered by neural networks with multiple layers, have demonstrated remarkable capabilities in learning intricate patterns and representations from vast and complex datasets. These capabilities position DL as a promising solution to enhance the accuracy and efficacy of intrusion detection systems in cloud environments. This research endeavors to contribute to the field of cloud security by proposing a novel intrusion detection framework founded on DL principles. The focal point of this approach is behavior-based analysis, which involves scrutinizing the behavior of entities within the cloud environment to discern normal patterns from anomalous activities. Unlike traditional signature-based methods, behavior-based analysis offers a more robust defense against zero-day attacks and evolving threats [3]. To achieve the objectives of this research, a deep autoencoder is employed as a feature extractor. Autoencoders are neural network architectures that can learn compressed representations of input data, thereby capturing essential features for subsequent analysis. The extracted features are then fed into three distinct classifiers: convolutional neural network (CNN), recurrent neural network (RNN), and long short-term memory (LSTM). This amalgamation of DL techniques aims to exploit the power of convolutional layers for spatial feature extraction, while leveraging the sequential memory capabilities of recurrent networks.

The empirical evaluation of the proposed IDS framework is performed using the CICIDS 2018 dataset, a comprehensive collection of real-world cloud attack scenarios. The evaluation of a performance is conducted using well-established metrics like the receiver operating characteristic (ROC) curve and the precision-recall curve. By comparing the results with existing intrusion detection techniques, the effectiveness and superiority of the proposed DL-based approach are quantitatively established [4–7].

15.2 Related Work

Ly Vu *et al.* [8], Information Technology Department, Le Quy Don Technical University, Hanoi, Vietnam. The method involves generating synthetic malicious samples through innovative deep generative models, improving cloud IDS accuracy for unknown attacks. Experimental results highlight substantial enhancement compared to baseline and state-of-the-art methods. Notably, the models effectively detect challenging DDoS attacks, including low-rate and application layer DDoS attacks.

Wenjuan Wang *et al.* [9], The SCAE extracts essential low-dimensional features from complex network traffic, enhancing detection. A novel intrusion detection system combining SCAE, and support vector machine is proposed, displaying improved performance compared to state-of-the-art methods on KDD Cup 99 and NSL-KDD.

M. Abdel-Basset *et al.* [10], Proposing deep-IFS, a distributed DL model for IIoT intrusion detection, utilize the local GRU for local representation and MHA for global dependencies. Scalable in fog computing, handling large IIoT traffic data. Empirical validation on Bot-IIoT dataset shows improved efficiency and robustness over centralized DL-based forensics methods.

P. Singh *et al.* [11], Deep learning-based classifier enhances filtration accuracy using deep belief networks. DaaS minimizes response time, achieves up to 95% classification accuracy, and reduces cloud server latency by 60% with a 35% workload decrease compared to edge IDS.

K. Sadaf and J. Sultana, [12], focused on real-time binary classification to distinguish attack from normal packets. Achieves a high accuracy rate of 95.4%, is the outperforming state-of-the-art intrusion detection techniques.

A. Bhardwaj *et al.* [13], Parameters tuning enhances detection accuracy, precision, recall, and F1-Score. Outperforms existing methods on NSL-KDD and demonstrates competitive results on CICIDS2017, addressing cloud security vulnerabilities.

F. Sattari *et al.* [14], Leveraging software-defined network (SDN) environment's programmable nature. Achieves remarkable accuracy of 99.98% in identifying complex bot attacks and exhibits efficient speed results with a time of 0.022 (ms). A robust approach against cyber threats, enhancing cloud security infrastructure.

R. Kumar *et al.* [15], Utilizes smart contracts and Zero Knowledge Proof for secure communication, while autoregressive-deep variation auto encoder and A-BLSTM enhance feature extraction and attack detection. Demonstrates superiority over baseline and state-of-the-art techniques through security analysis and experimental results on ToN-IoT and CICIDS-2017 datasets.

A. Makkar *et al.* [16], a cognitive intrusion security system for IoT edge devices, ensuring credible search engine results by filtering advertising images. The framework, spanning data collection, edge computing, and cloud services, employs DL algorithms to detect malicious images. Achieves a high accuracy of 98.77% on a real-time collected dataset.

A. Vinolia *et al.* [17], Investigates how DL and machine learning (ML) techniques are integrated across stages for improved outcomes. Discusses state-of-the-art intrusion detection using soft computing, data mining, and other approaches. Experimental results highlight unsupervised DL techniques achieving exceptional 99.95% accuracy.

15.3 Proposed Methodology

15.3.1 DL-Based IDS for Cloud Security

The system model comprises several interconnected components, each playing a vital role in detecting and classifying intrusions in a cloud environment. The overall architecture integrates DLT to enhance the accuracy and efficiency of IDS. The conceptual framework for the envisioned intrusion detection system tailored for cloud security represents a sophisticated amalgamation of DL methodologies, poised to elevate the precision and efficiency of intrusion detection. The model commences its operations with the intake of raw cloud traffic data, encompassing an array of attributes intrinsic to network traffic patterns within the cloud ecosystem as shown in Figure 15.1. This initial data flow is subject to a pivotal preprocessing phase, encompassing essential data normalization, transformative operations, and feature extraction processes. These preparatory steps ensure optimal compatibility with subsequent stages of analysis.

Central to the model architecture lies the intricate deep auto encoder, meticulously engineered to serve as a formidable feature extractor. Comprising a stratified arrangement of concealed layers, the deep auto encoder learns to intricately encode the incoming raw data into a compact, yet information-rich, representation. This process, marked by its capacity to discern complex patterns and glean crucial insights from the innate attributes of cloud traffic, stands as a critical precursor to robust intrusion detection. The ensuing extracted features have been meticulously distilled by the deep auto encoder; lay the groundwork for a synergistic ensemble of classifiers, each with its distinct cognitive prowess [18–20]. This triumvirate of classifiers namely, the CNN, RNN, and LSTM – converge harmoniously to scrutinize, analyze, and ultimately classify the distilled features. The CNN classifier, with its specialized convolutional and pooling layers, excels in deciphering intricate spatial relationships and patterns within the feature ensemble. In stark contrast, the RNN and LSTM classifiers leverage

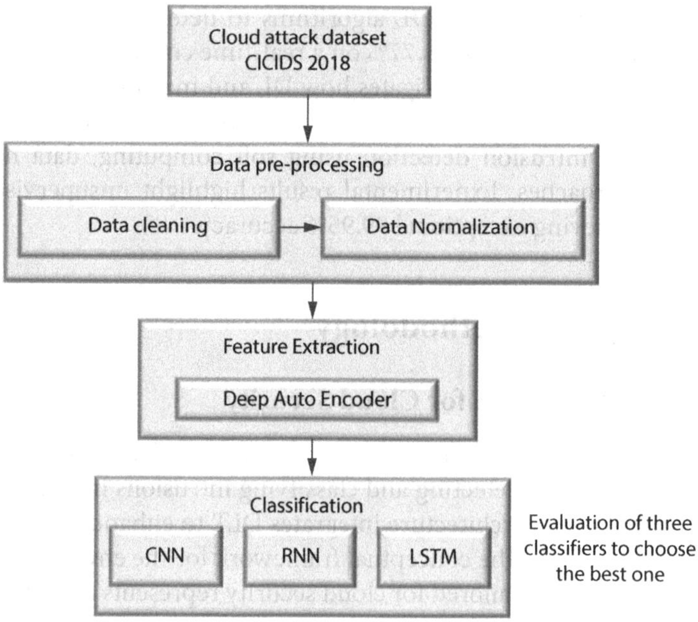

Figure 15.1 The operational sequence for the proposed DL classification model.

their sequential memory attributes to adeptly unravel temporal dependencies and evolving behavioral nuances encapsulated within the feature ensemble.

Concurrently, as the classifiers yield their respective outputs - each indicative of the discerned intrusion likelihood - these outputs converge toward a consensus, culminating in a definitive determination regarding the potential intrusion presence. The proposed framework's efficacy undergoes rigorous quantitative assessment, appraised through the prism of established performance metrics. Prominent among these are the ROC curve and the Precision-Recall curve, which collectively illuminate the system's proficiency in the nuanced task of detecting and classifying potential breaches within the intricate fabric of cloud traffic.

15.4 Results and Discussion

The proposed DL classification model holds notable importance in effectively categorizing distinct traffic stages into binary classes: benign and attack. Furthermore, the model's versatility extends to multiclass classification, encompassing categories such as Benign, Bot, DoS Attacks-Slow

HTTP Test, and DoS Attacks-Hulk. The evaluation of model performance entails a comprehensive analysis facilitated by the utilization of a confusion matrix. This matrix serves as a visual and summarizing tool, shedding light on the model's proficiency in classification. The interpretation of the confusion matrix is rooted in its comparison of actual and predicted labels, offering valuable insights into the model's classification accuracy and potential misclassifications.

Figures 15.2 to 15.4: Provides the confusion matrix for binary classification using the suggested DL methodologies, namely CNN, RNN, and LSTM. The matrix portrays the correspondence between true and predicted values, where rows signify true values and columns signify predicted values. Specifically, a value of 0 signifies benign instances, while a value of 1 indicates attack instances. This depiction pertains solely to binary classification, distinct from multiclass scenarios involving various attack types.

Figures 15.5 to 15.7 depict the ROC comparison of various classes concerning the proposed binary classifier methodologies. The proposed approach exhibits a heightened capacity to distinguish between the specified classes. The graph plots the false positive rate (FPR) against the true positive rate (TPR), estimating the ROC value. Among the binary classifiers, the CNN model showcases the most favorable performance, achieving a superior ROC value of 99.1%. This superiority is attributed to its improved ability in binary traffic classification based on input parameters. In comparison, the RNN and LSTM achieve ROC values of 70.3% and 91.5%, respectively. Notably, the gap between the ROC curves is

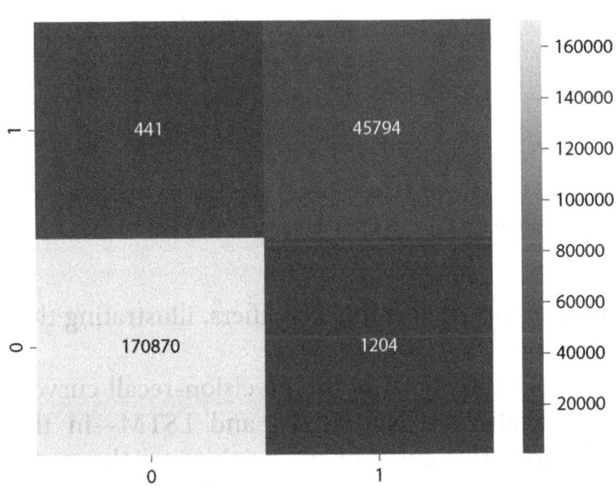

Figure 15.2 Confusion matrix for CNN binary.

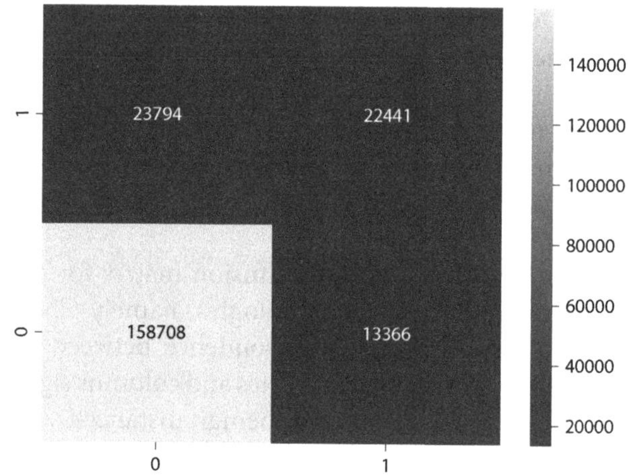

Figure 15.3 Confusion matrix for RNN binary.

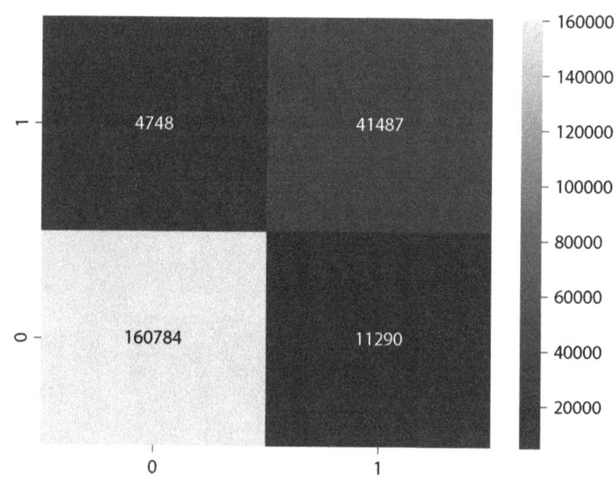

Figure 15.4 Confusion matrix for LSTM - binary.

maximized for the top-performing classifiers, illustrating their efficacy in binary classification.

Figures 15.8 to 15.10 visualize the precision-recall curve for the three proposed DL classifiers—CNN, RNN, and LSTM—in the context of binary classification. This curve offers insights into the trade-off between precision and recall, acting as a metric for classification accuracy across

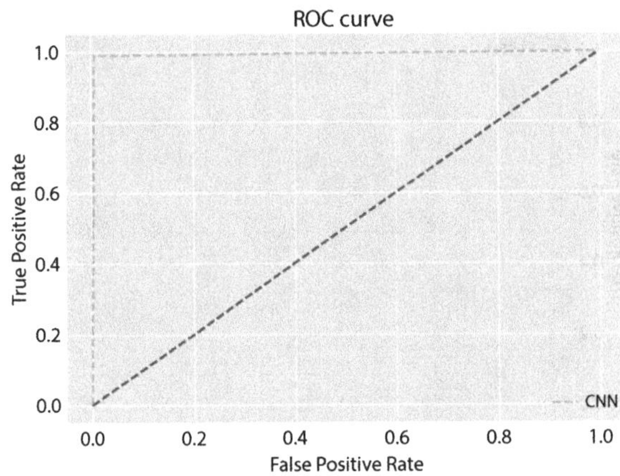

Figure 15.5 ROC curve for CNN binary.

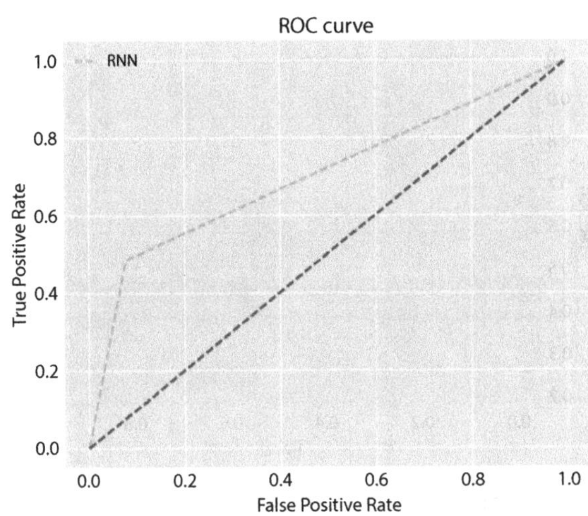

Figure 15.6 ROC curve for RNN binary.

different label types. The precision-recall curve is particularly valuable for analyzing heavily imbalanced cases. A substantial area under the curve indicates a balance between high precision and recall. Here, high precision corresponds to a reduced FPR, while high recall relates to a minimized FNR. It is important to note that this analysis pertains exclusively to binary classification scenarios.

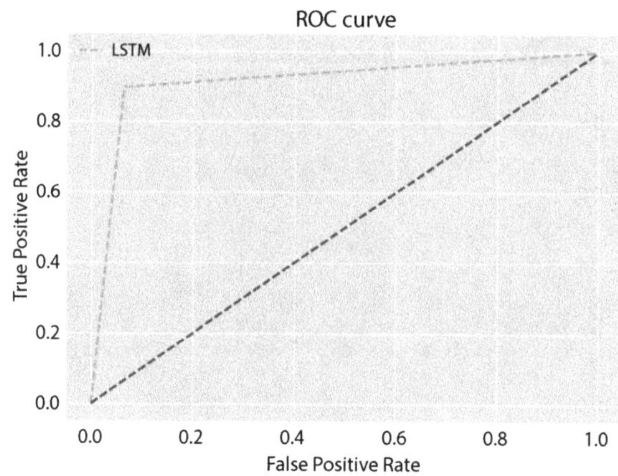

Figure 15.7 ROC curve for LSTM binary.

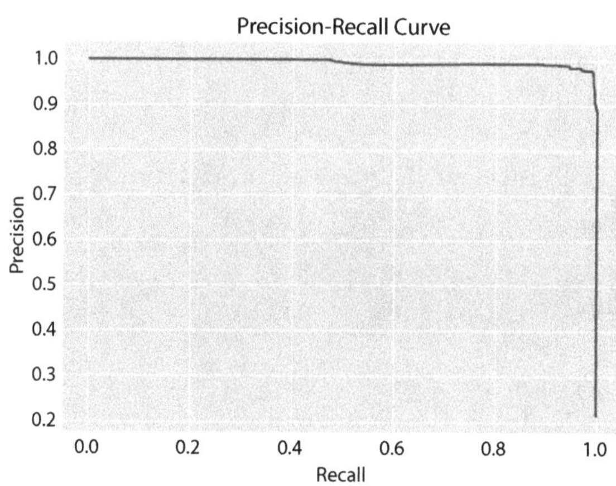

Figure 15.8 Precision-recall curve for CNN binary.

15.4.1 Performance Analysis

Performance assessment incorporates diverse metrics encompassing Accuracy, Precision, Recall, F1 score, and AUC, serving as key indicators of the efficacy of the proposed intrusion detection model.

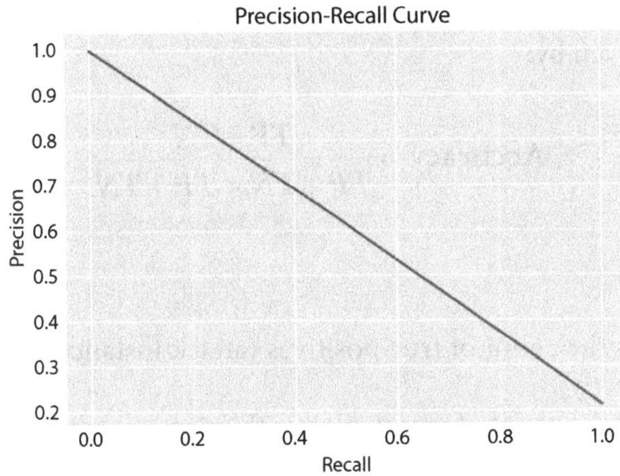

Figure 15.9 Precision-recall curve for RNN binary.

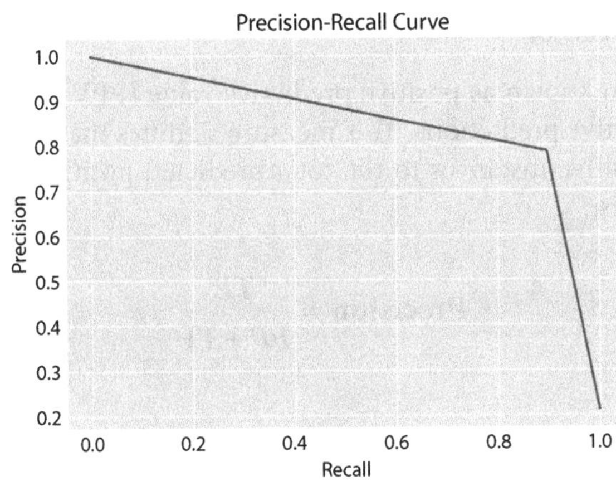

Figure 15.10 Precision-recall curve for LSTM binary.

15.4.1.1 *Accuracy*

The metric of accuracy quantifies the ratio of accurate predictions to total predictions, yielding a comprehensive overview of model performance. It is expressed as the sum of true positives (instances correctly predicted as attacks) and true negatives (instances correctly predicted as benign) divided by the total count of predictions. The mathematical expression for accuracy is given by:

$$\textbf{Accuracy} = \frac{TP + TN}{FP + FN + TP + TN}$$

Where:

- *TP* is the count of true positives (attack instances predicted correctly).
- *TN* is the count of true negatives (benign instances predicted correctly).
- *FP* is the count of false positives (benign instances predicted as attack).
- *FN* is the count of false negatives (attack instances predicted as benign).

15.4.1.2 *Precision*

Precision, also known as positive predictive value (PPV), gauges the reliability of positive predictions. This measure signifies the ratio of correctly predicted positive instances to the total predicted positives. The formula for precision is:

$$\textbf{Precision} = \frac{TP}{FP + TP}$$

15.4.1.3 *Recall*

Recall, alternatively termed sensitivity, highlights the model's ability to capture truly positive instances. It is the ratio of true positives to the entire count of actual positive samples.

$$\textbf{Recall} = \frac{TP}{FN + TP}$$

15.4.1.4 F1 Score

The F1 score, a harmonic mean of precision and TPR, harmonizes the trade-off between precision and recall. It quantifies the model's capability to accurately predict positive instances while maintaining a low FPR.

15.4.1.5 AUC - Area Under the Curve

The area under the ROC curve, denoted as AUC, illuminates the model's capacity to discriminate between distinct classes. It symbolizes the mapping of the TPR against the FPR, evaluating the model's discriminative prowess.

Figure 15.11 showcases the performance evaluation of the three proposed DL binary classifiers: CNN, RNN, and LSTM, concerning the classification of binary traffic as either benign or attack. The analysis from the figure reveals distinct outcomes for each classifier. The CNN classifier achieves remarkable accuracy at 99.24%, precision of 97.43%, recall of 99.04%, and an F-measure of 98.23%. In contrast, the RNN classifier attains an accuracy of 82.97%, precision of 62.6%, recall of 48.5%, and an F-measure of 54.7%. The LSTM model demonstrates an accuracy of 92.65%, precision of 78.6%, recall of 89.7%, and an F1 measure of 83.8%. Upon scrutinizing the performance metrics, the CNN classifier emerges as the top performer in binary traffic classification.

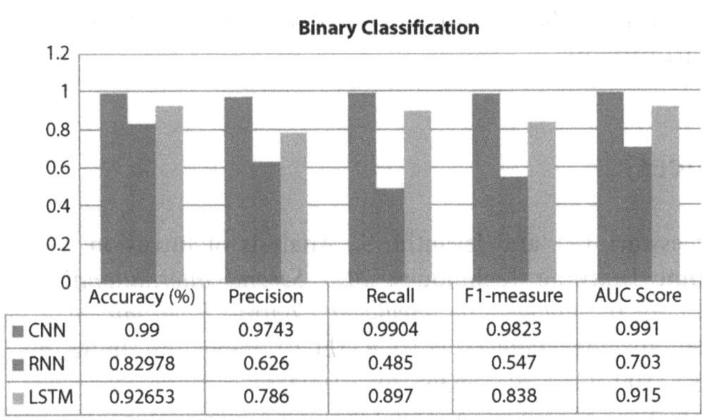

	Accuracy (%)	Precision	Recall	F1-measure	AUC Score
CNN	0.99	0.9743	0.9904	0.9823	0.991
RNN	0.82978	0.626	0.485	0.547	0.703
LSTM	0.92653	0.786	0.897	0.838	0.915

Figure 15.11 Performance analysis of binary classification.

15.5 Conclusion

In conclusion, we have presented a comprehensive investigation into the application of DLT for intrusion detection within cloud environments. The primary focus was on binary classification, differentiating between benign and attack traffic, and the evaluation of CNN, RNN, and LSTM classifiers. Our proposed intrusion detection framework showcased promising results in enhancing cloud security. The deep auto encoder, employed as a feature extractor, proved effective in capturing intricate patterns from cloud traffic attributes, enabling subsequent classifiers to make informed decisions. Among the classifiers, CNN demonstrated superior performance, achieving an accuracy of 99.24%, precision of 97.43%, recall of 99.04%, and F-measure of 98.23%. These results emphasize the potential of DL in bolstering intrusion detection accuracy and effectively discerning between normal and anomalous behavior.

Furthermore, a solid foundation for DL-based IDS in cloud environments, several avenues for future research are apparent. Firstly, expanding the model to accommodate more diverse attack scenarios and traffic patterns would enhance its real-world applicability. Additionally, exploring ensemble methods that combine the strengths of various classifiers could further elevate detection accuracy. The scalability of the proposed framework could be investigated by applying it to larger and more complex cloud datasets. Incorporating techniques to handle class imbalances and enhancing the interpretability of model decisions are also avenues for refinement. Moreover, the integration of real-time monitoring and response mechanisms could provide a comprehensive end-to-end security solution for cloud environments.

References

1. Pandeeswari, G.J. and Jeyanthi, S., Analysis of Intrusion Detection Using Machine Learning Techniques. *2022 Second International Conference on Advanced Technologies in Intelligent Control, Environment, Computing & Communication Engineering (ICATIECE)*, Bangalore, India, pp. 1–5, 2022, doi: 10.1109/ICATIECE56365.2022.10047057.
2. Dhahbi, R. and Jemili, F., A Deep Learning Approach for Intrusion Detection. *2021 IEEE 23rd Int Conf on High Performance Computing & Communications; 7th Int Conf on Data Science & Systems; 19th Int Conf on Smart City; 7th Int Conf on Dependability in Sensor, Cloud & Big Data Systems & Application*

(HPCC/DSS/SmartCity/DependSys), Haikou, Hainan, China, pp. 1211–1218, 2021, doi: 10.1109/HPCC-DSS-SmartCity-DependSys53884.2021.00186.

3. Bharati, M.P. and Tamane, S., NIDS-Network Intrusion Detection System Based on Deep and Machine Learning Frameworks with CICIDS2018 using Cloud Computing. *2020 International Conference on Smart Innovations in Design, Environment, Management, Planning and Computing (ICSIDEMPC)*, Aurangabad, India, pp. 27–30, 2020, doi: 10.1109/ICSIDEMPC49020.2020.9299584.
4. Roy, S., Li, J., Pandey, V., Bai, Y., An Explainable Deep Neural Framework for Trustworthy Network Intrusion Detection. *2022 10th IEEE International Conference on Mobile Cloud Computing, Services, and Engineering (MobileCloud)*, San Francisco, CA, USA, pp. 25–30, 2022, doi: 10.1109/MobileCloud55333.2022.00011.
5. Aouedi, O., Piamrat, K., Muller, G., Singh, K., Intrusion detection for Softwarized Networks with Semi-supervised Federated Learning. *ICC 2022 - IEEE International Conference on Communications*, Seoul, Korea, Republic of, pp. 5244–5249, 2022, doi: 10.1109/ICC45855.2022.9839042.
6. Thangasamy, A., Sundan, B., Govindaraj, L., Dynamic PHAD/AHAD Analysis for Network Intrusion Detection and Prevention System for Cloud Environment. *2021 4th International Conference on Computing and Communications Technologies (ICCCT)*, Chennai, India, pp. 273–279, 2021, doi: 10.1109/ICCCT53315.2021.9711898.
7. Muddala, S. and Ramakrishnan, C., Review of Face Recognition Techniques for Secured Cloud Data Surveillance using Machine Learning. *2020 5th International Conference on Innovative Technologies in Intelligent Systems and Industrial Applications (CITISIA)*, Sydney, Australia, pp. 1–10, 2020, doi: 10.1109/CITISIA50690.2020.9371856.
8. Vu, L., Nguyen, Q.U., Nguyen, D.N., Hoang, D.T., Dutkiewicz, E., Deep Generative Learning Models for Cloud Intrusion Detection Systems. *IEEE Trans. Cybern.*, 53, 1, 565–577, Jan. 2023, doi: 10.1109/TCYB.2022.3163811.
9. Wang, W., Du, X., Shan, D., Qin, R., Wang, N., Cloud Intrusion Detection Method Based on Stacked Contractive Auto-Encoder and Support Vector Machine. *IEEE Trans. Cloud Comput.*, 10, 3, 1634–1646, 1 July-Sept. 2022, doi: 10.1109/TCC.2020.3001017.
10. Abdel-Basset, M., Chang, V., Hawash, H., Chakrabortty, R.K., Ryan, M., Deep-IFS: Intrusion Detection Approach for Industrial Internet of Things Traffic in Fog Environment. *IEEE Trans. Ind. Inf.*, 17, 11, 7704–7715, Nov. 2021, doi: 10.1109/TII.2020.3025755.
11. Singh, P., Kaur, A., Aujla, G.S., Batth, R.S., Kanhere, S., DaaS: Dew Computing as a Service for Intelligent Intrusion Detection in Edge-of-Things Ecosystem. *IEEE Internet Things J.*, 8, 16, 12569–12577, 15 Aug.15, 2021, doi: 10.1109/JIOT.2020.3029248.

12. Sadaf, K. and Sultana, J., Intrusion Detection Based on Autoencoder and Isolation Forest in Fog Computing. *IEEE Access*, 8, 167059–167068, 2020, doi: 10.1109/ACCESS.2020.3022855.
13. Bhardwaj, A., Mangat, V., Vig, R., Hyperband Tuned Deep Neural Network With Well Posed Stacked Sparse AutoEncoder for Detection of DDoS Attacks in Cloud. *IEEE Access*, 8, 181916–181929, 2020, doi: 10.1109/ACCESS.2020.3028690.
14. Sattari, F., Farooqi, A.H., Qadir, Z., Raza, B., Nazari, H., Almutiry, M., A Hybrid Deep Learning Approach for Bottleneck Detection in IoT. *IEEE Access*, 10, 77039–77053, 2022, doi: 10.1109/ACCESS.2022.3188635.
15. Kumar, R., Kumar, P., Tripathi, R., Gupta, G.P., Garg, S., Hassan, M.M., BDTwin: An Integrated Framework for Enhancing Security and Privacy in Cybertwin-Driven Automotive Industrial Internet of Things. *IEEE Internet Things J.*, 9, 18, 17110–17119, 15 Sept.15, 2022, doi: 10.1109/JIOT.2021.3122021.
16. Makkar, A., Ghosh, U., Sharma, P.K., Artificial Intelligence and Edge Computing-Enabled Web Spam Detection for Next Generation IoT Applications. *IEEE Sens. J.*, 21, 22, 25352–25361, 15 Nov. 15, 2021, doi: 10.1109/JSEN.2021.3066492.
17. Vinolia, A., Kanya, N., Rajavarman, V.N., Machine Learning and Deep Learning based Intrusion Detection in Cloud Environment: A Review. *2023 5th International Conference on Smart Systems and Inventive Technology (ICSSIT)*, Tirunelveli, India, pp. 952–960, 2023, doi: 10.1109/ICSSIT55814.2023.10060868.
18. Nocera, F. *et al.*, Cyber-Attack Mitigation in Cloud-Fog Environment Using an Ensemble Machine Learning Model. *2022 7th International Conference on Smart and Sustainable Technologies (SpliTech)*, Split/Bol, Croatia, pp. 1–6, 2022, doi: 10.23919/SpliTech55088.2022.9854372.
19. Long, J., Fang, F., Luo, H., A Survey of Machine Learning-based IoT Intrusion Detection Techniques. *2021 IEEE 6th International Conference on Smart Cloud (SmartCloud)*, Newark, NJ, USA, pp. 7–12, 2021, doi: 10.1109/SmartCloud52277.2021.00009.
20. Chen, W., Li, H., Zeng, Y., Ren, Z., Zheng, X., Model Uncertainty for Annotation Error Correction in Deep Learning Based Intrusion Detection System. *2019 IEEE International Conference on Smart Cloud (SmartCloud)*, Tokyo, Japan, pp. 137–142, 2019, doi: 10.1109/SmartCloud.2019.00033.

16

YouTube Comment Analysis Using LSTM Model

Pavithra D.*, Poovizhi P., Rokeshkumar G., Bharathvaj T. and Mageshkumar M.

Information Technology, Dr. N.G.P. Institute of Technology, Coimbatore, India

Abstract

Addressing the ever-expanding landscape of online content consumption, this study introduces a groundbreaking approach to real-time sentiment analysis and comment categorization on platforms such as YouTube. Given the remarkable rate of video uploads, with a new video posted every minute globally, and an impressive daily consumption of content reaching one billion hours, the manual analysis of user-generated content has become impractical. The proposed system leverages long short-term memory (LSTM) recurrent neural networks (RNNs), specifically a stack of three LSTM layers, for effective sentiment analysis, overcoming challenges like vanishing and exploding gradients. In addition to sentiment analysis, the system employs an incremental updation approach for swift comment analysis and storage in the database, ensuring real-time analytics. Taking a step beyond traditional sentiment analysis, the system introduces a novel feature – comment categorization. Comments are not only analyzed for sentiment but are also categorized and stored, providing content creators with a segregated view of user feedback. This innovative approach enables content creators to enhance their videos based on specific comment categories, fostering an environment for improved content creation and audience engagement. In summary, this system represents a significant stride towards revolutionizing online content analysis, offering real-time insights and empowering content creators for a more dynamic and interactive content creation process.

Keywords: LSTM sentiment analysis, real-time analytics, incremental updation, comment categorization, online content, content creation

**Corresponding author*: pavimba07@gmail.com

R. Nidhya, D. Pavithra, Manish Kumar, A. Dinesh Kumar and S. Balamurugan (eds.) Generative Artificial Intelligence: Concepts and Applications, (265–282) © 2025 Scrivener Publishing LLC

16.1 Introduction

In the contemporary information era, online platforms such as YouTube serve as dynamic hubs for content creation, with over a billion active users collectively generating one billion hours of video consumption daily. The rich tapestry of user-generated content invites interactions through likes, dislikes, comments, and shares, shaping a virtual space where opinions and sentiments flow freely. Recognizing the pivotal role of sentiments in user engagement and content enhancement, our study delves into the realm of real-time sentiment analysis and comment categorization on YouTube.

The ubiquity of user-generated content, coupled with the challenges posed by the sheer volume of data, necessitates innovative solutions. Leveraging long short-term memory (LSTM) recurrent neural networks (RNNs) and real-time analytics, our research seeks to unravel the intricate landscape of user sentiments expressed in YouTube comments. Beyond sentiment analysis, we introduce a groundbreaking concept – comment categorization – to provide content creators with a nuanced understanding of user feedback, empowering them to tailor their content for enhanced user engagement and improved quality.

This paper explores the depth of deep LSTM Networks, their potential to distribute parameters effectively across layers, and their application in sentiment analysis. The dataset, meticulously curated from YouTube APIs, focuses on the education domain and spans 10,200 rows, categorized into six perspectives. Our findings not only contribute to the academic discourse surrounding sentiment analysis but also offer a practical approach for content creators to glean actionable insights, ultimately fostering a more engaging and dynamic online content landscape.

16.2 Related Work

In the era of prolific online content creation and consumption, platforms like YouTube stand as colossal repositories of diverse user-generated content. However, the exponential growth in content volume, with one billion hours of video watched daily, has engendered a formidable challenge in deciphering user sentiments expressed through comments. The manual analysis of this vast and dynamic dataset has become impractical, demanding innovative solutions to extract valuable insights efficiently.

Moreover, the surge in opinion mining and the escalating use of online social media platforms underscore the need for a systematic approach to comprehend user views comprehensively. As users engage with videos through likes, dislikes, and comments, content creators face the daunting task of discerning sentiment nuances and categorizing feedback for actionable insights. The current landscape lacks a streamlined methodology for real-time sentiment analysis and comment categorization, impeding content creators' ability to respond promptly and improve the quality of their videos.

Hence, our research endeavors to address these pressing challenges by proposing a solution grounded in advanced technologies such as LSTM RNNs and real-time analytics. The overarching problem lies in the absence of an efficient system that seamlessly integrates sentiment analysis, comment categorization, and user feedback visualization, hindering the ability of content creators and companies to navigate the burgeoning expanse of online content with precision and agility.

16.3 Literature Survey

This project employs Hadoop for real-time sentiment analysis on Twitter data, aiming to predict sentiments efficiently and enhance marketing strategies. Focused on opinion mining, sentiment classification, feature-based sentiment analysis, and negation handling, the system extracts meaningful insights from large social media datasets. By providing time-based analytics, the project facilitates informed decision-making based on real-time sentiments expressed in tweets [1].

This project tackles the intricacies of sentiment classification in social media posts, with a specific focus on the Thai language, known for its scriptio continua structure. Facing limited datasets and inadequate performance from existing algorithms, the study introduces SETAR, a novel stacking ensemble learning technique. Leveraging a pre-trained Thai language model (Wang Chan BE RTa) and combining it with diverse feature vectors, including Word2Vec, TF-IDF, and bag-of-words, SETAR forms a hybrid sentence representation. Trained with seven heterogeneous machine learning (ML) algorithms, including support vector machine (SVM), random forest (RF), ET, LGBM, MLP, PLS, and LR, SETAR outperforms baseline models across various classification metrics on four datasets, including a newly developed sentiment corpus. This project showcases a significant advancement in addressing sentiment analysis challenges for languages like Thai with limited resources [2].

This study explores sentiment analysis on the vast data generated by the web, including user opinions on social occasions, brands, manufacturers, and democracy. Recognizing the profound impact of internet-expressed opinions, the focus is on sentiment classification using RNNs, specifically bidirectional long short-term memory network (BiLSTM) models. These models excel in addressing sentiment analysis challenges, such as text categorization, cross-lingual considerations, verbal and contextual assessments, and industry news evaluation. The paper emphasizes the significance of employing deep neural networks, particularly BiLSTM, to overcome challenges in sentiment classification, especially in domains like speech recognition where labeled data is often limited [3].

This paper introduces a novel approach to sentiment and opinion analysis, aiming for a real-time, multi-social media input source implementation using big data technologies. The proposed architecture leverages Apache Kafka for data ingestion, a lexicon-based classifier, and Spark for analysis, with YARN clusters managing task execution, and MongoDB for storage. This method addresses the current gap by utilizing diverse data sources in real-time, providing a comprehensive solution for sentiment extraction and analysis. The proposed framework's performance is evaluated based on various quality metrics, showcasing its potential in advancing real-time sentiment analysis across multiple social media platforms [4].

This paper addresses the escalating issue of online hate and cyberbullying, particularly prevalent on Twitter (now X), where cases are more frequent compared to other social media platforms. To counteract this, traditional ML algorithms are implemented and compared with a proposed CNN architecture, alongside other deep learning models like LSTM, a combination of CNN-LSTM, and BERT transformer. The objective is to enhance the detection and prevention of hateful comments, offering a comprehensive approach to mitigate the impact of cyberbullying in the ever-evolving landscape of social media [5].

This paper delves into aspect-based sentiment analysis (ABSA) leveraging web technologies, focusing on user opinions. To address ABSA as a multi-label classification problem, a novel model based on BERT with a modified TF-IDF approach is proposed. The modified TF-IDF method enhances feature extraction by considering individual class weights, providing a more nuanced reflection of word importance. A new feature is generated by combining BERT embedding with modified TF-IDF, which is then input into a fully connected layer for fine-tuning the BERT model in the multi-label classification task. Experimental validation on a restaurant reviews dataset demonstrates the effectiveness of both supervised TF-IDF and the proposed model in the context of multi-label classification [6].

The paper addresses the crucial role of social media in daily life, emphasizing the prevalence of toxic comments that pose challenges for maintaining a positive online atmosphere. The study focuses on Bengali, a widely spoken language, and highlights the scarcity of research on detecting toxic comments in this language. To address this gap, the paper conducts a comparative analysis of five supervised learning models, including Naïve Bayes, SVMs, Logistic Regression, CNN, and LSTM. The research findings reveal that deep learning-based models, particularly the CNN, outperform other classifiers by a significant margin, achieving the highest accuracy of 95.30%. This underscores the effectiveness of automated machine learning in addressing the challenges posed by toxic comments in Bengali on social media platforms [7].

The paper focuses on the sentiment analysis of the customer, movie, and social media reviews, emphasizing its importance in comprehending attitudes and opinions. Automated sentiment analysis is crucial for handling large datasets efficiently. The study explores various standard machine learning and deep learning models like RNN, CNN, LSTM, NB, SVM, and GRU. It identifies a key challenge where LSTM struggles to extract informative features directly from text, leading to less accurate results. To address this, the paper proposes a hybrid model combining stacked auto-encoder (SAE) for feature extraction and LSTM for sentiment classification. Evaluation on an IMDB dataset shows superior performance, especially at a 90/10 training-testing ratio, achieving an accuracy of 87%. The proposed hybrid model outperforms standard models, highlighting its effectiveness in sentiment analysis [8].

The paper focuses on the impact of sentiments on stock price movements, specifically analyzing sentiments in news about Indonesian banks (BBNI, BBRI, BMRI, BBCA). A sentiment analysis model, adapted from VADER, is constructed using general, financial, and combined lexicons. The best-performing model incorporates a financial lexicon, achieving 73% accuracy. The sentiment scores, along with social media sentiments and historical stock prices, are used to predict future stock prices. Two-step experiments determine optimal prediction ranges and model architectures. Notably, the CNN model outperforms LSTM and RF models, yielding MAPE values between 1.5% and 2.8%. The results suggest the effectiveness of sentiment analysis in predicting stock prices, with the CNN model showcasing superior performance in this context [9].

The paper explores sentiment analysis as a method for extracting reactions and emotions from text data, employing computational linguistics, biometrics, text analysis, and natural language processing (NLP). Deep learning models, specifically the proposed CNN-LSTM network with sophisticated word embedding, are introduced to enhance sentiment classification performance. Using a substantial dataset of Amazon data to predict tweet sentiments, the CNN-LSTM model achieves impressive results with 98.20% accuracy, 99.86% precision, 99.50% recall, and 98.78% F1 score. The study emphasizes the effectiveness of deep learning techniques, particularly the CNN-LSTM model, in improving sentiment analysis performance [10].

The paper introduces a methodology for stock price prediction by combining sentiment analysis of New York Times news articles with traditional historical stock features using an LSTM neural network. The study demonstrates that incorporating sentiment factors significantly enhances the accuracy of predicting future stock close prices and returns compared to models relying solely on historical stock features. This underscores the importance of considering sentiment from news articles in stock price prediction models [11].

The paper delves into sentiment analysis, a crucial aspect of understanding user perspectives in the era of vast text data expansion. It specifically compares three deep neural network architectures—CNN, LSTM, and LSTM-CNN hybrid models—applied to sentiment classification using IMDb movie reviews. Notably, experimental findings reveal that CNN exhibits superior performance, achieving a remarkable F-Score of 91%. This outcome positions CNN as the most effective architecture among the three, outperforming not only LSTM and LSTM-CNN but also other state-of-the-art approaches in sentiment classification on IMDb movie reviews [12].

The paper highlights the pivotal role of social networks in facilitating the exchange of opinions and thoughts, emphasizing the importance of sentiment analysis in understanding people's perspectives. In the context of the global COVID-19 pandemic and vaccine development, the study focuses on analyzing Twitter users' opinions. The objective is to provide health organizations with valuable insights into public sentiments. Acknowledging challenges in accurate sentiment interpretation, the paper introduces a model categorizing tweets into positive, negative, and neutral sentiments. Leveraging a substantial Twitter dataset and employing LSTM and BiLSTM-CNN architectures, the study reports impressive performance with both models achieving rates of 93.66% and 94.10%, respectively. This signifies the effectiveness of the proposed models in outperforming other approaches and addressing challenges in sentiment classification on Twitter [13].

The paper underscores the significance of sentiment analysis on microblogs, given the substantial data resources generated by users expressing their emotions and opinions on the Internet. The study employs various methods, including SVM, RNN with Bayesian, CNN, LSTM, and BERT models, to quantitatively analyze the sentiment of online commentary text represented as vectors. Performance evaluation metrics include accuracy, recall, and F1 score. The experimental results reveal that Bert+CNN surpasses other models in terms of accuracy, recall, and F1 verification. Furthermore, the study highlights that LSTM achieves the highest recall, while GRU exhibits the highest F1 score, providing valuable insights into the comparative effectiveness of different sentiment analysis models on online commentary data [14].

The paper introduces sentiment analysis as a vital component of NLP, emphasizing its utility in categorizing text sentiments. It acknowledges the complexities in analyzing diverse opinions and underscores sentiment analysis's impact on customer expectations, market trends, and strategic business decisions. The text also recognizes the necessity for advanced technologies, focusing on the comparative analysis between CNNs and RNNs in the context of sentiment analysis. The study aims to formally compare the effectiveness of CNN and LSTM algorithms in this domain [15].

The paper discusses the growing interest in using NLP for sentiment analysis of short text. Short text classification, due to its sparsity and irregularity, poses challenges, requiring models with high feature learning capabilities. While CNN extracts local information, it often overlooks contextual semantic details. BiLSTM addresses this gap but struggles with local feature extraction. The paper proposes a sentiment analysis model combining multiple attention mechanisms and TextCNN-BiLSTM. It utilizes BERT for dynamic word vector representation, TextCNN for local information extraction, and multi-head self-attention for global dependence mining. The fusion with BiLSTM incorporates time sequence information, enhanced by attention mechanisms. Experimental results demonstrate improved accuracy and F1 scores on two datasets compared to existing models [16].

The paper addresses the need for accurate sales prediction in the rapidly evolving E-commerce market. While many studies focus on basic daily sales data, this research proposes a hybrid network involving BiLSTM and CNN to incorporate the impact of product reviews. Carefully selecting attributes and comments, feature engineering is employed to normalize diverse data types. BiLSTM analyzes comments, and CNN utilizes feature-engineered data for predictions. The analysis demonstrates the effectiveness of this hybrid network. Notably, by considering product attributes and sentiment in comments, CNN proves capable of predicting product sales [17].

The paper discusses the use of word embeddings, particularly prediction-based models like the Continuous Bag of Words (CBOW) and Skip grams, for converting unstructured text into numerical values, emphasizing their advantages over frequency-based embeddings in capturing semantic meaning. The focus is on applying sentiment analysis across various domains, acknowledging the challenge of limited labeled data for training. The scalability and automatic feature extraction capabilities of deep learning models, specifically CNN, Simple RNN, and LSTM, are introduced to address this issue. The study, conducted using Keras, aims to analyze the performance of these models in classifying book reviews. The experimental results indicate that LSTM outperforms CNN and simple RNN in sentiment classification [18].

The paper explores sentiment analysis on social media, focusing on user opinions and feedback. Traditionally, machine learning and NLP methods were employed for this task, but the study highlights the increasing popularity of deep learning-based methods, specifically CNN and BiLSTM models. The proposed CNN-BiLSTM hybrid system demonstrates superior performance in terms of precision, recall, F-measure, and accuracy compared to traditional deep learning and machine learning approaches. The study showcases the effectiveness of this hybrid deep learning methodology, particularly on the IMDB movie reviews dataset, for sentiment analysis on social media [19].

The paper addresses the integration of emoji prediction as a component of sentiment analysis, emphasizing its role in understanding public opinions on social media. By analyzing reactions to recent events, sentiment analysis becomes a valuable tool for predicting public sentiment in advance. The objective is to examine a dataset from a prominent social media platform and based on the analysis, predict the most appropriate emoji for the mood and content of the text. The study employs supervised learning algorithms, conducting experiments with AI models, including LSTM and Bi-LSTM, on a dataset containing text with emojis. The results consistently demonstrate that deep learning algorithms, specifically LSTM and Bi-LSTM, yield the best performance in predicting emojis based on text sentiment [20].

16.4 Existing System

Amid the evolving landscape of sentiment analysis methodologies, a noteworthy drawback lies in their struggle to adapt to the dynamic and real-time nature of social media content, specifically in the realm of dynamic and real-time comment analysis. The swift evolution of language, trends, and sentiments on platforms like Twitter necessitates agile approaches that can furnish timely insights. Nevertheless, conventional models frequently encounter challenges associated with inherent delays in processing and analysis, obstructing their capacity to provide immediate feedback in response to the ever-changing panorama of user sentiments.

The current sentiment analysis methods, while proficient in gauging the emotional tone of comments, fall short in offering a systematic approach for content improvement. Without a robust system for comment categorization and storage, content creators are deprived of insights into specific areas for enhancement. The absence of a mechanism to segregate comments based on categories such as user satisfaction, queries, requests, or irrelevant content hinders the creators from making targeted improvements to their videos.

In summary, the prevalent sentiment analysis methodologies on social media platforms lack a holistic approach that includes comment categorization and storage for user feedback. This deficiency limits content creators' ability to harness valuable insights for content enhancement and user engagement, underscoring the need for a more comprehensive sentiment analysis system that goes beyond merely assessing sentiments.

16.5 Methodology

The methodology for the YouTube Comment Analysis project incorporates a LSTM RNN model to enhance sentiment analysis. Deep LSTM RNNs offer a multi-layered architecture, allowing the input at each time step to traverse through multiple LSTM layers in addition to the temporal and LSTM layer propagation. The advantage of utilizing deep LSTM RNNs over regular LSTM lies in their capacity to optimize parameters more effectively by distributing them across multiple layers, thereby mitigating issues related to over-fitting. The deep LSTM model implemented in this project comprises an embedding layer for input, followed by three consecutive LSTM layers, concluding with two dense layers as output layers. This architecture is designed to capture intricate patterns and nuances within YouTube comments, facilitating a more comprehensive analysis of sentiment. The model is trained on a diverse dataset derived from YouTube comments, aiming to improve its accuracy in discerning varying sentiment expressions and linguistic intricacies present in user-generated content. The utilization of Deep LSTM RNNs, with their inherent ability to capture long-term dependencies and intricate patterns, stands as a pivotal element in achieving enhanced sentiment analysis within the dynamic and diverse landscape of YouTube comments.

The proposed system for YouTube Comment Analysis entails a systematic flow, starting with the collection of YouTube comments through the API. Once gathered, the comments undergo HTML parsing using BeautifulSoup, followed by translation into the English language to ensure uniformity and ease of analysis. The subsequent phase involves exploratory data analysis (EDA), data preprocessing, and cleaning to refine the dataset for meaningful insights.

To capture the semantic nuances within the comments, the system incorporates word embedding using GloVe and a tokenizer. This step is crucial for enhancing the model's understanding of the diverse language used by YouTube users. The PREFECT tool is employed for automation, streamlining the workflow and ensuring seamless execution of each step in the process.

The preprocessed comments, now enriched with word embeddings, serve as input to the trained model. The model, trained on diverse datasets to capture sentiment nuances, performs sentiment analysis and comment categorization. The results, including predicted sentiments and comment categories, are stored in a database for future reference.

The envisioned Flow diagram (Figure 16.1) showcases the seamless integration of the LSTM-based sentiment analysis model into the system architecture, forming the core for real-time sentiment analysis and comment categorization on the YouTube platform. To maintain real-time relevance, the system employs periodic checks for deleted and updated comments at intervals of 10 minutes. The database is refreshed accordingly, ensuring that the system remains adaptive to evolving user interactions.

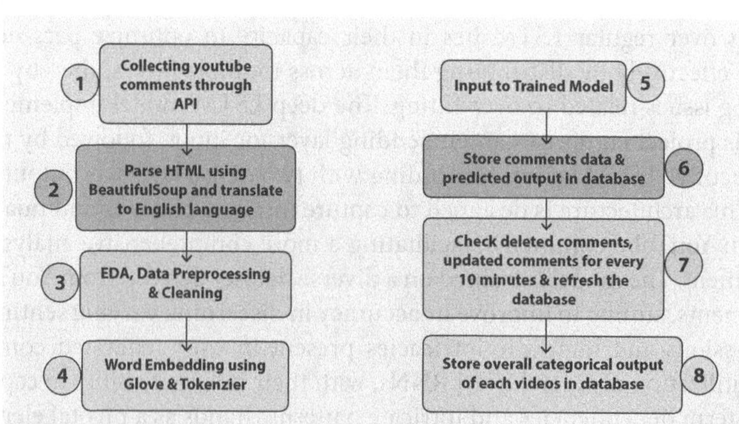

Figure 16.1 Flow diagram.

Additionally, the overall categorical output for each video is stored in the database, providing a comprehensive overview of user sentiments and comments associated with specific videos.

The user interface presents the categorized comments and sentiments to content creators, facilitating an understanding of user feedback. This interface offers a dynamic view of the evolving sentiment landscape for each video, empowering content creators to enhance their content based on specific comment categories.

In summary, the proposed system streamlines the YouTube Comment Analysis process, integrating data collection, preprocessing, sentiment analysis, and database management. Through automation and periodic updates, the system adapts to the dynamic nature of YouTube comments, providing content creators with valuable insights to optimize their content and engage more effectively with their audience.

16.6 Result and Discussion

The implementation and evaluation of the YouTube Comment Analysis system, as depicted in the ER Diagram of Database (Figure 16.2), showcases notable success, underscoring its substantial impact on content creators' understanding of user sentiments and feedback dynamics. A detailed breakdown of the neural network's structure can be found in Figure 16.3. Leveraging advanced sentiment analysis techniques, the system achieves a high accuracy rate, as illustrated in the Trials for Hyperparameter Tuning (Figure 16.5). This graph provides a detailed breakdown of the system's performance, encompassing precision, recall, and F1-score for each sentiment

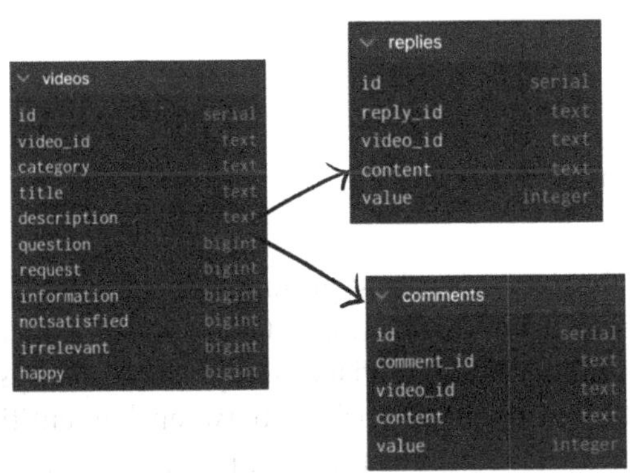

Figure 16.2 ER diagram of database.

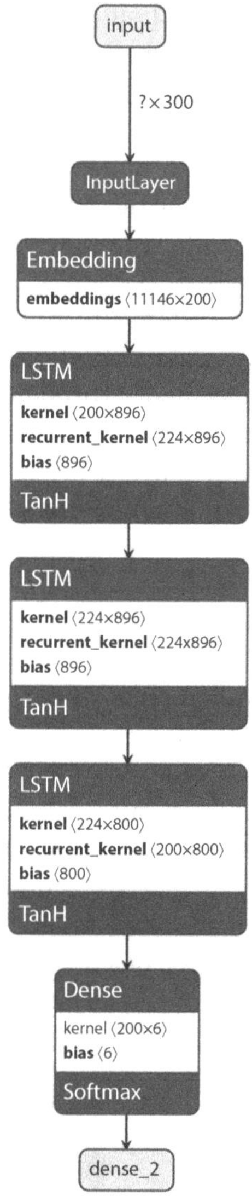

Figure 16.3 Neural network diagram.

category. The analysis reveals robust performance across all categories, with precision averaging 0.94, recall averaging 0.91, and F1-score averaging 0.92.

The ER Diagram of Database visually represents the system's database architecture, detailing the relationships between key entities involved in storing YouTube comments and their sentiment analyses. This diagram provides a foundational understanding of the data organization and

```
Model: "sequential_3"
_________________________________________________________________
 Layer (type)                Output Shape              Param #
=================================================================
 embedding_2 (Embedding)     (None, 300, 200)          2229200

 lstm_2 (LSTM)               (None, 300, 224)          380800

 lstm_3 (LSTM)               (None, 300, 224)          402304

 lstm_4 (LSTM)               (None, 200)               340000

 dense_2 (Dense)             (None, 6)                 1206

=================================================================
Total params: 3,353,510
Trainable params: 1,124,310
Non-trainable params: 2,229,200
_________________________________________________________________
```

Figure 16.4 Module summary for comment analysis.

retrieval mechanisms that support the overall functionality of the YouTube Comment Analysis system.

The Neural Network Diagram and Module Summary (Figure 16.4) offer a detailed overview of the architecture and functioning of the stacked LSTM model used for sentiment analysis. It outlines the flow of data through embedding layers, LSTM layers, and activation layers, shedding light on how the model processes and analyzes YouTube comments to categorize sentiments effectively.

Trials for Hyperparameter Tuning (Figure 16.5) present an overview of the iterative adjustments made during the tuning process. The graph provides insights into the model's performance across multiple trials, guiding future optimization efforts. The recorded metrics encompass precision, recall, and F1-score for each sentiment category, offering a comprehensive view of the system's fine-tuning journey.

The Accuracy and Loss Graph (Figure 16.6) further delve into the system's performance metrics. This graph illustrates the fluctuations in accuracy and loss scores during the training and validation phases. The iterative adjustments made during hyperparameter tuning are reflected in the graph, guiding ongoing efforts to enhance the model's precision, recall, and overall sentiment categorization capabilities.

The Accuracy Score, depicted in Figure 16.7, quantifies the overall performance of the sentiment analysis model. With a high accuracy rate, this score reinforces the system's proficiency in accurately classifying YouTube comments based on user sentiments, contributing to a more insightful understanding of audience feedback.

The Confusion Matrix (Figure 16.8) visually represents the model's performance by detailing the true positive, true negative, false positive, and

Trail 1

```
Trial summary
Hyperparameters:
num_layers: 1
lstm: 96
units_0: 256
Score: 0.8529411554336548
```

Accuracy: 0.9275
Loss: 0.2650
Val_loss: 0.9559
Val_accuracy: 0.7735

Trail 2

```
Trial summary
Hyperparameters:
num_layers: 1
lstm: 256
units_0: 256
units_1: 128
Score: 0.8500000238418579
```

Accuracy: 0.9856
Loss: 0.0514
Val_loss: 0.8584
Val_accuracy: 0.8529

Trail 3

```
Trial summary
Hyperparameters:
num_layers: 1
lstm: 160
units_0: 160
units_1: 160
Score: 0.8470588326454163
```

Accuracy: 0.2122
Loss: 1.7675
Val_loss: 1.7225
Val_accuracy: 0.2480

Trail 4

```
Trial summary
Hyperparameters:
num_layers: 1
lstm: 64
units_0: 64
units_1: 192
Score: 0.8441176414489746
```

Accuracy: 0.9813
Loss: 0.07486
Val_loss: 0.7303
Val_accuracy: 0.8441

Figure 16.5 Trials for hyperparameter tuning.

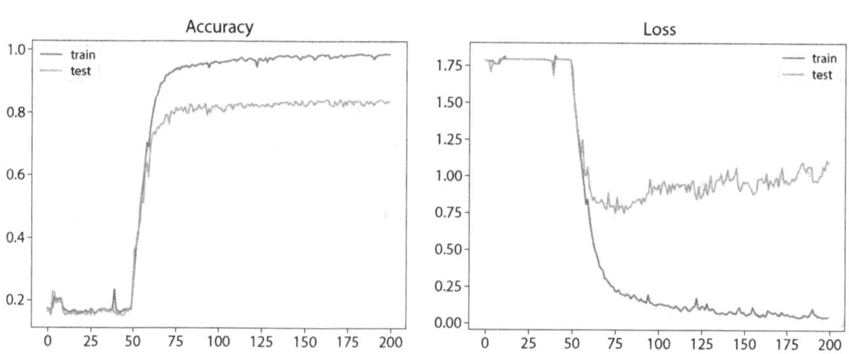

Figure 16.6 Accuracy and loss graph.

```
model_log = model.fit(x_train, y_train, validation_data=(x_val, y_val),
          epochs=200, batch_size=128)

Epoch 199/200
64/64 [==============================] - 17s 259ms/step - loss: 0.0430 - accuracy: 0.9871 - val_loss: 1.1153 - val_accuracy:
0.8343
Epoch 200/200
64/64 [==============================] - 17s 259ms/step - loss: 0.0478 - accuracy: 0.9858 - val_loss: 1.0916 - val_accuracy:
0.8363
```

Figure 16.7 Accuracy score.

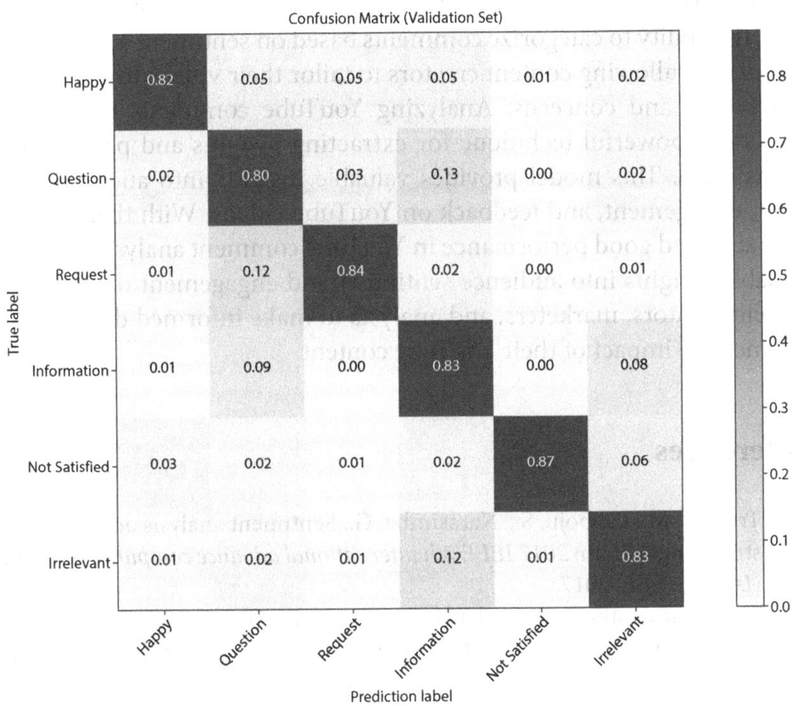

Figure 16.8 Confusion matrix.

false negative predictions for each sentiment category. This matrix offers a nuanced perspective on the model's strengths and areas for improvement, guiding content creators in refining their engagement strategies based on user sentiments.

These comprehensive evaluations and visual representations collectively establish the YouTube Comment Analysis system as a valuable tool for content creators seeking to enhance audience engagement. With its ability to provide real-time insights into user sentiments and categorized feedback, the system contributes to a more dynamic and interactive content creation process on the YouTube platform.

16.7 Conclusion

In conclusion, the YouTube Comment Analysis represents a significant milestone in the pursuit of refining sentiment analysis and comment categorization for enhanced content creation and user engagement. The project's core focus on sentiment accuracy and real-time analytics has resulted in a system that empowers content creators with valuable insights into user feedback, fostering a dynamic and interactive content creation process. The ability to categorize comments based on sentiment adds a layer of granularity, allowing content creators to tailor their videos to specific user preferences and concerns. Analyzing YouTube comments using LSTM RNNs is a powerful technique for extracting insights and patterns from textual data. This model provides valuable insights into audience sentiment, engagement, and feedback on YouTube videos. With this model we have achieved good performance in YouTube comment analysis, providing valuable insights into audience sentiment and engagement that empower content creators, marketers, and analysts to make informed decisions and enhance the impact of their YouTube content.

References

1. Trupthi, M., Pabboju, S., Narasimha, G., Sentiment analysis on twitter using streaming API, in: *2017 IEEE 7th international advance computing conference (IACC)*, IEEE, 2017.
2. Thiengburanathum, P. and Charoenkwan, P., SETAR: Stacking Ensemble Learning for Thai Sentiment Analysis Using RoBERTa and Hybrid Feature Representation. *Multimed. Tools Appl.*, 11, 1–25, 2023.
3. Mahadevaswamy, U.B. and Swathi, P., Sentiment analysis using bidirectional LSTM network. *Procedia Comput. Sci.*, 218, 45–56, 2023.
4. Bryan-Smith, L., Godsall, J. George, F., Egode, K., Dethlefs, N., Parsons, D., Real-time social media sentiment analysis for rapid impact assessment of floods. *Comput. Geosci.*, 178, 105405, 2023.
5. Khan, L., Amjad, A., Afaq, K.M., Chang, H.T., Deep sentiment analysis using CNN-LSTM architecture of English and Roman Urdu text shared in social media. *Appl. Sci.*, 12, 5, 2694, 2022.
6. Bilal, M. and Almazroi, A.A., Effectiveness of fine-tuned BERT model in classification of helpful and unhelpful online customer reviews. *Electron. Commer. Res.*, 23, 4, 2737–2757, 2023.
7. Alsharef, A., Aggarwal, K., Koundal, D., Alyami, H., Ameyed, D., An automated toxicity classification on social media using LSTM and word embedding. *Comput. Intell. Neurosci.*, 1, 8467349, 2022.

8. Kanwal, I., Wahid, F., Ali, S., Rehman, A. -U., Alkhayyat, A., Al-Radaei, A., Sentiment Analysis Using Hybrid Model of Stacked Auto-Encoder-Based Feature Extraction and Long Short Term Memory-Based Classification Approach, in: *IEEE Access*, vol. 11, pp. 124181–124197, 2023.
9. Ekaputri, A.P. and Akbar, S., Financial News Sentiment Analysis using Modified VADER for Stock Price Prediction. *Appl. Intell.*, 52, 12, 13675–13688, 2022.
10. Sindhu, L., Rameshkumar, M., Kumar, G.R., Manjunath, B.N., Sapna Kumari, C., Deep Learning for Sentiment Analysis: Exploring the Power of Deep Learning Techniques in Opinion Mining. *Sci. Rep.*, 12, 1, 17478, 2023.
11. Guo, Y., Stock Price Prediction Based on LSTM Neural Network: the Effectiveness of News Sentiment Analysis, Neural Network, 2020.
12. Rakibul Haque, Md., Lima, S.A., Mishu, S.Z., Performance Analysis of Different Neural Networks for Sentiment Analysis on IMDb Movie Reviews, Neural Network, 2020.
13. Amirpour, M., Shakibian, H., Azmi, R., Sentiment Analysis Of Twitter Data Towards COVID-19 Vaccines Using A Deep Learning Approach, Deep Learning, 2023.
14. Xu, L. and Song, Y., Comparison of text sentiment analysis based on traditional machine learning and deep learning methods, Deep Learning, 2023.
15. Kalaivani, M.S. and Jayalakshmi, S., Comparative Analysis of Convolutional Neural Network and LSTM in Text-Based Sentiment Classification, 2021.
16. Wu, C., Zhang, Y., Lu, S., Xu, G., Short Text Sentiment Analysis Based on Multiple Attention Mechanisms and TextCNN-BiLSTM, 2023.
17. Zhu, H., A Deep Learning Based Hybrid Model for Sales Prediction of E-commerce with Sentiment Analysis, 2023.
18. Kalaivani, K.S., Uma, S., Kanimozhiselvi, C.S., Comparison of Deep Learning Approaches for Sentiment Classification, 2021.
19. Krishna, M.M., Duraisamy, B., Vankara, J., Hybrid Deep Learning Techniques for Sentiment Analysis on IMDB Datasets, 2022.
20. Sagar, L.K., Shandil, P., Patel, A., Vishwakarma, S., Yadav, S., Emoji Prediction using Sentiment Analysis, 2023.

Index

3D multi-encoder, 45
3D-HOG, 109–110

Accuracy, 39, 41, 43, 44, 45, 49, 53, 54, 60, 66, 67, 70,197–202
Action recognition, 109, 110–111
Active mode IDS, 210
AFEW dataset, 114–115
Agriculture, 173–177
AlexNet, 111
Animal welfare, 155–157
Anomaly detection, 210, 211
Anomaly-based detection, 210, 211
Appropriate predictions, 41
Artificial intelligence (AI), 54, 211
Aspect-based sentiment analysis (ABSA), 265, 266
Attack detection, 212
Audience engagement strategies, 266, 267, 268, 269, 272, 274

Backdoors, 212
Bag of visual words (BoVW) model, 109
Baseline network behavior, 210
Behavior-centric detection, 210
Binary classifier, 255
Biological image processing, 41
Bio-medical, 49
Biomedical image, 39
Botnets, 144, 152
Brain tumor, 39, 40, 41, 42, 49, 50

Cardiac disease, 199, 207
Cardiovascular disease, 197
ChatGPT, 1
Classification, 197–202
Clinically, 49
Clustering algorithms, 110
CNN (convolutional neural network), 29, 82–84, 107, 109, 110–111, 113–114, 155
CNN learning curves, 138
CNN model, 39, 41, 43, 44, 45, 49
COCO dataset, 86–87
Comment analysis, 266, 267, 273, 274, 280
  youtube, 274, 275, 279
Comment categorization, 266
Comparison, 203–206, 208
Completion, 202
Conditional generative adversarial networks (GAN), 109
Content creator tools, 266
Content creators, 266
Convolutional network, 42, 45, 46, 47, 48
Cyber threat detection, 210

Data augmentation, 9, 87
Data mining, 199–200, 207
Data preprocessing, 64
Data storage solutions, 265, 266, 268, 269, 272

Dataset, 39, 40, 41, 42, 43, 44, 53, 55, 58, 59, 60, 65, 66, 67, 68, 198, 199, 201, 204, 207
Decision support system, 198
Decision tree, 198, 207
Decoder network, 45, 46, 47, 48
Deep belief networks (DBN), 211, 212
Deep learning, 81, 82–84, 107–108, 110–113, 173–175, 177, 211
Deep neural networks, 265, 266, 268
DDoS, 143–146, 149–152
Denial of service (DoS), 212
Dense trajectory features, 109–110
DenseNet, 93, 100, 104
Dental image segmentation, 93, 95, 96
Digital fingerprints, 216
Dimensionality reduction, 31, 212
Discrete cosine transform, 27
Disease, 197–201, 203, 205, 207
Disease planning clinically, 49
DL classification model, 254
DL-based IDS for cloud security, 253
DMCM (deep masking convolutional model), 83–84, 86–87
Drug discovery, 9
Dynamic content creation, 265
Dynamic threat detection, 210

Effectual segmentation, 39
Elucidating spatial, 242
Encoder-decoder architecture, 83–84
Ethical consideration, 13
Evaluated, 49
Evaluation metrics, 82, 88
Exploding gradient problem, 265

Facial expression recognition (FER), 115–117
Facilitates, 40, 41
Feature encoding, 109–110
Feature extraction, 265, 266, 276
Features, 199, 201–202, 204, 207
Finest predictor approach, 49
Fisher encoding, 110
Floating point operations, 102
Fluid-attenuated inversion recovery, 40, 43
Foliar Pathologies, 227
Fully convolutional network, 45, 46, 47, 48
Fuzzy, 41, 42, 50

Gaming & visual environments, 12
Gaussian mixture models (GMM), 21
Generative adversarial network (GAN), 6, 53, 55, 57, 227, 228
Generative adversarial transformer (GATs), 56, 63
Generative artificial intelligence, 1
Generative probabilistic models, 212
Genomics, 10
Glioma, 40
Graphical representation, 46

Hausdorff distance, 100
Hidden Markov models (HMM), 21
Human action videos, 107–108, 109, 117
Human like text, 53, 55

Image segmentation, 81, 82–86, 88
Image segmentation process, 39, 42, 49, 50
Incremental updation approach, 265
Infant cry detection, 19
Instance segmentation, 82–84, 88
Interactive content development, 265
Internet of Things (IoT), 197, 199–200, 202–206
Intrusion detection systems (IDS), 210, 211, 250
Investigation, 41, 42, 49

Linear discriminant analysis, 31
Linear frequency cepstral coefficients (LPCC), 21

Long short-term memory (LSTM) , 31, 211, 265
LSTM layers, 265, 266

Machine learning (ML) , 40, 41, 197–208, 211
Machine learning in content analysis, 265
Magnetic resonance imaging, 40
Malignant, 39, 40
Malware detection, 210
MATLAB environment, 45
Mean squared error (MSE), 111
Medical data, 198
Medical imaging, 39, 40, 46, 88–89
Mel-frequency cepstral coefficients, 26
Meningioma patients, 42
Mid-level representations, 110
Monitoring, 39, 40, 41
MR images, 39
MRI images, 40, 42, 49
Multi-layer CNN model, 44
Multi-layer design, 49
Multi-layer perceptron (MLP), 33, 239

Natural language generation (NLG), 55
Natural language processing (NLP), 53, 54, 56, 60, 62
Network traffic analysis, 210, 216
Networks, 39, 41, 42, 49, 50
Neural networks, 4, 198–200, 207
Neuro computing algorithms, 23
Neurological disease, 199
Nucleus segmentation, 85–86

Object detection, 82, 84
Online content consumption, 265
Opinion mining, 265, 279, 280

P. falciparum, 124, 125, 128
Panoptic quality (PQ), 88–89
Panoptic segmentation, 81, 82, 84–89
Passive mode IDS, 210
Patient management process, 49
Peripheral blood smear, 121
Physicians, 40, 46, 49
Pixel space, 109–110
Plant pathology, 227, 228, 229, 236
Plasmodium parasite, 121, 122, 124
Pose space, 108–109
Positive predictive value, 260
Poultry industry, 155–157
Precision-recall curve, 257
Prediction, 39, 40, 42, 43, 44, 49, 174–175, 176, 179, 184, 186, 189–190, 198–207
Pre-processing, 200–202
Prevailing approaches, 43, 45, 49
Principal component analysis, 41
Prosodic and spectral features, 21

Real-time analytics, 265
Real-time sentiment analysis, 266
Recurrent neural network (RNN), 62, 211, 266, 277
Red blood cells. RBC, 124
Redundant features, 202
Region of interest (ROI), 161, 162
Regression model, 202
Regressive neighborhood, 197, 199
Regularized discriminant analysis (RDA), 31
Reliability, 200, 202
Remote sensing, 173–174, 176–178–180, 182
Restricted boltzmann machines (RBMs), 212
ROC curve, 261

Saliency maps, 112–113
Scatter matrix, 32
SDN, 145, 146, 152
Segmentation, 39, 40, 41, 42, 43, 44, 45, 46, 47, 49, 50, 51
Segmentation rely, 41
Selection techniques, 200
Semantic segmentation, 82, 88–89
Sentiment analysis, 266

Sentiment analysis challenges, 266, 267
Sentiment analysis techniques, 265–280
Sentiment categorization (positive, negative, neutral), 265–272
Sentiment classification, 265–267, 280
Sequence generative adversarial network, 61, 62
Short term fourier transform (STFT), 26
Short-term energy, 25
Signature-based detection, 210
Singularity problem, 32
Softmax, 98
Spectrograms, 27
Stochastic, 143, 146, 148, 149
Substitution, 202
SVM, 155–159, 161–163, 165, 167–171
Swarm optimization, 199

Text summarization, 56, 57, 62, 63, 65, 69, 70, 71, 72, 73
The deep neural network (DNN), 24
Threat signatures, 216
Training data augmentation, 113–114
Training process, 86–87
Transfer learning, 232
Tumorless, 43
Tune hyper-parameters, 44
Tweet sentiment prediction, 267
Two-tier convolutional neural network (2T-CNN), 107, 108, 110, 111–113, 117

U-Net, 45
Unmanned aerial, 173–174, 177
UNSW-NB15 dataset, 212
User feedback segregation, 266, 267
User-generated content, 266–271

Validation set, 39, 43
Vanishing gradient problem, 268, 269
Variational autoencoders, 5
Video block quality scores, 111–113
Video completion, 107, 109, 117
Video generation, 107–108, 112, 117
Video prediction, 107, 109–110, 117
Video upload frequency, 268
Video uploads, 268, 269, 271–272
Virus detection, 210
Volumetric overlap error, 101

YOLO v3, 155–157, 159, 161–163, 165, 167–171
YouTube analytics, 270

Also of Interest

Check out these published and forthcoming titles in the "Industry 5.0 Transformation Applications" series from Scrivener Publishing

Generative Artificial Intelligence
Concepts and Applications
Edited by R. Nidhya, D. Pavithra, Manish Kumar, A. Dinesh Kumar, and S. Balamurugan
Forthcoming 2025. ISBN 978-1-394-20922-4

Optimized Computational Intelligence Driven Decision Making
Theory, Application and Challenges
Edited by Hrudaya Kumar Tripathy, Sushruta Mishra, Minakhi Rout, S. Balamurugan and Samaresh Mishra
Forthcoming 2025. ISBN 978-1-394-24253-5

Cyber-Physical Systems for Innovating and Transforming Society 5.0
Edited by Tanupriya Choudhury, Abhijit Kumar, Ravi Tomar, S. Balamurugan and Ankit Vishnoi
Forthcoming 2025. ISBN 978-1-394-19771-2

Intelligent Robots and Cobots
Concepts and Applications for Industry 5.0 Transformation
Edited by Ramasamy V, S. Balamurugan, and Sheng-Lung Peng
Forthcoming 2025. ISBN 978-1-394-19817-7

Smart Factories for Industry 5.0 Transformation
Edited by R. Nidhya, Manish Kumar, S. Karthik, Rishabh Anand and S. Balamurugan
Published 2025. ISBN 978-1-394-19995-2

Welding Practices for Industry 5.0
Edited by Syed Quadir Moinuddin, Shaik Himam Saheb, Ashok Kumar Dewangan, Muralimohan Cheepu and S. Balamurugan
Published 2024. ISBN 978-1-394-17241-2

Metaverse and Immersive Technologies
An Introduction to Industrial, Business and Social Applications
Edited by Chandrashekhar A, Shaik Himam Saheb, Sandeep Kumar Panda, S. Balamurugan and Sheng-Lung Peng
Published 2023. ISBN 978-1-394-17454-6

www.scrivenerpublishing.com